Service Breakthroughs

Service Breakthroughs

Changing the Rules of the Game

James L. Heskett
W. Earl Sasser, Jr.
Christopher W. L. Hart

THE FREE PRESS
A Division of Macmillan, Inc.
NEW YORK

Maxwell Macmillan Canada
TORONTO

Maxwell Macmillan International
NEW YORK   OXFORD   SINGAPORE   SYDNEY

The Free Press
A Division of Macmillan, Inc.
866 Third Avenue, New York, N.Y. 10022

Maxwell Macmillan Canada, Inc.
1200 Eglinton Avenue East
Suite 200
Don Mills, Ontario M3C 3N1

Macmillan, Inc. is part of the Maxwell Communication Group of Companies.

Printed in the United States of America

printing number

5 6 7 8 9 10

Library of Congress Cataloging-in-Publication Data

Heskett, James L.
    Service breakthroughs: changing the rules of the game / James L. Heskett, W. Earl Sasser, Jr., Christopher W. L. Hart.
        p.   cm.
    Includes bibliographical references (p.   ).
    ISBN 0–02–914675–5
    1. Customer service.   2. Sales management.   I. Sasser, W. Earl.
II. Hart, Christopher W. L.   III. Title
HF5415.H43   1990
658.8'12—dc20   90–34202
                                                                      CIP

Contents

Preface

Services have replaced used car and aluminum siding salespeople as the most frequent butt of jokes and complaints. Who doesn't have a favorite bad service war story? In fact, the abysmal quality of services in America has been made out by some to be a national scandal.

And yet, a number of firms have been successful at designing and activating what we call breakthrough services. These are services that revolutionize an entire industry's rules of the game by setting new standards for consistently meeting or exceeding customers' service needs and expectations. In some cases, these services are perceived by customers as being of exceedingly high quality, whether that is defined in terms of speed, accuracy, or other features. In other cases, the services produce unusually high value by delivering consistent quality at low prices.

A breakthrough service is significantly differentiated from competition both on matters important to customers and the manner in which it achieves its results, whether that be through a well-defined, focused, and positioned service concept; a high-commitment organization; a comprehensive database; a hard-to-duplicate network or technology; clever financing arrangements; or other methods.

We're concerned here not so much with the competitive strategies elected by service firms, but with the ways in which those strategies are implemented. This takes us to the very core of the service firm, to its human, technological, and financial resources and the way they are marshaled and brought to bear on delivering a service concept.

It requires attention to detail. At a meeting several years ago, a senior executive of the Trust House Forte hotel chain related how it had taken the English-based company 18 months just to implement a program in which its receptionists regularly greeted prospective guests with ``———hotel, how may we help you?'' This executive was quite pleased when, during a break in the program, a member of the audience called a local Trust House Forte hotel and received the proper response.

It also requires that as much attention be given to the server as to the served. In a service, the two are much more closely linked than in most manufacturing processes.

Our concerns are selfish. Most of us, as citizens of post-industrial societies, live and work in a service economy, one in which services provide a vast and increasing majority of the jobs and national income.

Technology, in particular communications and information systems, has brought us to a point in time for services that is comparable to the era of the industrial revolution in manufacturing. It is a point in time when the nature of work and relationships among service workers are being transformed. In implementing service strategies, managers have a choice. They have an opportunity to benefit from the mistakes of their manufacturing forbears. Or they can make the same mistakes that led to worker alienation, the decline of product quality, militant union organization, and, according to many political economists, Marxist leadership in some parts of the world.

Consequently, the major objectives of this book are to: (1) identify elements common to methods that successful service firms adopt for activating strategies, (2) examine the implications that these methods have for the long-term benefits to servers as well as the served, and (3) suggest ways in which service-producing companies can avoid the mistakes of the industrial revolution as they bring modern technology to bear in creating a service revolution.

Our emphasis is on those things that are particularly critical to service-producing organizations and set them apart from their counterparts in manufacturing or extractive industries. They include:

1. The skillful organization and integration of marketing, operations, and human resource management critical to a successful service enterprise

2. The "real-time" nature of many service production and delivery ("marketing") processes, with the profound implications it has for the training, compensation, and motivation of people; the design of information support systems for them; the design of other elements of the service delivery system, many of them associated with the place where both work is performed and customers are encountered; and the control of quality and productivity.

3. The management of people working simultaneously and often in an interactive mode in geographically far-flung networks connected only by a communications system, a marketing program, and whatever culture-building activities management may design and implement.

4. The fact that customers of many service-producing organizations have direct access to or contact with *most* of the members of those organizations, including people associated with *most* of the financial departments of the service-producing firm.

5. The demands that all of this places on the management of the service firm, particularly in the implementation and ongoing management of efforts to maintain a knowledge of customer needs and the way they are or are not being met; to design work and workplaces in ways intended to meet those needs most profitably; to select, develop, and assign people suitable to various tasks; and to devise ways of insuring that the service and the way it is produced and delivered will change to reflect new customer and server needs, technologies, and competitive dynamics.

We first examine in Chapter 1 ways in which successful firms orchestrate the service encounter between a customer and employee to create what we've called a "self-reinforcing service cycle." This, in addition to the strategic service vision reviewed in Chapter 2, provides the framework with which we organize our thoughts in the remainder of the book.

Customer and employee loyalty are at the heart of all service breakthroughs. In addition to reporting important new research results concerning the value of customer retention, Chapters 3 and 4 discuss ways in which a service strategy can be focused to foster such loyalty.

Service quality and productivity are our concerns in Chapters 5 through 7. This material reflects our conclusions that: (1) service quality is a positive force for attracting and retaining both the most desirable customers and employees, leading directly to superior productivity, (2) the starting point for the upgrading of quality is the measurement of costs and benefits, (3) nothing less than total customer (and employee) satisfaction should be the goal, and (4) the task is complex and never-ending.

A great deal of available service capacity often is wasted because it is perishable and must be held in reserve for just those moments when customers need it. But service demand and supply can be managed in ways described in Chapter 8.

Important building blocks of outstanding service—networks, information technology, and especially people—are addressed in Chapters 9 through 12. The creation and management of networks comprising physical facilities (such as routes), information (communications), and relationships (between people and organizations) will receive increasing attention in the coming decade, something we've tried to anticipate in Chapter 9. Many hopes for increasing service quality and productivity are centered around the potential for and capabilities of information technology, the subject of Chapter 10. Chapters 11 and 12 address the ways in which people in leading service organizations are being energized through truly innovative methods of selection and development, rewards and recognition, and organizing work itself. These are methods that provide high levels of satisfaction to service personnel as well, a significant goal in societies in which as many as 80% of all jobs are in services.

The future holds the prospect for delivery of more services anywhere and any time, a condition that has been called "future perfect." In Chapter 13 we discuss forces underlying the trend toward future perfect as well as possible limits on management efforts to achieve it.

The final chapter reviews the major themes of the book by comparing breakthrough and what we have termed "merely good" service organizations on a number of dimensions. The time-constrained reader can thus obtain a good sense of the book by reading Chapter 14 and then sampling in greater depth those chapters of greatest interest.

The organization of the book parallels that of a companion volume, *The Service Management Course,* which contains in-depth case studies of many of the companies referred to here.

This book conveys deep convictions. They are ours, but they have been influenced and fueled by managers who have found them essential in the development of service breakthroughs.

James L. Heskett

W. Earl Sasser, Jr.

Christopher W. L. Hart

Boston, Massachusetts

Acknowledgments

In November 1987, we had the extraordinary opportunity to spend an evening and the following day on the Harvard Business School campus with CEOs of 15 of the leading service firms in their respective industries. It was a chance of a lifetime for three students of service management. The purpose of our CEO Workshop was to discuss broad-ranging issues confronting service companies which members of the group might identify. But because their firms spanned most service industries, we were apprehensive about whether members of the group could settle on an agenda of mutual interest. We need not have worried. Much of this book, especially those sections concerning organization, human resources, and strategies for becoming an "employer of choice," was inspired by that meeting. Furthermore, we were challenged to go beyond those discussions to identify other characteristics of breakthrough services in a broader spectrum of firms.

We are indebted to Rand Araskog; William W. Bain, Jr.; Edward H. Budd; M. Anthony Burns; Donald C. Clark; J. Michael Cook; James R. Emshoff; Thomas P. Fagan; Mitchell S. Fromstein; Ray J. Groves; Bruce Henderson; Paul H. Henson; J. Willard Marriott, Jr.; Joseph Neubauer; and William E. Phillips for a memorable experience and the inspiration for many of the ideas developed in this book.

Other executives have read and commented on portions of the manuscript. They include Eugene Arbaugh, Vice President, Corporate Marketing, PHH Corporation; Adam Aronson, Chairman Emeritus, Mark Twain Bancshares, Inc.; G. Edmond Clark, Manager of Investor Relations, Federal Express Corporation; Robert Horner, Chairman, Citicorp Mortgage Corporation; Charles W. McCall, President, CompuServe, Inc.; John B. McCoy, Chairman and Chief Executive Officer, Banc One Corporation; C. William Pollard, President and Chief Executive Officer, The ServiceMaster Company L. P.;

Christopher Swan, General Manager, British Airways, Inc.; Martin Trust, President, Mast Industries, Inc.; and Wilson Wilde, President and Chief Executive Officer, The Hartford Steam Boiler Inspection and Insurance Co. They helped us check our facts while supplementing our ideas.

Former colleagues have influenced and enriched our thinking. They include David H. Maister and Christopher H. Lovelock, both of whom are now pursuing consulting careers; Richard B. Chase, Professor of Operations Management at the University of Southern California; William Fulmer, Floyd D. Gottwald Professor of Business at William & Mary College; and Hervé Mathe, Associate Professor at ESSEC in France.

Our all-too-brief association with the late D. Daryl Wyckoff had a significant impact on our work as well as that of practicing managers in leading service firms. Daryl had a discerning eye; he could spot emerging service breakthroughs. He wrote cases on Federal Express, Singapore Airlines, and Stanford Court Hotels long before these firms became models for service excellence in the popular press. Daryl had the ability to make the complicated seem very simple with a cleverly done diagram or chart; he used data very effectively to make his points. He contributed a great deal to our thinking.

Among our current associates, Regina E. Herzlinger, Dwight B. Crane, Leonard A. Schlesinger, Minette E. Drumwright, and Timothy B. Blodgett have been particularly willing to share ideas and time with us.

Research leading to the book has been supported by the Division of Research at the Harvard Business School in general and the UPS Foundation in particular. This arms-length support has been particularly helpful.

Sarah Markham was instrumental in supervising the production of the manuscript.

As always, Marilyn Heskett, Connie Sasser, and Joan Livingston have provided support and encouragement whenever it was needed.

Whatever their source, we're certain that few of the ideas in this book are ours alone. Many of them are being tested in the real laboratory, the one where services actually are being delivered. But since we've done the sorting and organizing of other people's work in an effort to discover and communicate significant patterns in it, we obviously bear the responsibility for the contents of this book. It's a small burden to bear for the stimulation and enjoyment of being able to spend so much time with managers of breakthrough services.

J. L. H.
W. E. S.
C. W. L. H.

1

Creating
Breakthrough Services

Outstanding service organizations are managed differently from their merely good competitors. Missions are stated differently. Managers act differently. Actions are based on totally different assumptions about the way success is achieved. And the results show it, both in terms of conventional measures of performance and the impact these services have on their competitors.

Recently one of us visited the Tyson's Corner Mall in northern Virginia. The visit resulted in one surprise after another as salespeople in large stores and small exhibited unusual interest in providing unexpectedly outstanding service. At first we attributed it to Southern hospitality. But the experience wasn't consistent with others we've had in the same area. And then it dawned on us. Among the four department stores which the huge mall contained, one was Nordstrom. And Nordstrom's level of service exceeded even that provided by other retailers that same day. The experience was a clear reflection of a strong conviction often expressed by Nordstrom's service managers that a store manager's primary responsibility is to satisfy customers.

Naturally, we had seen many of the things written about the high level of service provided by this fashion retailing organization. But we had not witnessed the impact it could have on an entire shopping center, one of the largest in the United States. The experience triggered a line of thinking about those one or two firms in every service industry that stand out from the pack. Firms that seem to gain momentum, almost as if they are propelled by an added force not available to their competitors. Firms that seem to have broken through some sort of figurative ''sound barrier,'' that have passed through the turbulence that precedes the barrier into the relatively quiet, smooth zone beyond in which a management action produces exaggerated results, results that often exceed reasonable expectations. Firms that alter the very basis of competition in their industries.

We began to think of the offerings of these firms as breakthrough services and set out to try to capture in words, numbers, and diagrams the essence of what managers do to break the figurative sound barrier.

We started with three simple beliefs: (1) it is possible to manage a good firm through the barrier that distinguishes the good from those that are moving beyond Mach 1; (2) outstanding services and the firms that provide them are made, not born; and (3) breakthrough services managers don't think like their merely good counterparts in competing organizations.

Having tested these ideas through numerous field observations, we are convinced more than ever that our starting beliefs hold up. But we have found out a great deal more along the way about how managers think and act in designing and delivering breakthrough services. They invariably start with the service encounter.

THE SERVICE ENCOUNTER

At the heart of every service is the service encounter. Everything flows from it. A service encounter is the event at which a customer comes into contact with a service provider, its people, its communications and other technology, and the services it provides. It is the point in time at which especially marketing, operations, and human resource management are brought to bear on the process of creating and delivering a service that meets customers' needs, perceived risks, and expectations. It has been termed by Jan Carlzon, CEO of SAS (Scandinavian Airlines System), the "moment of truth" at which the representatives of a service company must prove to their customers that their company is the best alternative.[1]

The most important relationships in a service encounter, based on research done to date, are summarized in Figure 1–1. We have purposely been selective in choosing elements of this model. The first is based on research findings; the others follow from it. They are:

1. The quality of service (customer satisfaction) = service quality delivered − service expected.
2. The value of a service to a customer = service quality (both the results realized and process by which they were achieved) divided by (price and other customer costs of acquiring the service).

FIGURE 1-1 The Service Encounter as a Set of Trade-Offs

3. Potential profit "leverage" in providing the service = value to the customer − cost to the service provider.

4. The profitability of a service to its provider = margin × repeat usage ÷ investment.

It occurred to us that most service managers understand these relationships. Why then do so few use this understanding to produce services that achieve true competitive superiority? The primary reason, we've concluded, is that most view these relationships as a set of trade-offs to be designed and managed in traditional ways that have been handed down from one generation of operating manager to the next for years. This is the view that assumes that nearly all decisions involve trade-offs. That higher quality requires greater investment or higher costs, or that lower costs naturally are associated with lower quality. That higher prices naturally reduce demand. And that the primary avenue to higher profits is higher margins. While these assumptions ignore the way in which customers assess the value of a service, they represent conventional, accepted management thinking.

Breakthrough managers look at the same relationships and see something else. They see the service encounter as a dynamic force with a potential for fueling a set of self-reinforcing relationships shown in Figure 1-2. They take advantage of relationships that propel a firm through the competitive sound barrier, often by defying conventional logic concerning trade-offs. These managers spend less to achieve higher value and higher margins. They lower prices to increase margins. They raise prices and sell more. They understand customer value, quality, and ways of leveraging value over cost. Most important, they understand how to develop fanatical loyalty among customers, employees, suppliers, and investors, loyalty that produces the flow of results bordering Figure 1-2. In short, they frequently astound and often confuse their merely good competitors, who work just as hard but end up being second- or third-best.

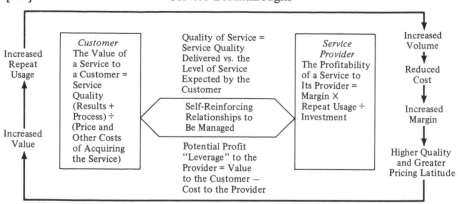

FIGURE 1–2 The Service Encounter as a Self-Reinforcing Process

Consider, for a moment, the underlying policies of Nordstrom and how management implements them. As we said earlier, everything flows from the mission of providing outstanding service to customers. The way this is achieved is by stocking fashion merchandise in greater depth and breadth than competitors; having pleasant, well-located stores; providing incentives to salespeople and managers to deliver superior service to customers; and then leaving it up to individual store managers and salespeople as to how superior service is to be achieved.

Merely good competitors whose managers practice by the "trade-off" philosophy look at Nordstrom and shake their heads. Because Nordstrom has more complete stocks of fashion merchandise, its inventory carrying costs should be higher than industry averages, right? Wrong. Nordstrom's inventory carrying costs in relation to sales are not higher. Well-designed stores in good locations featuring such amenities as live music performed on a grand piano in each store have to result in higher overhead and occupancy costs than for competitors, right? Wrong again. Nordstrom's overhead and occupancy costs in relation to sales are not higher. Because Nordstrom relies heavily on sales commissions, paying successful salespeople roughly twice as much as they could make at its most serious competitors' stores, it must have the highest labor costs in the industry, right? Still wrong. In relation to sales, Nordstrom's labor costs are at or below industry averages. Delegating the control of service quality to the point of sale must involve risks of achieving highly uneven service quality, right? The evidence suggests not. Nordstrom has one of the most fiercely loyal group of customers of any firm anywhere. Most are recruited by word-of-mouth referrals, thus reducing advertising costs to one of the lowest levels of all fashion retailing firms.

The results of Nordstrom's breakthrough service are mirrored not only in the company's loyal customers but also in its high productivity of assets and personnel; in its ability to retain experienced, capable people; and in its substantial profit on investment even while growing rapidly. At the heart of Nordstrom's success is an understanding of not just how to deliver value to customers or how to control costs, but rather how to leverage value over cost to achieve profit.

LEVERAGING VALUE OVER COST TO ACHIEVE PROFIT

The difference between the value of a service to a customer and the cost of providing it determines profit potential. It is what we call profit leverage. The extent to which it is fully captured by the service provider depends on its pricing policy.

VALUE OF SERVICE

What we receive for what we pay is the basis for measuring value in services as well as products. Our perception of what we receive in a service, however, is based both on results obtained and the manner in which the results are achieved.

Quality of Service. Results and the process by which they are delivered are the components of what we call service quality.

Results from a service often are difficult to assess. As Valarie Zeithaml has pointed out, it is hard to know the results even after we have purchased many services.[2] In contrast, we see the result immediately when we try on a piece of clothing or wear it in public for the first time. We can get some idea of the potential result before we buy. Other goods and many services are harder to assess in advance. For example, we have to have our hair styled to know whether we received good results from the hair stylist. It's nearly as hard to correct a bad haircut in process as it is to reverse it after the fact.

With many services, including almost all educational (this book, for example), medical, legal, and other professional services, the problem is even more extreme. We don't know the results even after the service has been performed. Astute service providers understand this and take measures to assure us that the result will be a good one, often through the process by which the service is delivered.

While we may not be able to assess results before, during, or even after some services, we frequently are able to observe how a service is delivered.

This is why outstanding service organizations devote as much attention to the manner of service delivery as to the achievement of desired results.

Quality = *Actual Service* − *Expected Service*. Results and process, and thus quality, are evaluated by customers in terms of what they actually receive in relation to what they expected. Because needs and expectations vary by customer and situation, service quality is a highly subjective matter. Clearly, the customer defines quality.

Absolute measurements of service quality that do not include customer expectations miss the point. Customers have different expectations of the quality they can expect from different types of service providers, competitors within the same industry, and the same providers at different points in time and under varying conditions. This helps explain why customers regularly rate auto service quality at such chain organizations as Sears, Firestone, and Midas Muffler higher than at their authorized General Motors, Ford, or Toyota dealers. They expect more from the latter. And because they save their complex auto "medical" problems for the authorized dealer, they do not always come away satisfied. They expect only to get a muffler replaced at a certain price at Midas and it happens.

Customers often expect more rapid response from a Federal Express representative than they do from their doctor. Why? They have been conditioned to believe that the doctor is busier and a scarcer resource, whether it is true or not. One organization, Au Bon Pain, a French bakery café chain featuring sandwiches made with croissants, organized a "Moments of Truth" quality excellence program. As a result, it established several standards, including one borrowed from McDonald's, that no customer should wait more than two minutes in line to place an order. This standard, however, was modified to three minutes when customers indicated that they didn't expect Au Bon Pain to be as fast as a McDonald's because the food being served obviously took longer to prepare.[3]

Customers expect better service from a firm that has provided good service in the past than one that has not, suggesting the importance of a series of service encounters and results over time. And customer expectations may or may not take into account the impact of peak or slack business times on the quality of service or the fact that they may buy different classes of service from the same provider from time to time. Thus, airlines serving travelers who use first class on business but who are traveling coach class with families on vacation regularly run the risk of being perceived as offering poor service, suggesting the need to find ways of making available some form of "first-class" vacation travel to those customers and their families.

Breakthrough service managers understand that a high-quality service encounter raises expectations for future encounters, not only those involving a customer with the same service company, but also those of its competitors. Thus, it is both a competitive weapon and a prod for continued service improvement. In a sense, high-quality service is its own best competition. The term "personal best," sought by competitive track and field athletes, applies in successful service firms as their customers' expectations are ratcheted upward and they strive to meet or exceed them with new features, variety, and positive service "surprises."

This ratchet effect may vary from one targeted customer segment to another, however. For years, the success of McDonald's has been based in part on the fact that one of its primary customer targets, children, typically do not want change from one encounter to another. They want the successful experience repeated exactly as it was the last time, whether or not their dutiful parents concur.

Perceived service quality can be enhanced both through efforts to improve results produced for customers and through efforts to condition their expectations about the nature of the service encounter and the results it might produce. Both are important.

One of the major themes of this book is service improvement. But we shouldn't overlook the fact that many services are enhanced through the conditioning of expectations. The medical profession, for example, has done a masterful job of enhancing value of service perceptions by conditioning prospective patients to expect to be treated like small children, told little, accept much of what happens to them on faith, and not be disappointed with failures to correct medical problems.

One progressive hospital manager, Erie Chapman, CEO of the U.S. Health Corporation, compares the situation of hospital patients unfavorably to that of prison inmates. In his view, both are subjected to excessive questioning, stripped of their usual clothing and possessions, placed in a subservient, dependent relationship to those attending to them, and allowed visitors only during certain hours.[4] His organization is trying to do many things to correct this, including the creation of patient advocates and the designation of liaison people between staff and patients. But the fact is that today medical practitioners who exceed even by a small margin minimal expectations which have been established are regarded as delivering outstanding service.

In a less critical service encounter, a restaurant customer may be told to expect a 30-minute wait and then called to a table in only 20 minutes. Given the conditioning of expectations, the result can be a positive perception of service quality even at the end of a 20-minute wait.

Firms that raise customers' expectations before developing the ability to meet them may experience short-term sales gains and long-term customer losses. This may help explain why Delta Air Lines modified its slogan, "Delta is ready when you are," and why Holiday Inn did the same with its advertising campaign stressing, "No excuses. Guaranteed."[5]

High-value service results in part from high quality. But service value has another component, cost. This includes both the price of the service and the less easily measurable costs of acquiring it.

Costs of Service to Customers. The traditional view of service acquisition costs is that they are all viewed negatively by the customer and thus have to be "traded off" against increased quality for the same or lower prices.

For example, Levitz Furniture pioneered the concept of the furniture warehouse store, one in which customers purchase from displays set up adjacent to a large warehouse stocked with crated furniture. In addition, customers may carry out their own purchases, thus reducing some of the most onerous costs of the furniture business, delivery and setup, with attendant damage to the product. This perhaps explains why Levitz offers a significant price incentive to customers to cart away their own purchases from the "warehouse."

Breakthrough services, in contrast, have been designed around the proposition that customers' perceptions of service acquisition costs are not all negative. Some of the most imaginative applications of this are provided by managers who understand that acquisition costs include the costs of delayed gratification, noninvolvement in the service, and lack of customer control over the result. This has led to the design of services incorporating more and more self-service, but at higher rather than lower prices of full-service competitors. In the case of furniture retailing, we are beginning to learn that for many customers, immediate access to their furniture has value. Further, they often ignore or underestimate acquisition costs, thus resulting in positive perceptions of the cost of self-service.

As one observer put it:

> Many consumers are so convinced that self-service is the height of good service that they are willing to pay extra for the privilege— witness the people who pay fees for using teller machines in New York, or who pay extra to tap into data systems through their own computers.[6]

The Subjective Nature of Service Value. We have just observed that quality in services is subjective, defined by individual customers. At the same time, customers attach different costs to the same process of acquiring a service. As a result, service value, the difference between service quality and cost, for an identical service may vary a great deal from one customer to the next.

Excellence in service requires an understanding of customer needs and expectations. That perhaps explains the growing number of efforts to measure them. Even though these efforts have not all had the same objective, the results contain common patterns. British Airways, through such efforts, has found for example that nearly all travelers have the usual basic needs for convenient schedules, on-time service, and other physical elements of air travel service. But assuming these basic common needs are met, some travelers respond most positively to the care and concern shown to them in the delivery of the service. Others value highly the spontaneity with which front-line service staff deal with problems and requests. And still others look for and value the ability of service agents to solve problems and the skill with which they and their company respond when things go wrong.[7]

Many differences in the value attached to services by customers are explained by the level of risk perceived by a customer in purchasing the service and the degree to which such risks can be minimized by the service provider. As humans, we are sensitive to many kinds of risks, including economic, social, medical, and legal risks. Our assessment of risk is based both on the likelihood and consequences of service failure. The likelihood of failure we perceive may result from the complexity of the service itself. Most of us view auto repairs involving mechanical problems as carrying higher perceived risks than an elevator ride. The consequences of failure might actually be greater in an elevator ride. But the likelihood of failure in repairing an auto is so much higher than riding an elevator that it may be viewed as riskier.

Breakthrough service designers and managers understand further that perceived risks also help explain why two customers value the same service differently. The difference often is explained by the amount of self-confidence, often associated with knowledge and expertise, that a customer brings to the service encounter. Thus, those with little mechanical ability often value auto repair services more highly than "weekend auto tinkerers." At the same time, auto repair value varies directly with the newness of the vehicle, its cost when purchased, and the value of time of its owner, reflecting both perceived economic and social risks.

Why is all of this important? Because customers associate value with efforts on the part of service providers to reduce economic, social, medical, legal, or other risks in achieving results that customers seek. That's why breakthrough services often make complex services seem simpler, help build customer self-confidence, and in the process achieve a level of reliability that helps insure that expectations regarding both service quality and cost are met.

This suggests the importance of managing customers' perceived risks designed to produce a range of expectations that the service provider can meet. It also suggests reducing customers' perceived risks and thus increasing their expectations in ways competitors cannot match, thus creating competitive advantage.

Outstanding service providers also seek consistency in the way basic elements of a service are provided. They meet and perhaps by a small margin exceed customers' expectations for the level of service provided. At the same time, they build expectations about the consistency with which the service is delivered. In addition, an effort may be made to enhance service over time by adding "surprises," in the form of noncritical service elements. For example, while the two commandments of the in-flight catering service business are: (1) thou shalt not cause a flight's departure to be delayed, and (2) thou shalt not damage the aircraft, efforts to upgrade the appearance of planeside personnel or assist in carrying out the on-board review of the accuracy of the delivery may help differentiate a superior, high-value in-flight kitchen.

COST OF SERVICE TO ITS PROVIDER

The cost of a service to its provider is influenced by, among other things: (1) the nature of the service offered to the customer, (2) the operating strategy of the service company, (3) its service delivery system, (4) the degree to which the server's capacity is utilized, and (5) the needs and attitudes of servers.

The first of these factors establishes a range of costs within which a service may be delivered. The development of an operating strategy and the design of a service delivery system further define the range of cost incurred, assuming a given level of capacity utilization. It then falls to the management of the service firm to both manage capacity and stimulate demand for it. But unless servers' needs are met and their attitudes toward service delivery developed, the finest operating strategy and service delivery system mean little. This underlines both the importance of the relationship between design and activation and the role of the manager in making it work. Because it is the subject of much of this book, we will only set the stage for our later discussion here by underlining one particular feature of Figure 1–2. It is the set of relationships between quality, productivity, cost, margin, price, value to customers, and increased repeat customer usage suggested by the arrows bordering the figure.

CREATING A SELF-REINFORCING SERVICE CYCLE
VERSUS MANAGING TRADE-OFFS

Those who design and deliver service excellence are exposed to the same ideas as their less successful competitors. What is it, then, that they see and do that enables them to more successfully leverage value to customers over the cost of delivering a service? It is embodied in the relationships explaining the clockwise arrows around the border of Figure 1–2.

Service excellence is built first around an understanding that:

1. The value associated with the results a service provides and the quality of the way it is delivered depends on the extent to which a provider can reduce a customer's perceived risks.
2. Increased value in relation to the costs of acquiring a service leads to a higher probability that a customer will become a repeater.
3. Repeat customers, because they have established expectations, growing respect for the provider, and greater knowledge of what is expected of them in the service delivery process, are less expensive, and therefore more profitable to serve, than new customers.
4. The value of service to a repeat customer grows with the reliability of the way it is delivered and the results it achieves.

This leads rapidly to the conclusion that investments intended to build service reliability actually reduce the costs of service delivery while building value to customers. Investments in higher service reliability may take the form of greater care in the selection and training of employees, higher rewards for employees, the acquisition of superior technology or other elements of the service delivery system, and a single-minded emphasis on customer satisfaction, among others. The resulting improvements in both server satisfaction and motivation in turn are reflected in the quality and value of service to the customer, thus completing the "drive wheel" for the self-reinforcing service cycle, as shown in detail in Figure 1–3.

Why are so many of these investments made to attract and retain superior human resources? An important factor differentiating most service industries from manufacturing is the greater impact of the needs and attitudes of the service firm employee (the server) on the quality and value of the service delivered as well as its cost. Wages and salaries represent a much higher proportion of total costs in most service industries than in the manufacturing sector. Of greater significance, though, is the fact that in most service industries a much higher proportion of the total labor complement comes

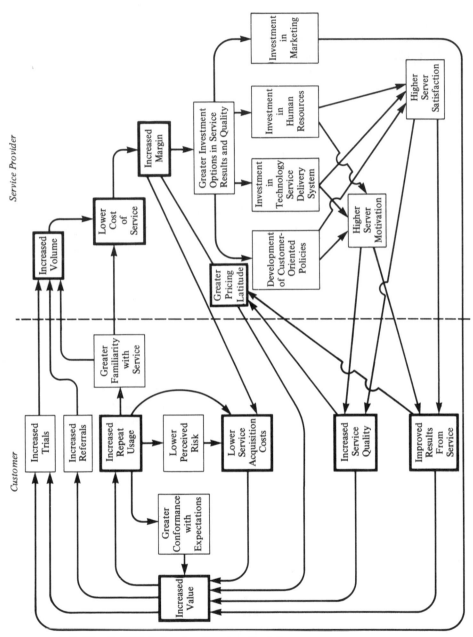

FIGURE 1–3 The Self-Reinforcing Service Cycle[a]

[a] Boxes with heavy borders relate to those shown in Figure 1–2.

into direct or indirect (by telephone) contact with the customer than in the traditional manufacturing firm. For example, Robert Eccles and Dwight Crane have observed that in investment banking firms, "nearly all of the firm's professionals are directly involved with its environment, including customers, competitors, and experts in accounting, law, and taxes."[8] The point of contact, of course, is the service encounter.

There is a growing body of evidence that suggests direct links between the satisfaction of the server, motivation to provide good service, the satisfaction of the customer, repeat sales, and profits.[9] Contributing to the satisfaction of the server in this "cycle," pictured in Figure 1–3, are the satisfaction of the customer (thus completing the loop) as well as the service firm's policies concerning selection, development, and assignment of personnel; its efforts to measure performance, reward, and recognize people; and the physical and personal support services and facilities made available to the server at the time of the service encounter.

Nordstrom attracts managers and salespeople who want to work hard and get rewarded for it. Recruiting costs are very low because an unusually high proportion of applicants come to Nordstrom through referrals from current employees. Most training is on the job, carried out by successful employees. Because compensation of salespeople is by commissions on sales, the unsuccessful or those unable to stand the pace of work leave, and not always quietly.[10] Those who stay communicate their enthusiasm to customers, a process that generates sales and reinforces Nordstrom's employee enthusiasm.

This self-reinforcing cycle of behavior is one of the reasons Nordstrom's customers get superior service. Another is that its salespeople and managers are charged with the mission of providing outstanding customer service and given the latitude to do so, in the process developing undying customer loyalty. Recently, for example, Nordstrom's senior managers at Seattle headquarters noted that hosiery sales at a West Coast store were several times those at other West Coast Nordstrom stores. Upon investigation, they found that an enterprising department manager had taken it upon herself to have her sales staff begin calling local offices during slack sales periods to inquire whether Nordstrom could deliver hosiery to busy secretaries who may have forgotten to replenish their supplies. Hosiery thus sold by telephone was immediately delivered by existing Nordstrom personnel. In the process, the precious time of salespeople was leveraged and the costly retail space in the store made much more productive. This is summed up in another of the frequently told stories that have made Nordstrom's service truly legendary. This one is told by a customer.

The customer pointed out to the Nordstrom salesperson that she had bought a pair of shoes at Bloomingdales that were too small for her. She liked the style, but Bloomingdales didn't have her size. After being fitted with the same shoe of the proper size, the customer started to pay for the shoes. The salesperson instead suggested that she merely take the too-small shoes in exchange for the new purchase. When the customer reminded the salesperson that she hadn't bought the first pair at Nordstrom, the salesperson said to her: "If I take these shoes for you, you won't have any reason to return to Bloomingdales."

Stocking broad selections of merchandise in attractive, well-located stores and providing incentives and the latitude to managers and salespeople to serve result in extraordinarily high sales productivity, both in terms of space and labor, at Nordstrom. This is the way that value is leveraged over cost at Nordstrom through a series of "margin-growing" activities.

These "margin-growing" activities pave the way for higher or lower prices, depending on competitive conditions. As a recent television advertisement for United Parcel Service says, "when you run at peak efficiency, you not only perform a better service but you have the luxury of charging less for it." Nordstrom's policy is not to charge less but to be competitive on all comparable merchandise, always meeting lower prices at competitors' stores. Both of these approaches can produce higher margins than those realized by merely good competitors.

Repeat customer usage of a service is central to the "drive wheel" shown in Figure 1–3. Much of what we've described results from it. Ordinary service providers take it for granted. Breakthrough companies give it unusual attention, carefully track it, and extensively nurture it.

CONCLUSION

The simple set of relationships that describe a service encounter as a positive self-reinforcing dynamic force in Figure 1–2 represents the result of a large number of "behind-the-scenes" decisions required to enhance the server's chances of achieving results desired by the customer. A successful service is the product of many small details, only some of which are the result of design and to some degree controllable. We are reminded of this every time we see a potentially disastrous customer relationship rescued by a remarkably perceptive and responsive human being exercising good judgment in a difficult situation. But wait a minute. How did that individual come to be affiliated with the service firm in the first place? How was the selection and assignment made? What part did training play in a seemingly fortuitous if difficult situation?

Interestingly, a successful service encounter most often appears to have less to do with compensation than a combination of loyalty to and belief in a company's service concept by a server and a reciprocal amount of trust in the server's ability to manage a service encounter effectively on a real-time basis by the company's management.

Such things as reciprocal loyalty and trust are built over time. They often are associated with both high quality and high productivity, in part resulting from the establishment of long-standing customer relationships and the sizable revenue stream they may represent. Just as important, they contribute to and result from close attention to the personal development of the server and resulting low turnover of staff, reinforcing high productivity and presenting added opportunity for high-quality customer encounters. In fact, service excellence is in large measure due to loyalty. The loyalty of employees to their customers, their company, and the service concept they are delivering. The trust of employees by a service company's management. And the loyalty of customers, employees, suppliers, and investors to a service provider.

This is the stuff of which breakthrough services are made for both customers and those who serve them. In exploring ways they are achieved in the remainder of the book, we'll be citing a number of examples drawn from firms we regard as breakthrough service providers in their respective industries, many of which are listed in Table 1–1. These firms provide evidence that service excellence pays off. As a group, they have achieved significantly higher rates of growth and higher returns on assets than the average for the largest firms in their industries, as shown in Table 1–2.

The major challenge to service firms that have achieved breakthrough performances is to meet the increasingly high expectations that they generate. They are held to a different standard than their "merely good" competitors. They risk becoming high-profile targets of potential criticism. Recently, for example, the Nordstrom organization has been found by a Washington state agency to have failed to pay employees for a variety of duties (a practice not altogether unusual in an organization paying a large proportion of its employees on the basis of commmissions on their sales).[10] How Nordstrom handles these kinds of challenges may well determine its ability to maintain breakthrough status, which in part is based on its ability to be very selective in its choice of employees. For this reason, we will be concerned here not only with ways in which outstanding service organizations have achieved service breakthroughs but also ways in which they have sustained them. How do they do it?

Table 1–1 SELECTED FIRMS PROVIDING EXAMPLES OF
BREAKTHROUGH SERVICE MANAGEMENT

Industry	*Firm*
U.S. Airlines	AMR Corp. (American Airlines, Inc.), Delta Air Lines, Inc.
European Airlines	British Airways PLC, Scandinavian Airlines System
Small Package Transportation	Federal Express Corp., United Parcel Service of America, Inc.
Highway Freight Transportation	J. B. Hunt Transport Services, Inc.
Money-Center Banking	Citicorp
Regional Banking	Wells Fargo & Co., Banc One Corporation, Mark Twain Bancshares, Inc.
Diversified Financial Services	American Express Company
Savings Institutions	Guardian Savings & Loan Association
Insurance	Progressive Corporation, The Hartford Steam Boiler Inspection and Insurance Co., The Paul Revere Insurance Co.
Hospitality	Marriott Corporation, Club Mediterranee S.A.
Retailing	McDonald's Corp., Nordstrom, Inc., L. L. Bean, Inc., Au Bon Pain, Inc., Wal-Mart Stores, Inc.
Utilities	Wisconsin Electric Power Co., FPL Group, Inc. (Florida Power & Light)
Oil Service	Schlumberger Ltd.
Information Services	CompuServe, Inc. (a subsidiary of H & R Block, Inc.)
Diversified Services	The Walt Disney Company, PHH Corporation, The ServiceMaster Company Limited Partnership, Manpower Inc.

Table 1–2 PERFORMANCE OF BREAKTHROUGH SERVICE FIRMS[a]

Industry and Names of Selected Firms Providing Examples of Breakthrough Services in This Book	Compounded Sales Growth, 1983–1988		Return on Assets 1983–1988	
	Breakthrough Service Firms	Composite of Largest Competitors[b]	Breakthrough Service Firms	Composite of Largest Competitors[b]
U.S. Airlines		18.5		1.8%
AMR Corp. (American Airlines)	13.1%		6.0%	
Delta Air Lines	13.8		7.0	
European Airlines		9.7		2.3[c]
British Airways PLC	8.5		6.1	
Scandinavian Airlines System	11.1		12.2	
Small Package transportation		N.A.[d]		N.A.[d]
Federal Express Corp.	29.2		3.9	
United Parcel Service of America, Inc.	12.9		14.3	
Highway freight transportation		13.3		7.2
J.B. Hunt Transport Services, Inc.	44.2		13.9	
Money-Center Banking		9.0		0.38
Citicorp	13.5		0.41	
Regional Banking		14.6		0.55
Banc One Corporation	29.8		1.37	
Wells Fargo & Co.	10.2		0.65	
Diversified financial services		12.2		0.94
American Express Company	18.6		0.95	
Savings institutions		10.7[e]		0.63[e]
Guardian Savings & Loan Association	43.2[e]		0.97[e]	
Fire and Marine Insurance		10.8		1.3
The Hartford Steam Boiler Inspection and Insurance Co.	14.3		7.9	
Progressive Corporation	37.4		5.5	
Hospitality		2.0		5.4
Club Mediterranee S.A.	14.3		5.0	
Marriott Corporation	19.4		4.6	
Merchandise Retailing		8.3		3.5
Nordstrom, Inc.	24.2		8.4	
Wal-Mart Stores, Inc.	34.6%		13.6%	
Food Retailing		11.7		8.0
McDonald's Corp.	13.0		9.0	
Utilities		4.1		4.8
FPL Group, Inc. (Florida Power & Light)	11.8		4.6	
Oil Service		−3.6		−3.9
Schlumberger Ltd.	−2.2		−0.8	
Entertainment		1.7		6.1
The Walt Disney Company	21.3		9.1	

[a] Breakthrough service firms listed here do not include all of those referred to in the book where the latter were subsidiaries of larger firms, privately held companies, or companies for which there were no directly relevant companies for comparison.

[b] The number of competitors comprising the comparison group in each case ranged from 4 (international airlines) to 13 (regional banking).

[c] Data for return on assets available for only two major competitors.

[d] Data for relevant competitors was not available.

[e] Data is for the years 1984 through 1988 only.

2

Developing a
Vision of the Business

Leaders of breakthrough services do not think about their businesses the way their competitors do.

Insurance company executives look at motorcycle owners and operators and see little but high risk. Peter Lewis, CEO of the Progressive Corporation, looks at them and sees nothing but opportunity. He has built one of the most profitable casualty insurance companies by, among other things, targeting sales of insurance to motorcycle owners. However, many of these are mature "bikers" who garage their motorcycles at night.

When he talks about Banc One, CEO John B. McCoy cannot remember precisely how many assets or even how many banking subsidiaries his rapidly growing regional bank holding company has. His interest is in ideas for extending his firm's financial and information services.

Jan Carlzon, CEO of Scandinavian Airlines System, tells of a visit to a number of CEOs of major U.S. airlines, which he divided into two types, "one type belonging to history." It took these CEOs "five minutes to start discussions about . . . aircraft planning." As Carlzon puts it:

> The other type of managers were those who, even if you pushed them after one hour, . . . didn't want to talk about . . . aircraft. They talked about the business in the marketplace, the customer. They talked about human resources in their companies as their tool to create . . . good service. . . .[1]

When he checked on the financial performance of the airlines he had visited, Carlzon found that only the latter had been consistently profitable.

Some sound, successful service strategies have been built on the idea of emulating an outstanding competitor. For example, more than one fast-food chain has substituted such a strategy for its real estate department. They merely locate as closely as possible to McDonald's outlets.

But breakthrough service design often involves a comprehensive view of the business and, in many cases, a counterintuitive, almost contrarian approach to developing and operating a business. Some of this can be attributed to the genius of individuals or the Eureka factor of accidental discovery or serendipity. But much of it is summed up by what we call the strategic service vision.

THE STRATEGIC SERVICE VISION[2]

Peter Lewis has a strategic service vision. John McCoy and Jan Carlzon have them too. But one of our favorite strategic service visions was successfully developed by Adam Aronson, founder and now Chairman Emeritus of Mark Twain Bancshares, Inc., headquartered in St. Louis. A brief description of Aronson's idea of banking is a better introduction to the strategic service vision than any dry definition we could provide.[3]

First, it is important to understand Aronson's motives for setting forth in banking the way he did. Already successful in two previous ventures, he wanted to fashion a business in which he could spend his time with interesting, trustworthy customers and colleagues in surroundings no less pleasant than his very comfortable home. As Aronson puts it:

> I don't think that you should be in business if it isn't fun. . . Why should you be less careful during your working hours where you spend most of your time than you are at home? . . . I don't want to eat less well and I don't want to be with less interesting people. Why should I have to subject myself to boring clods, even if they are smart or can make money for the bank . . . I am perfectly willing to work hard but I want it to be enjoyable.[4]

From this somewhat unconventional starting point, he was to fashion a highly successful banking venture.

To start with, Mark Twain Bancshares knows who it does and does not want to serve. Its *market targets* are: (1) the managements of preferably dynamic, medium-sized companies, the so-called "middle market" targeted by nearly every bank in the United States worth its salt, and (2) private individuals of substantial means, some of whom may be owners of targeted companies. Among the most important needs of managers and individuals targeted by Mark Twain are custom-designed financing on short notice, often without the credential provided by an audited accounting statement, and under conditions that suggest that they are getting preferred, "first-class" attention because of relationships they have established and maintained over time with their lender.

Mark Twain's response to these needs is to provide the timely, hassle-free responses that enable its customers to carry out transactions ranging from the advance purchase of inventory at favorable terms to the opportunistic acquisition of another business unexpectedly offered for sale. This is the *service concept* that the bank's customers value highly enough to willingly pay a premium to get.

It is able to respond because its *operating strategy,* dictated originally by Missouri banking laws which prohibited branch banking, is centered around the belief that each of the 35 locations from which it provides banking services should be a separately operated bank with its own president and board of directors. This requires that the bank in total have more than 300 directors, all of them members of the targeted market segments. As a result, Mark Twain has little difficulty obtaining character references for new customers it desires from one or more of its directors, most of whom are additionally motivated by the fact that they also own shares in the bank.

The facilities from which Mark Twain's managers do business are more than a little different from many other banks. Comfortable chairs and desks replace half the usual tellers' windows. The banks are unusually quiet, without the large number of depositors flocking to their competitors' facilities. Expensive art pieces purchased by Adam Aronson himself decorate the walls. And eleven of the banks have their own kitchens and gourmet chefs. All in all, it doesn't resemble the *service delivery system* of other banks.

BASIC ELEMENTS

Adam Aronson went by the book, at least our book, in assembling the basic elements of a strategic service vision essential to a winning business strategy. He clearly targeted two of many possible *target market segments* for banking services, middle-market firms and high-net-worth individuals, and made sure he understood the needs of members of those segments. Then he developed a *service concept,* defined not in terms of products or services but in terms of results produced for customers, the kinds of results they can achieve with fast-response, creative lending decisions. Next he put together an *operating strategy* comprising organization, controls, and financial, marketing, and operating policies that ensured that he could deliver on the promise of the service concept. And he complemented the operating strategy with a *service delivery system,* the service equivalent of the "plant" that provided the facilities from which service could be both marketed and delivered.

These are what we call the basic elements of a strategic service vision, as diagrammed in Figure 2–1 along with questions helpful in their development. They are complemented by other concepts we call integrative elements.

INTEGRATIVE ELEMENTS

In going after medium-sized companies, Mark Twain Bancshares faces competition from nearly every other of its local and regional competitors as well as lending representatives from several of the huge New York and other "money center" banks. The so-called "middle market" is a popular target. How does Mark Twain manage to compete? The answer is without much trouble, given the way it has *positioned* itself in relation to competitors and desired customers.

Mark Twain's close relationships with its director-owner-customers provide the core of a strategy that enables it to make what are often unsecured loans on short notice without the documentation of an audited financial statement. Its larger, more traditionally managed competitors, whether from

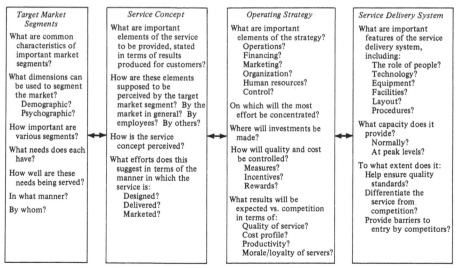

FIGURE 2–1 Basic Elements of a Strategic Service Vision
SOURCE: James L. Heskett, *Managing in the Service Economy* (Boston: Harvard Business School Press, 1986), p. 8.

St. Louis or New York, either can't or won't do the same because of standard corporate policies regarding lending risk and security. Such policies are understandable in large organizations comprising many levels of management in which the lending decisions of relatively low-level officers typically assigned to "middle-market" accounts must be carefully controlled in order to avoid excessive risk. But such policies are of little help to "middle-market" and large individual borrowers. In spite of repeated warnings of overwhelming competition from banks with much more clout than Mark Twain's, the latter's competitive position appears quite secure in the market segments it has targeted.

The operating strategy followed by Mark Twain, requiring the creation of the equivalent of many local "clubs," is not inexpensive. But in pushing the responsibility for such tasks as lending and even pricing certificates of deposit (a primary way the bank acquires capital) to the local level, Mark Twain eliminates several levels of approval required for smaller loans. It allows a relatively small headquarters staff to concentrate on decisions involving the largest dollar amounts as well as providing the management information system and other staff support required by the company's satellite banks. The value of the responsiveness to customer needs that this operating strategy produces is reflected in the premium prices that the bank receives for many of its services. In short, the value of the service to customers (quality in relation to price) is *leveraged* over the cost of providing it, yielding substantial margins and profits to Mark Twain's shareholders.

Customers always know when they are in a Mark Twain bank. The contemporary design and color and the presence of fine art everywhere may confuse or repel other bankers. But to the degree they attract clients in Mark Twain's targeted market segments and repel others, they signal a service delivery system well *integrated* with the bank's operating strategy.

Positioning, leverage, and integration are the three integrative elements that provide the glue that holds together an effective strategic service vision among outstanding service firms we have observed. They are shown, along with questions which help define them, and the basic elements they "glue together," in Figure 2–2.

At this point, you may be thinking, "These are elements that characterize any service strategy. What differentiates truly inspired breakthrough service strategies from all others?"

BREAKTHROUGH VISIONS

Adam Aronson uses personal adjectives in describing Mark Twain's *targeted customers*. The business firms that are the bank's clients are not

Target Market Segments	Positioning	Service Concept	Value-Cost Leveraging	Operating Strategy	Strategy-System Integration	Service Delivery System
What are common characteristics of important market segments?	How does the service concept propose to meet customer needs?	What are important elements of the service to be provided, stated in terms of results produced for customers?	To what extent are differences between perceived value and cost of service maximized by:	What are important elements of the strategy?	To what extent are the strategy and delivery system internally consistent?	What are important features of the service delivery system, including:
What dimensions can be used to segment the market?	How do competitors meet these needs?	How are these elements supposed to be perceived by the target market segment? By the market in general? By employees as a whole?	Standardization of certain elements?	Operations?	Can needs of the strategy be met by the delivery system?	The role of people?
Demographic?	How is the proposed service differentiated from competition?		Customization of certain elements?	Financing?	If not, what changes must be made in:	Technology?
Psychographic?	How important are these differences?	How do customers perceive the service concept?	Emphasizing easily leveraged services?	Marketing?	The operating strategy?	Equipment?
How important are various segments?	What is good service?	What efforts does this suggest in terms of the manner in which the service is:	Management of supply and demand?	Organization? Human resources?	The service delivery system?	Layout? Procedures?
What needs does each have?	Does the proposed service concept provide it?	Designed?	Control of quality through—	Control?	To what extent does the coordination of operating strategy and service delivery system ensure:	What capacity does it provide?
How well are these needs being served?	What efforts are required to bring customer expectations and service capabilities into alignment?	Delivered?	Rewards? Appeal to pride? Visibility and supervision?	On which will the most effort be concentrated?	High quality?	Normally? At peak levels?
In what manner?		Marketed?	Peer group control?	Where will investments be made?	High productivity?	To what extent does it:
By whom?			Involving the customer?	How will quality and cost be controlled?	Low cost?	Help ensure quality standards?
			Effective use of data?	Measurements? Incentives? Rewards?	High morale and loyalty of servers?	Differentiate the service from competition?
			To what extent does this effort create barriers to entry by potential competition?	What results will be expected versus competition in terms of:	To what extent does this integration provide barriers to entry by competition?	Provide barriers to entry by competitors?
				Quality of service? Cost profile? Productivity? Morale and loyalty of servers?		

FIGURE 2–2 Basic and Integrative Elements of a Strategic Service Vision

thought of so much in terms of their size as the mentality with which they are managed—conservatively, aggressively, or opportunistically. Above a certain threshold level of assets, Aronson feels it's more important how a person thinks about risk, return, and life-style than the amount of assets, education, or age he or she might have. Demographics, what or who businesses or individuals are, are put aside for the psychographics, how they or their managers think and live their personal or business lives. Psychographics are harder to obtain, often requiring closer relationships. Breakthrough service managers get and use them.

The service concept offered by other banks is to provide depository, lending, and trust services for customers. Mark Twain, on the other hand, offers a membership in a club where financial needs can be met as a means to achieving business or personal gain. The *service concepts* are not the same.

Operating strategies are viewed by most service managers as being synonymous with operations. In breakthrough services, they are viewed as ways of leveraging value over cost, prime determinants of profit. They include strong beliefs about the kind of people to be employed, the way they are organized, controlled, and given latitude to manage as well as the marketing, operating, and financial policies employed by management. Thus, the development of 35 bank boards at Mark Twain Bancshares is as much a marketing effort as it is an important aid to operations. The staffing of banks with relatively young managers from the president on down not only reflects Mark Twain's desire for operating vigor but also the fact that many of its customers are relatively young entrepreneurs or professionals who like to bank with people who think like they do.

The *service delivery system* in most service firms is viewed as a facility where the service is produced and sold. At Mark Twain Bancshares, as in other breakthrough service firms, the service delivery system is conceived as an opportunity to enhance and control the quality of results achieved for customers. Some regard Mark Twain banks as second offices, where they can conduct affairs privately and in agreeable surroundings. Those who are directors undoubtedly achieve results made possible in part through their association with the bank and its other directors as well as the use of its facilities.

Turning to integrative elements, *positioning* is a concept that has become a household word with advertising and marketing managers. But in the breakthrough strategic service vision, all of a firm's resources are devoted to and designed around the competitive position that the firm seeks in a customer's mind. Mark Twain Bancshares' services, policies for delivering them, controls on individual bank presidents, bank locations, people, bank decor, and mode of dress are all selected with a particular position in mind relative to customers and competitors. Its operating, financial, and human resource as well as its marketing strategies are designed with positioning in mind.

Heavy emphasis is placed on achieving profits by increasing productivity and efficiency in many service organizations. The break-through firm seeks profit *leverage,* first and foremost, through ways of enhancing value through quality while simultaneously reducing cost. It's possible. As at Mark Twain Bancshares, this objective may be achieved by appealing to a customer's need for involvement in actually helping to perform the service (through references for acquaintances seeking loans) or the need for a membership relationship that produces a stream of income for the bank without the high costs associated with frequent customer turnover.

In achieving the *integration* of operating strategy and service delivery system, a breakthrough service firm like Mark Twain Bancshares achieves it through people, policies, and facilities that are carefully coordinated to complement one another. In a superior strategic service vision, it is difficult to sort out policies and even people by function, to know where marketing ends and operations begin, to identify what part of the success of a service is due to people and the way they are rewarded and what part due to the facility in which they work. The result is what we like to think of as a "seamless" service in which the customer deals with a single person seemingly able to put all of the resources of the organization at the customer's disposal.

This is true of only a handful of service firms today. Too often reliance is placed on the individual service provider to figure out and attempt to deliver a service concept with little positive, consistent support from top management, company policies, organization, or the physical service "plant." Contrasts between all-too-typical and breakthrough views of elements of the strategic service vision are shown in Figure 2–3.

So far in our discussion of the strategic service vision we haven't said much about Mark Twain's people, other than Adam Aronson. While he is a formidable person, he didn't build the bank alone. But he did have a great deal to do with putting in place an internal strategic service vision that has attracted capable young managers to Mark Twain Bancshares and kept them there. Without an internal vision, all we've said so far about breakthrough service strategies would be impossible.

THE INTERNAL STRATEGIC SERVICE VISION

Mark Twain Bancshares attracts the most capable MBAs from the best business schools who elect to go into banking, period. How does it do it? In the same manner that it targets and serves its customers. It knows what type

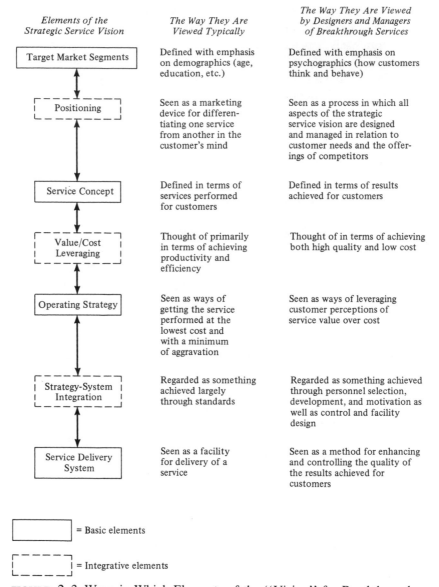

Elements of the Strategic Service Vision	The Way They Are Viewed Typically	The Way They Are Viewed by Designers and Managers of Breakthrough Services
Target Market Segments	Defined with emphasis on demographics (age, education, etc.)	Defined with emphasis on psychographics (how customers think and behave)
Positioning	Seen as a marketing device for differentiating one service from another in the customer's mind	Seen as a process in which all aspects of the strategic service vision are designed and managed in relation to customer needs and the offerings of competitors
Service Concept	Defined in terms of services performed for customers	Defined in terms of results achieved for customers
Value/Cost Leveraging	Thought of primarily in terms of achieving productivity and efficiency	Thought of in terms of achieving both high quality and low cost
Operating Strategy	Seen as ways of getting the service performed at the lowest cost and with a minimum of aggravation	Seen as ways of leveraging customer perceptions of service value over cost
Strategy-System Integration	Regarded as something achieved largely through standards	Regarded as something achieved through personnel selection, development, and motivation as well as control and facility design
Service Delivery System	Seen as a facility for delivery of a service	Seen as a method for enhancing and controlling the quality of the results achieved for customers

□ = Basic elements

⌐ ¬ = Integrative elements

FIGURE 2–3 Ways in Which Elements of the "Vision" for Breakthrough Services Are Different

of MBA it wants. And it offers a service concept that promises the greatest amount of responsibility in the shortest period of time under circumstances and with a title designed to satisfy a person's ego.

After two or three years as understudy, a young graduate can become a bank president at Mark Twain before reaching the age of 30. The special treatment begins at the first meeting; until recently, Adam Aronson personally was involved in recruiting all candidates. Now his successor CEO does the same thing.

How can the bank give so much responsibility to a freshly minted MBA? It has designed its operating strategy to limit the range of authority of its bank presidents to loans of a size often delegated to the middle managers of larger competitors. It restricts pricing authority over depository offerings such as CDs to narrow limits, all the while providing support services and management guidance from headquarters. But the young presidents with their own banks, boards of directors, clientele, and first-class facilities do not feel controlled to the extent this might suggest. And the best of them respond to encouragement from above to build their businesses in a variety of ways, sometimes even competing with a Mark Twain sister bank in the process.

In short, the bank has replicated the elements in its external strategic service vision for its own people. The enthusiasm created among its employees matches the natural enthusiasm of the clients the bank targets. As a result, counter to dire warnings that the bank is about to be engulfed by competitors with more clout, its shares of markets it has targeted in both St. Louis and Kansas City continue to grow while it maintains some of the highest margins in the banking industry. The only way Mark Twain's larger competitors will engulf it appears to be through acquisition. But that will happen only at the healthy market premium commanded by all breakthrough services organizations with carefully thought-out external and internal strategic service visions.

COMMUNICATING THE VISION

The strategic service vision is understood by employees at every level in leading service organizations. This requires either employees of outstanding intellect or a clear, compelling memorable vision. Reginald Jones, former CEO of General Electric, has said that he "expected every SBU (strategic business unit) manager to be able to stand before a peer group and, without benefit of visual aids, give a clear and concise statement of his strategic plan."[5] The same is true for a strategic service vision.

The heart of any vision is the result to be achieved for the customer. As someone once said, "People buy quarter-inch holes, not quarter-inch drills." Anyone who thinks he is in the drill business is deluding himself.

In services, the vision has to be extended to include the way in which the results are to be achieved, often a more complex set of ideas.

But written or even spoken statements are often only a starting point. The real message is communicated to employees through signals sent by management attitudes, policies, rewards, and supporting facilities. Adam Aronson or his successors can speak or write about comprehensive, responsive, financial services provided on a personal basis to customers and the importance of enjoying doing it. But it comes alive when young bank presidents are encouraged to assemble their own boards of directors, establish their own networks of contacts in the community, and take responsibility for the profits generated by their banks. And it is communicated by example as they see the active involvement of top managers in community affairs and are encouraged to provide amenities that make their banks more pleasant places in which to do business both for their customers and themselves.

Conflicting signals rapidly negate a carefully designed service vision. Research has suggested that one of the most frustrating experiences of service providers is to work in an organization that stresses total customer satisfaction and then imposes controls or provides facilities that make it difficult or impossible to deliver it.[6]

A vision formulated by an organization's leadership can be lost in the telling by successive levels of middle managers. Even the simplest, clearest of visions are blurred by middle-management interpretation that communicates a conflicting message. This requires that leaders determine those elements of a vision which are not negotiable at other levels of management, particularly where decentralization and the empowerment of first-line service personnel are stressed. Once determined, these elements are then repeated constantly and demonstrated by action in day-to-day contacts with operating personnel.

At Nordstrom, the chain of retain fashion stores that stresses superior service through complete assortments of merchandise, careful inventory control, and extraordinary personal responses to customer needs, James Nordstrom, the company's president, has said that he repeatedly has confronted the problem of communicating the organization's vision. According to Nordstrom:

> . . . there have been signs in stores which said we don't take merchandise back unless accompanied by receipt. This is just not true. It is our policy to take back merchandise if the customer says they bought it from us, unless we had a valid reason to reject it. I have taken down the signs personally and told several people that this is not our policy . . .[7]

Even though Nordstrom stresses maximum latitude for its employees in serving customers, some things are not negotiable.

By now it should be apparent that there are profound differences from the ordinary in the way that breakthrough service managers view each element of the strategic service vision. They have suggested to us that the basic elements of the vision are important for strategy development, but that the integrative elements—positioning, leveraging, and integrating—and the internal application of the vision are "where the action is" in putting a strategic service vision to work. We'll turn next to these integrative elements, applied both externally and internally, beginning with positioning.

3

Building Customer Loyalty

Customer loyalty is the cornerstone of a successful service. It influences employee and supplier loyalty. And it produces the profits that induce shareholder loyalty.

Few argue with the importance of customer loyalty. Only breakthrough service leaders, however, go two steps further to first calculate the extent to which loyalty spells profits through increased volume and reduced costs and, second, do what is necessary to develop intensely loyal customers.

DETERMINING THE VALUE OF A CUSTOMER

Typically, service managers don't know the value of a customer, even though nearly all have calculated the margin on sales of their services. They see a customer in terms of the profit potential represented by a sale. A story is told about a visit that Bernard Garber, the chairman of a successful New England regional travel service, Garber Travel, paid to the head of another chain of travel agencies based in Manhattan. According to the story:

> One agency owner in New York amazed Bernie by his lack of concern for (repeat) clients. He took Bernie over to his window on 42nd Street and pointed down to the crowds and said, "Do you see that mass of humanity down there? I only want a crack at each one of them once."[1]

Breakthrough services are based on the concept of customers as sources of streams of profitable revenue, resulting from both their own increasingly knowledgeable usage and the patronage of others to whom they recommend their service supplier.

CUSTOMER LOYALTY AND PROFITABILITY

Customer loyalty and profitability go hand in hand. The most common examples of this are insurance contracts in which the insurer usually does not recover selling costs until the third or fourth year, losing money if the insured cancels or switches policies before then. But the relationship extends to other services as well.

It costs less to serve repeat customers. There is a start-up cost associated with most new customers. This may be in the form of a reduced price as an incentive to try a service or costs associated both with learning about the characteristics and wishes of a new customer and acquainting that potential customer with the service. For example, the costs of collecting information about new hospital patients are incurred largely on the first visit. Luxury hotel chains such as Four Seasons Hotels collect information over time about the preferences of each guest to insure high levels of service that encourage loyalty. This effort must be amortized over repeated guest visits to its hotels.

Because repeat customers know a service, they are less costly to serve. Expectation levels are established. But, more important, customers know the role they are expected to play in the service delivery process and how to play it. Thus, weekly users of the Trump Shuttle air services between New York and Washington require less orientation time and information than first-time Shuttle flyers.

Loyal customers are the most vocal in telling others about their successful, long-standing "love affairs" with services, particularly in a world where service excellence may be hard to find. Nordstrom's fashion goods customers are the chain's most effective form of advertising. In fact, they allow Nordstrom stores to spend a smaller proportion of sales dollars on media advertising than any of their major competitors.

Holding on to existing customers costs less than attracting new ones. One study by the Forum Corporation shows that the cost of retaining a loyal customer is only one-fifth that of attracting a new one.[2]

A more recent study by Fred Reichheld and Earl Sasser has documented the dramatic impact of customer retention on profits in a sample of service-producing firms.[3] They argue that the pattern of profits over the life of a customer relationship resembles that shown in Figure 3–1 for a hypothetical service business. If a firm can document such a profitability pattern for its customers, it can then answer the question, "What's it worth to increase our retention rate by five percentage points?" Reichheld and Sasser calculated the impact of five-point retention rate increases for a sample of service firms. While the power of retention depends upon the shape of the curve in Figure 3–1 in the cases tested, and the point on the curve at which a company finds

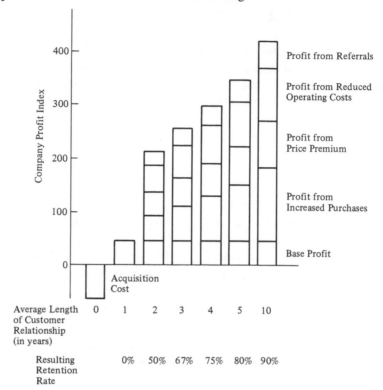

FIGURE 3–1 The Impact of Customer Retention on Profits
SOURCE: Frederick F. Reichheld and W. Earl Sasser Jr., "Zero Defections: Quality Comes to Services," *Harvard Business Review*, September–October 1990, pp. 105–111.

itself, the percentage increases in profits ranged from 25% to 125%, as shown in Figure 3–2. As a result of this work, they argue that retaining customers should be a strategic focus of most service forms.

Those who recognize the increasing value of a loyal customer over time devote unusual effort to understanding customer needs and behavior patterns and ways of addressing them.

NEW INSIGHTS INTO CUSTOMER BEHAVIOR

Jan Carlzon, CEO of Scandinavian Airlines System, tells of the efforts of the management of a charter airline under his direction, Vingresor, to develop the ideal resort in the Canary Islands for Swedish senior citizens. The concept involved apartment-type suites in a secluded spot with a shallow pool located away from noisy beaches; equipped with social rooms and

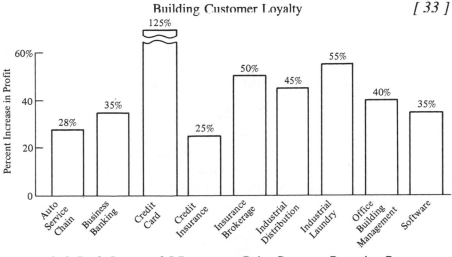

FIGURE 3–2 Profit Impact of 5 Percentage Point Customer Retention Rate Increase

SOURCE: Frederick F. Reichheld and W. Earl Sasser Jr., "Zero Defections: Quality Comes to Services," *Harvard Business Review*, September–October 1990, pp. 105–111.

familiar Swedish appliances and products; and staffed with matronly, down-to-earth people with medical training. Arrangements would be made for brief excursions from the facility (with frequent restroom stops), and with local restaurants to prepare certain Scandinavian items for their menus.

The concept was described to members of a Stockholm retirement club. One objected to the idea of a remote location near a pool, preferring instead the excitement of people and the beach. Another suggested that he would visit a place for a week, return home, and immediately begin looking for a new place to go, largely based on price. Yet another suggested that Vingresor instead add Mexico to its list of tours, having already visited other fascinating places such as Sri Lanka and Gambia. One by one, differences between responses and Vingresor managers' assumptions were considered and somehow rationalized by the managers as surely not being typical. As Carlzon described it:

> And so it continued, until finally not a single retiree there expressed interest in our wonderful product. We thanked them for coming to Vingresor and promptly dismissed all of their options. We stubbornly invested $100,000 in beautiful, tabloid-size brochures with huge block letters. And our matronly nurses were left waiting for pensioners who never showed up.[4]

Vingresor's management didn't commit every mistake in the book. At least they asked potential customers what they wanted. But they didn't listen to what people were saying. And they probably committed a common error of assuming that anyone of a certain age would have roughly the same needs and preferences. Once again, they were trapped by a reliance on customer demographics (such as age, location, education, or wealth) rather than the psychographics of customer life-styles, perceived risks, and thought patterns.

This vignette suggests again the importance of knowing not only what services customers want where, when, and at what prices, but also learning about why they want these services and how they want them delivered in order to be able to design truly differentiated service capabilities. This can lead not only to an understanding of customer needs, service evaluation processes, and demand patterns, but also better knowledge of the intensity of customer loyalty.

UNDERSTANDING CUSTOMER NEEDS

Too many managers view their customers in terms of things such as their sales volume or location (for commercial services) or their income or educational status (for consumer services). These so-called demographic measures are easy to obtain but of limited value because they tell us next to nothing about what people think about purchases and use of services.

Emphasizing Psychographics. It is often necessary to explore more basic aspects of their needs with customers. This quickly establishes the importance of psychographics—the way people think, feel, and behave—in identifying potential profitable market segments and estimating demands.

Consider, for example, one of the most maligned services in the United States, auto maintenance and repair. At the very heart of the problem are the franchised, authorized auto dealers who service the products they sell. Traditionally, of course, the dealer system in the United States, through which authorized, warranted service has been delivered, is organized by brand. This implicitly assumes that everyone who drives a Chevrolet, for example, has the same set of needs. They drive the same product and therefore must experience the same problems, both in operation and service. This perhaps explains, but doesn't excuse, why both manufacturers and dealers have made such little effort to find out much about the needs of owners of the autos they make and sell.

Small, so-called "focus" groups of customers provide excellent ways of exploring the expectations, fears, and needs for which numbers can be developed by subsequent survey research. Auto owners in every focus group that we have observed within minutes have suggested that service has little to do with the brand of the auto under discussion. Instead, people approach the universal service problem differently depending on their knowledge of autos, their experience and interest in fixing their own auto, whether they are men or women negotiating what is essentially a male-dominated minefield, the age and value of the autos they drive, and the pleasure that they derive from driving high-performance vehicles.

Identifying Perceived Risks. Human beings are walking bundles of perceived risks, whether on the job or in their daily personal lives. These risks are born out of a lack of adequate information, knowledge, and resulting self-confidence. Risk may be economic (especially for ''big-ticket'' purchases such as insurance), social (characteristically involving decisions about services affecting personal appearance or image), medical (usually involving high personal risk), or legal (either resulting from action or failure to act).

Research told us long before auto dealers began to alter their product-oriented service programs that, increasingly, automobile service was being requested by less-experienced owners with a wider range of more intensively perceived risks. These perceived risks arose in large part from insecurity resulting from a lack of control of the process and the absence of clues to the likely quality of the complex service being purchased. As a result, a large proportion of the people, both male and female, seeking auto repair service have both high risk perceptions and low expectations for quality of service they are likely to receive, as suggested in the lower left-hand quadrant of Figure 3–3. Invariably, this situation suggests a significant opportunity for a breakthrough service.

Changes on the part of auto dealers have resulted slowly from the realization that the service system can no longer be designed primarily for customers who are presumed to have considerable knowledge of the product and are comfortable dealing with someone with mechanical but not human

Customer Needs

		Complex	Simple
Customer Knowledge of the Service Process	High	Moderate Perceived Risk and Expectations	Low Perceived Risk and High Expectations
	Low	High Perceived Risk and Low Expectations	Moderate Perceived Risk and Expectations

FIGURE 3–3 The Effects of Customer Needs and Knowledge on Levels of Perceived Risk and Service Expectations

skills. Such research has led to the design of auto repair services centered, to a growing degree, around full disclosure of pricing methods, so-called posted "menu" prices for basic jobs, more accessible facilities, and service personnel with the ability to discuss potential work with increasingly unknowledgeable owners.

Watching "Migration" Patterns. An understanding of customer needs can be gained too from a study of critical events in the service consumption process, such as a switch by the customer from one competitor's service to another's or from one type of service to another. When confronted by the fact that consumers in large numbers increasingly patronize auto service chains and continue to seek out corner garages for "unauthorized" repair work, we have tried to find out why customers have sought these other alternatives. We have been told that the chains provide dependable, fast service at predetermined prices at convenient locations, often with little need for interaction with people who are used to dealing with "amateur" customers. On the other hand, corner garages, often with one or two mechanics, are patronized because of the ease with which customers can communicate with the mechanic, the visibility of the service, the integrity of the mechanic, and in some cases the convenient location of the garage.

There are many cues here to aid in the development of breakthrough services for automobiles. Many are being heeded by entrepreneurs who have introduced us to Speedy Muffler changes, Jiffy Lube lubrication services, and Aamco Transmissions replacements, and in the process have produced one of the most marked of all "migrations" in service patterns in recent years. The cues exist for all services if only we seek them out.

For example, many professions have been enhanced in part through the obfuscation of the service process and the service encounter to the buyer by means of incomprehensible language, the use of mysterious tools and documents, and other means. But breakthrough service providers are attempting to reduce perceived risk both through the simplification of seemingly complex services as well as the education of the buyer. For example, most legal services are relatively routine, thus providing an opportunity for organizations such as Hyatt Legal Services to open store-front, walk-in offices where perfectly acceptable wills and contracts can be prepared efficiently and in a "low-risk" environment.

UNDERSTANDING CUSTOMER EVALUATION PROCESSES

Any exploration of customer needs, expectations, and fears associated with a service suggests immediately the importance of helping customers evaluate services. This is reinforced by work setting forth basic differences between goods and services from a customer's viewpoint.

Economist Philip Nelson has categorized products as possessing search qualities and experience qualities.[5] Search qualities are qualities that a consumer can determine prior to purchasing a product; experience qualities are those that can be determined after the purchase. M. R. Darby and E. Karni subsequently added credence qualities to this topology, those that a customer can't determine even after purchase and use.[6] An analysis of any set of goods and services suggests that the former possess search qualities to a larger degree. Services, on the other hand, largely are associated with experience and credence qualities, as suggested in Figure 3–4.

As a result, Valarie Zeithaml has proposed and is exploring a number of hypotheses associated with the manner in which customers evaluate their prospective use of various services as opposed to products. Among others, she advances the following propositions.[7]

1. Customers perceive greater risks when buying services than when buying products.

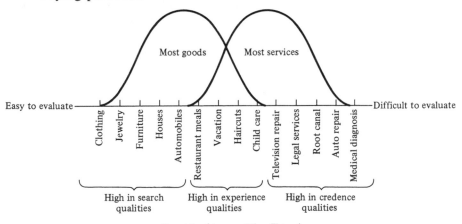

FIGURE 3–4 Implications of Product and Service Qualities for Their Marketing and Delivery
SOURCE: Reprinted from Valarie A. Zeithaml, "How Consumer Evaluation Processes Differ Between Goods and Services," in James H. Donnelly and William R. George, eds., *Marketing of Services*, pp. 186–189 at p. 186. Published by the American Marketing Association, Chicago, 1981.

2. Customers seek and rely more on information from personal sources than from impersonal sources when evaluating services prior to purchase.

3. Customers use price and physical facilities as the major cues to service quality.

4. For many nonprofessional services, the customer's set of alternatives include self-provision of the service.

5. The customer set of competing options is smaller for services than for products, largely because of the difficulty of obtaining exposure to a wide array of competing service alternatives.

6. Consumers engage in greater post-purchase evaluation and information-seeking with services than with products.

Clearly, these hypotheses are more important for some services than for others, and for some customers, as we saw earlier in our examination of concerns about auto repair service. But they provide a starting point for the design and delivery of many services. They are of particular importance for services high in the experience or credence qualities diagrammed in Figure 3–4. They help us understand both challenges faced by Hartford Steam Boiler Inspection and Insurance Company (HSB) and the substantial barriers which that organization has built against competition.

ADDRESSING PERCEIVED RISKS

Both inspection and insurance services are high in credence qualities. The customer doesn't know how good the services are even after they've been performed. Inspection by an HSB engineer often leads to recommendations for changes in the configuration or use of a boiler. These changes may be required prior to the issuance of an insurance policy. The customer has little way of knowing whether they are necessary. Only the breakdown of a boiler shortly after inspection might provide evidence of poor service quality. It requires that HSB's engineers communicate visible signals of their expertise and professionalism, including the way they act, talk, and even dress on the job. (Some always show up for an early morning inspection with coffee and doughnuts for the equipment operators.) And it requires prompt preparation and clear communication of recommendations for change, along with reasons why the changes are important.

Similarly, the quality of insurance is never tested until it is needed. It requires that insurance policies be issued in a timely fashion in an easy-to-understand format. It requires that needs for changes in insurance, perhaps dictated by law, be brought to a customer's attention in a timely fashion by HSB underwriters. And it requires that claims processes be responsive, prompt, and reasonable. These are the only tangible cues that the customer has that the service is satisfactory.

Having achieved a reputation for high-quality inspection and insurance services, however, HSB can rely on its large network of satisfied customers to sell its service to new accounts. If referrals have the impact that Zeithaml attributes to this kind of service, they represent a significant barrier to the entry of would-be competitors who cannot provide similar evidence of service excellence.

One might assume that it would be difficult to build customer loyalty for these types of services. But Zeithaml suggests that loyalty for services may be greater than that for products.[8] While there may be many exceptions to this general statement, the experience of Hartford Steam Boiler Inspection and Insurance Company is not one. As the service manager of an HSB customer told one of us, "If I tried to replace that insurance contract, my operating people in the plant would let me know about it."[9]

Similarly, consider the challenges facing the provider of cleaning services, particularly to hospitals. This is the service that many of The ServiceMaster Company's people manage for many organizations. Theoretically, good cleaning service is invisible. If results become visible in the form of dust, they are evidence only of poor service. In hospitals, confronted with their own problems of offering services that are high in credence qualities, it is important that the facilities pass inspection not only by staff, but also by patients and their visitors. This requires that evidence of good service be provided for a largely intangible service high in credence qualities both before and after a sale to a new customer.

For this reason, one of the most critical events in ServiceMaster's sales process to hospital administrators is a visit to the company's headquarter offices and laboratories in Downers Grove, Illinois. Here a prospective customer not only has an opportunity to meet the senior management of the company, but also observe what is one of the world's most extensive laboratories for the development of industrial cleaning processes, products, and materials. These, along with the references from other satisfied customers, are the tangible pieces of evidence needed to sell a service with high credence qualities.

Another important event in the post-sale service delivery process is the "break-in" cleanup. On the eve of a new contract, ServiceMaster's management descends on the facilities of a new account and leads, often by example, the hospital's custodial staff through a thorough cleaning of the premises. A focal point of the effort is the stripping and refinishing of the floors of the hospital's lobby, the first thing noticed by everyone entering the facility on the first day of a new contract. This, along with the continuing professionalism and expertise of the company's management assigned to the facility, provides tangible evidence of service quality where little may have existed before.

Breakthrough services provide assurance where little is obvious from the nature of the service itself. They make the intangible tangible and the invisible visible for customers. In the process, they reduce customers' perceived risks.

WOWING CUSTOMERS ON THE FIRST ENCOUNTER

Good service organizations set out to meet customers' expectations. Outstanding service companies specifically seek to impress customers in ways they will never forget. They do it by managing first (and last) impressions and by balancing attention to substance and "style" in designing and delivering services.

MANAGING THE "SERVICE BOOKENDS"[10]

First impressions count. That's why ServiceMaster's management team devotes so much attention to the "break-in" hospital cleanup and especially the stripping and refinishing of hospital lobby floors. It explains in part why Nordstrom, the stand-out fashion department store chain, employs a live pianist outfitted with formal attire and a grand piano instead of "canned" music in its stores. And it explains why the Lex Service Group in England assigns its best people as service advisors to diagnose problems in automobiles brought in for service at its repair shops. It has concluded that the diagnosis of the problem is the most critical element of good service. But it also creates a great first impression in customers' minds.

The stage for the service experience is set in the first few minutes of the situation. Once the tone has been established, it is difficult to change a customer's impression of what follows.

Last impressions count too. The last few minutes of a service experience may cement the final impression of the event, which influences a customer's willingness to make a repeat purchase or provide positive "word-of-mouth" selling to a potential customer. These first and last parts of the service encounter are the "service bookends." Great service organizations get the service bookends right, as well as the part in the middle.

For example, Rusty Pelican Restaurants' management formed what it called the ''90-second committee'' to study the first and last seconds of a guest's experiences at their restaurants. As a result of this committee, the valet parking and reception were substantially changed to be much more sensitive to the customers. Likewise, promptness and clarity of bill presentation were reorganized to be excellent at even the most busy periods.

In the same spirit, Beth Israel Hospital in Boston, with a reputation for quality medical services, has a doorman who receives patients and helps with parking and other arrival problems. The patient is escorted to a private, quiet zone where both medical tests and financial formalities for admission are carried out very quickly in a calm and convenient manner away from the high traffic. The patient is required to move only a few feet during the process and is unlikely to see any other patients. The preliminaries completed, the patient is introduced to the nurse from the care unit to which he or she is assigned who escorts the patient to a room in a matter of a few minutes. Checkout at Beth Israel Hospital is similarly orchestrated to minimize anxiety and hassle. The doorman arranges transportation and transfer to the vehicle. Follow-up calls from the hospital assure the patient that the caring continues after checkout.

At the Lex Service Group in England, all autos brought in for repair are washed. This practice is based on the well-known fact that clean cars run better than dirty ones. (Do you doubt it?)

BALANCING SUBSTANCE AND STYLE

Outstanding service may begin and end with a good measure of style. But without substance, first and last impressions alone will not create customer loyalty. That's why the Lex Service Group combines substance and style in the first contact with customers. A good service advisor not only creates a good impression; he or she can provide the proper diagnosis that enables (1) an ailing auto to be assigned to the right mechanic; (2) the availability of necessary parts to be checked immediately; (3) work to be scheduled realistically; and (4) an accurate estimate of the time and cost required for repairs to be made for the customer.

The first impression is merely the promise of the impressive service that is designed to follow at ServiceMaster, Nordstrom, Beth Israel Hospital, and other outstanding service firms. In fact, it establishes the standard to be lived up to by the day-to-day service delivery activities in ways that we will describe throughout the remainder of the book.

DEVELOPING BETTER CUSTOMERS

Truly innovative service firms have made better customers of us by both measuring and managing our expectations, making us more enlightened users of services, encouraging habitual usage patterns, and forcing us to change everyday practices to make us more successful. In the process we become more satisfied and more profitable customers.

MEASURING EXPECTATIONS

Customers often are much better able to articulate expectations about results to be achieved from a service than they are about the way services are delivered and the kinds of encounters they involve. As customers, we want our car fixed when we take it for repairs. But we are less articulate in expressing ourselves about how we expect to be treated and the relative importance of process and results in our evaluation of service quality.

Customers may be able to express expectations about some kinds of service processes more clearly than others. Even then it is often done indirectly. Several companies that measure continually and carefully, for example, find that five minutes in a line is the breakpoint between acceptable service for banking transactions or the purchase of airline tickets (although probably too long for the purchase of a lottery ticket just prior to the deadline for purchases). Although it has been found that customers are not good judges of time, they can tell a questioner whether the time spent in line was too long, leaving it to the questioner to measure the actual time.

Expectations and perceptions of the personal interaction that takes place in the encounter are much more difficult to elicit from customers. This does not deter breakthrough service providers who attempt to elicit such information through efforts ranging from focus group interviews to simulated transactions. They design services that err on the safe side of presumed expectations of most customers. It was through these kinds of efforts, for example, that British Airways, in the example cited in Chapter 1, learned that beyond basically reliable air transport, its passengers wanted from British Airways employees an expression of care and concern, spontaneity, problem solving, and the ability to recover from mistakes. The last of these items, recovery ability, was perhaps the greatest surprise to the airline's management and compelled it to focus on recovery as a distinct area of service management.[11]

MANAGING EXPECTATIONS

Customers often don't know what to expect or have the wrong notion of what they should expect from a service. Given our previous conclusion that service quality is what is delivered in relation to what is expected, inadequate information about what to expect often represents a root cause of perceived poor service. As we saw earlier, this is particularly critical where customers have high perceived risks and need some degree of control over the service process.

Such things as posted prices for auto repair and step-by-step instructions about what acquiring firms should expect from an investment banker's merger and acquisition services not only alleviate perceived risks, they make better customers.

Every effort is made by breakthrough service providers to instruct customers in what to expect. Patients at Shouldice Hospital in Toronto, Canada, are told on arrival exactly what to expect at each stage of the treatment for their hernia afflictions. This includes when they might expect their bowels to begin moving after the operation.[12] Similarly, American Airlines flight attendants on flights to American's largest hub at busy and potentially confusing Dallas–Fort Worth International Airport attempt to inform passengers in advance through on-board maps and flight information what to expect in changing planes at the hub.

Developing expectations in advance is not risky if a service is designed to fulfill the promise this implies. It can be a form of control if it is done publicly and directly to customers. However, this requires advance notice and training for employees if they are to feel that they've been given proper opportunity to deliver on their company's promise.

CREATING ENLIGHTENED USERS

Enlightened users often are regarded with some amount of suspicion by many service providers. Too often, it is thought, they are the ones who find ways of "beating the system." Frequent long-distance telephone users, for example, for years have developed ways of signaling by placing person-to-person calls to people who they knew were not at the receiving end of the call. Not only was this used as a way of placing a free call, it consumed valuable operator time at the telephone company. Because much of the problem resulted from the high minimum cost of a long-distance call, rates keyed to the actual "connect" time used for a call have alleviated the problem. (Given the operator time required for the practice, one could argue that a breakthrough service offering 15-second free calls might actually have saved telephone companies money.) The new rates have been accompanied by advertising campaigns designed to teach customers how to make the most effective use of the new rates.

Enlightened users are critical to the success of self-service. A growing list of companies, including Dun & Bradstreet and TRW in commercial credit services and CompuServe and The Source in consumer information services, are allowing customers to gain access to a central database from which they can extract the particular information they seek.[13] Experience has shown that the more adept customers become at using the service, the heavier their usage becomes. The inability to educate customers has proven to be a barrier to the development of some services. For years, Chemical Abstracts, a computerized information service for scientists, has sought a way to educate individual researchers in the use of its service. In many cases, it had to settle for a program to educate librarians who are most often asked for assistance in researching published materials by scientists less adept in the use of the service.

Service leaders help their customers learn how to use the service to the mutual benefit of both, regardless of the short-term impact on revenues. For example, leading utilities supplying everything from water to electricity have launched programs showing customers how to conserve such resources. In the short run, this has enabled utilities to avoid adding expensive capacity. In the long run, however, this will make what service is available more valuable, providing justification for higher rates to customers who have learned how to do more with less. The same philosophy could be applied effectively by suppliers of other forms of resource-based products and services, especially petroleum companies.

INCREASING SWITCHING COSTS

Loyalty to a service results from positive incentives as well as the natural desire to avoid learning new service "routines." Economists have termed the phenomenon the development of switching costs.

Positive incentives often involve the creation of some kind of "membership" mentality in customers. Frequent travelers need only sort through their wallet cards designating membership in airline, hotel, rental auto, and other "clubs" to verify the increasing use of incentives to encourage the repeated use of a service. Such incentives make each repeated use more valuable by moving the customer closer to some promised payoff at a specified service level. They are most often used where it is otherwise difficult to differentiate one competing service from another. However, experience has shown that they are not powerful enough to encourage continued usage of poorly performed services. Rather they provide a service firm an opportunity to show what it can do over a prolonged period of time rather than during a single encounter.

Habits die hard among both individual customers and commercial users of services. Because services so often involve customers in some kind of routine, these routines have to be learned over time as we get better in the usage of the service. This helps explain why the Eastern Airline Shuttle between New York, Boston, and Washington was able to develop such a loyal following. Even though passengers complained about the "bare bones" nature of the service that originally substituted in-flight ticketing for beverage service, they nevertheless were willing to forgo any amenities for the guarantee of a seat without a prior reservation, and the time-saving nature of the boarding process and other elements of the service. More important, frequent users developed a set of habits that were an extension of their early morning toilet and breakfast routines. Many probably felt they could walk the route to the shuttle blindfolded if necessary.

Even though repeated competitors, including Pan American Airlines and New York Air, sought to penetrate the Northeastern U.S. shuttle market by offering reserved seats, on-board amenities, and even half-priced tickets, the Eastern Shuttle maintained a remarkably high market share, discouraging such competitors for years. It was only after repeated references in the press to labor unrest, allegations of unsafe practices, and the potential sale of the Eastern Shuttle that customers became willing to learn a new routine, learning how to get to the Pan American gates, and remembering their new parking locations in the airport garage. Once customers invest in switching costs, they are hard to entice back to their former service. That's why outstanding service performers invest so much effort in building switching costs in the first place.

MAKING CUSTOMERS BETTER AT WHAT THEY DO

The very best service providers are able to require that their customers become better at what they do, and at the same time, become better customers, as a condition of supplying their service. They are like the U.S. Marines, looking only for a few good men and women. Only the most effective services can command this kind of customer obeisance.

Hartford Steam Boiler's customers are not the same after they've bought the company's inspection and insurance services. Unless they are already operating their boiler and related equipment in flawless fashion, HSB's engineers invariably spot potential improvements in management practice and often make them the condition of most favorably rated (priced) insurance coverage.

Similarly, hospitals utilizing The ServiceMaster Company's management of hospital support services become better places to work for everybody, but especially for support personnel, particularly if quality of work life is measured in terms of clear supervision, individual development, and fair appraisal and compensation for work performed.

The Malcolm Baldrige National Quality Awards that were recently established in the United States appear in themselves to represent a breakthrough service in this respect. The awards offer the promise of recognition for excellence to only two manufacturing, two service, and two small business firms each year. However, many competitors have entered the competition just to benefit from the learning process and possible improvement in practice which may result from the rigorous auditing process by the Baldrige Committee, which in itself is highly instructive.[14]

Many breakthrough services that we will be describing throughout the book change their customer's management practices forever as a central element of their respective strategies.

The most effective efforts to build loyalty have focused on the needs of selected customers that form the target for a service that we say is consciously "positioned" to meet such needs. It is our next concern.

4

Focusing and
Positioning the Service

The "pizza restaurant syndrome" is the scourge of the service sector. Its symptoms are an entrepreneur with a burning passion to develop a new service business and the certainty that his or her concept for the venture is the most ingenious and satisfying ever devised. Invariably, when described in detail, it turns out to be one more "pizza restaurant" started on a shoestring, undifferentiated in any important way from a million competitors, and doomed to failure.

When challenged to describe the "hook," the innovation (often counterintuitive) that provides unusual leverage of customer value over cost, the victim of the pizza restaurant syndrome can provide none. Invariably, the would-be entrepreneur has been overcome by the attraction of low-cost entry, the attractiveness of entrepreneurial independence, or the certainty that the new service will be the finest ever seen in the industry. Once again, the entrepreneur has succumbed to the siren song of the service business, forgetting the all-important concepts of focus and positioning.

ACHIEVING STRATEGIC FOCUS

Focus can create significant competitive advantage. It may be achieved by offering a wide range of services to a targeted group of customers (à la The ServiceMaster Company), a focused, "limited menu" service to a wide range of customers (à la United Parcel Service), or a limited range of services to a highly targeted set of customers (à la Hartford Steam Boiler Inspection and Insurance Company), as suggested in Figure 4–1. Regardless

Targeted Customer Segment

	Narrow		Broad	
Narrow ("Limited Menu")	*A la Hartford Steam Boiler*		*A la United Parcel Service*	
	Greatest Advantage:	Extreme focus	Greatest Advantage:	"Ownership" of an operating process
	Greatest Potential Problem:	Insufficient market potential	Greatest Potential Problem:	More comprehensive service concepts
	Primary Influence on Customer Behavior:	Low cost and good service	Primary Influence on Customer:	Good value for price
Broad	*A la ServiceMaster*		*A la Sears Roebuck*	
	Greatest Advantage:	"Ownership" of customers	Greatest Advantage:	Large potential and "one-stop shopping"
	Greatest Potential Problem:	Lack of operational focus	Greatest Potential Problem:	Lack of focus (being "all things to all people")
	Primary Influence on Customer Behavior:	Outstanding service based on knowledge of customer needs	Primary Influence on Customer Behavior:	?

Service Concept/ Operating Strategy

FIGURE 4–1 Focus on a Means of Influencing Customer Buying Behavior for Services

of the nature of focus, it facilitates the accumulation of information about customers, service offerings, or both which can be used to influence customer demand in ways that lead to benefits for customers and outstanding long-term performance for service providers. But enough of the abstract. Let's see how ServiceMaster, Nordstrom, United Parcel Service, Shouldice Hospital Limited, Hartford Steam Boiler, and Schlumberger use focus to influence customer behavior.

CUSTOMER-ORIENTED FOCUS

Understanding thoroughly and serving the needs of a targeted group of customers often requires the development of a customer-centered database and the growth of the service business through new offerings to existing customers.

The base on which The ServiceMaster Company's business is built is the management of custodial services performed for hospitals, in which it has become a worldwide leader since acquiring its first customer in 1962. Gradually, the company developed an "experience curve" for hospitals through what a former chairman, Kenneth Hansen, described as "listening."

When we began our hospital housekeeping management business we
. . . founded it on the cornerstone of hard listening. . . . From 1957 to
1959 Ken Wessner (the company's current chairman) and I worked in
tandem in a series of hearing sessions with individuals and groups of
men and women who were a direct part of hospital managements. . . .

As we listened, we thought we heard administrators saying that their
time could be better used if they could have professional help for some
of the more nonpatient-related functions of their hospitals. . . .

As we listened, we seemed to hear administrators saying that the
hospital community was ready for the services of a specialist organization . . . one that would build itself on the hospital's objectives, and
blend itself into their needs.

At the same time, other companies heard there was going to be a lot
of money spent by hospitals for contract housekeeping. They
approached this job as some more buildings to clean. This is not what
we heard at all . . .[1]

Through this process, the company developed its capabilities for managing not only custodial activities but also food service, transportation, purchasing, and equipment maintenance. As its service package to hospitals has
grown to include most of the support services performed in hospitals, the
company's managers increasingly have sought to become regarded as members of their respective customers' management teams. Through this process, ServiceMaster has been able to influence customers' decisions in ways
that make their hospitals cleaner, safer, more congenial places in which to
carry out their primary objective, effective health care.

Many airlines target the business traveler as opposed to the leisure trav-
eller. The management of Fairfield Inn, the budget lodging chain operated
by the Marriott Corporation, carries this one step further by targeting the
"Road Warrior," the sales representative on a limited budget probably
driving from place to place and seeking a uniformly good lodging experience.

Similarly, Nordstrom in the fashion retailing business has targeted upscale shoppers of fashion goods by providing an array of "soft" goods
(apparel, shoes, cosmetics, and accessories) in abundant depth of assortments and maintaining twice the inventory per square foot of selling space
as the average of its competitors.[2]

Nordstrom places great emphasis on service to this targeted group of
customers, paying not only its salespeople but also its department managers
and buyers to an unusual degree in commissions based on sales. As a result,
all are found from time to time on the retail selling floor. Salespeople thus

get the idea that they are part of a buying-selling team. Buyers pick up valuable information from customers. And customers enjoy the benefits of the attention they receive. According to one account, "In Alaska, Nordstrom employees have been known to warm up cars while drivers spend a few more minutes shopping."[3] At the same time, of course, customers provide information to Nordstrom's "database." It's common practice at the store, for example, for salespeople to keep logs of customers' purchases and preferences so they can phone them about new merchandise they might like as it arrives at the store. Unlike their competitors, Nordstrom's salespeople keep these logs in all departments ranging from high-fashion evening wear to hosiery. This is truly a "learning curve" in action, as potent as any in manufacturing.

A strategy of focusing on and meeting an array of needs of one group of customers may be costly, but it often produces high margins associated with high value created for customers. In the case of Nordstrom, it has also led to productive use of expensive fixed facilities, with Nordstrom's sales per square foot regularly exceeding those for other major fashion store chains.

SERVICE-ORIENTED FOCUS

The service itself may be the most important source of focus. Companies that do one thing very well often enjoy cost and service advantages over less well-focused competitors. This realization has spawned an industry of firms specializing in servicing one part of an automobile. In the process, Jiffy Lube, Midas Muffler and Brake Shops, Aamco Transmissions, and others have achieved dominance over franchised auto dealers in their specialties. They offer their services to all comers desiring a particular type of auto service.

United Parcel Service (UPS) concentrates on doing one thing better than any other firm in the world. It will transport anyone's package between any two points in the United States as long as the package does not exceed length and size limits. Its eventual objective is to be able to do this between any two points in the world. (Think of that for a moment.) It offers the ultimate in "limited menu" service.

It is probably safe to say that no organization has so thoroughly analyzed and engineered such a relatively simple production process, enjoying its own "learning curve" benefits. The ability to focus attention on a narrow range of package-handling activities and capabilities has produced such good value, in terms of dependable service at low cost, that customers are willing to "play UPS's game," adhering to its limits of 70 pounds and 130 inches combined length, width, and height per package; putting up with its limited package-tracing capability; and even transporting their own packages to UPS's receiving depots where necessary.

Patients are willing to play Shouldice Hospital's game too, even though for years it has required that they get up from the operating table after an operation and walk to the door of the operating room with their surgeons, not without a certain amount of discomfort.[4] After a couple of hours' rest in a "semi-private" room shared with another patient, they are told to start exercising, possibly by making the trek required to get to a commercial television set, radio, or even telephone. Why do they do it? For any of a number of reasons associated with this Toronto hospital's focus.

Shouldice Hospital Limited only performs hernia operations, but not all kinds. Its staff of surgeons limits itself to inguinal hernias, for which there are perhaps three million operations in the world each year. Of those, nearly 8,000 are performed at Shouldice by surgeons who have logged as many as 30,000 such operations *each*. This tends to develop expertise, both in operating and recovery procedures. The more exercise immediately following the operation, the faster the recovery, of importance to busy people. And operating practice tends to make perfect, so much so that the hospital pioneered a completely different approach to the surgery. Even though Shouldice has many emulators among hospitals that are even performing the operation on an out-patient basis with no hospitalization, Shouldice's operations have a default rate (requiring a second operation) roughly twelve times better than the average for North American hospitals and carrying a price about one-third that of their competitors. This is all offered in a country club-like setting with good food and the opportunity to interact with "classmates" who have endured the same affliction. Little wonder that its patients are willing to travel long distance just to be "managed" by Shouldice's staff.

CUSTOMER- AND SERVICE-ORIENTED FOCUS

Truly outstanding service firms utilize several or all of these sources of focus. McDonald's, for example, built its core vision around fast food of good value (the service concept) aimed at families with small children and others attracted to time-saving dining (targeted market segments) achieved through an extremely limited menu of offerings with few options, especially in pre–Chicken McNuggets days (the operating strategy) and delivered through stores equipped to take the guesswork out of quality fast-food preparation and located near targeted customers (the service delivery system).

Hartford Steam Boiler directs its inspection and insurance services toward just a few industries, primarily utilities, papermakers, oil refiners, and food processors, those that make the most extensive use of boilers. As we saw earlier, it concentrates an army of engineers on these customers, an army that has collected a wealth of information and experience applicable to a narrow service concept, the inspection and insuring of steam boilers and closely related equipment.

Given this information, HSB's "experience curve" is difficult for competitors to duplicate, and the company's engineers are able to influence potential clients to alter their work sites in ways that make them more effective as well as lower the likelihood that they will ever produce an insurance claim. Ongoing preventive maintenance programs assure that the equipment insured remains a low risk. HSB pays fewer claims per thousand insured than its competitors. But its customers are not concerned. They are willing to let themselves be "managed" by HSB's engineers to achieve better results in their respective plants.

Similarly, Schlumberger's "wire-line service" engineers literally direct their oil company customers' drilling efforts at times.[5] Using the world's largest data base of oil drilling experiences under all conditions, combined with delicate sensing and computing equipment hauled to the drilling site, Schlumberger's engineers command respect even from the largest drillers' geologists and drilling crew chiefs. They help produce results by assisting in decisions both about drilling direction and when to quit a probable dry hole and cut losses at a site. Their influence is strong and is reflected not only in the results of their customers but in Schlumberger's profits from the business as well.

COPING WITH PROBLEMS OF FOCUS

Companies attempting to be all things to all people, which by plan or default is what Sears, Roebuck appears to be doing in its retailing business, rarely achieve competitive advantage over their more focused rivals, at least not in terms that get translated into economic performance. Nor do they find effective ways of influencing customer buying behavior.

But their more focused rivals have problems of their own. Chief among these is that, with continued success, they achieve such high relative shares of limited markets that further significant growth is impossible without diversification. This explains why ServiceMaster has greatly broadened its targeted markets to provide a similar package of support services to schools and industrial firms as well as hospitals. In addition, it has expanded a franchised rug cleaning service to include additional services provided in the home, such as house cleaning and extermination services.

United Parcel Service has achieved such a high share of the market in the United States that it is now rapidly building new markets for the same service outside the United States. Hartford Steam Boiler has introduced a new "all-risk" insurance coverage that insures items other than boilers against various kinds of catastrophes.

If the experience of manufacturers is instructive here, all too rarely do new service products or markets meet or exceed the profit expectations of their developers. Further, firms offering expanded services to targeted markets they know (such as Hartford Steam Boiler) have a higher probability of meeting or exceeding expectations than those offering current services to newly developed markets (such as ServiceMaster or United Parcel Service). But all will achieve a higher frequency of success (though not necessarily a higher payoff) in their new endeavors than competitors who seek to grow through the simultaneous development of new services for new customers.[6]

POSITIONING

In the 1970s, two advertising executives, Al Ries and Jack Trout, coined the term "positioning" to signify the use of advertising and other promotional efforts to establish a place in, and a share of, a customer's mind.[7] Shortly thereafter, we learned and remembered that Avis tried harder (because it was No. 2), United flew the friendly skies, and *Sports Illustrated* was the third newsweekly.

Scholars and practitioners interested primarily in the marketing of services quickly broadened the concept. Christopher Lovelock, for example, expressed a concern "with the role of positioning in guiding development of marketing mix strategy for services that compete on more than just imagery. This entails decisions on substantive attributes that are known to be important to customers and that relate to product performance, price, and service availability (distribution)."[8]

More recently, Lynn Shostack and others have begun to point out that the effective positioning of a service involves much more than marketing efforts. At its heart, it includes the very design of the service itself and the way it is delivered.[9] Some years ago, Marshall McLuhan perhaps put it most succinctly when he asserted that the medium (the process) is the message (the product).[10]

When we withdraw money from a bank, we are concerned not only about getting our money but the nature of the transaction required to get it, whether or not it involves interacting with a human teller or a machine, and the positive or negative nature of the interaction itself. Our perception of quality is a combination of sensual responses to the service and the person or machine delivering it.

In a service, the concept of positioning is expanded to include not only the "product" (or service concept) itself, but also the "policies and practices" by which it is delivered (the operating strategy), the "place and plant" in which it is delivered (the service delivery system), the "provider" delivering it, and the "procurer" (or customer), who may be both changed by the service and play an important role in its delivery.[11] These "Ps" can be used to describe the profile of one firm's competitive position against others', as suggested in Figure 4-2.

Methods used for establishing a distinctive position suggest a rich pallet of alternatives available to firms in each of the several service industries. No one by itself is strong enough to support a position or fuel a positioning strategy. All are not available to players in every industry. But there are common threads running through many of these efforts.

Some of the most successful positioning efforts have included:

1. Careful attention to understanding results desired by potential customers, life-styles producing needs for such results, strengths and weaknesses of alternative methods available to customers in achieving the results, and the frustrations commonly encountered in attaining them. This involves paying as much attention to psychographics (how people think and behave) as well as demographics (where they live, how much they earn, and how well-educated they are).

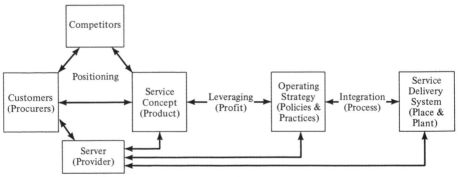

FIGURE 4-2 The "Ps" of Service Positioning[a]

[a] Adapted from J. L. Heskett, "Rethinking Strategy for Service Management." In D. E. Bowen, R. B. Chase, and T. G. Cummings (eds.), *Serving Management Effectiveness: Balancing Organization and Human Resources, Operations, and Marketing.* San Francisco: Jossey-Bass, 1990.

2. Based on this information, the coordinated positioning of a service around the Ps of product, policies, practices, process, place, plant, provider, procurer, and not least, profit.
3. "Myth-breaking" initiatives, built around the launching of a direct alternative to the "sacred cow" of a particular industry, often on some aspect of operations that is considered generic to the industry.
4. The design of services that "change" customers and the way they feel, live, or do business.
5. The design of the strategic service vision around a dramatic premise, often in the form of an unconditional promise to the customer.
6. As much close attention to servers, their personal development, and their shared values, as to customers.
7. Last (not first), communicating the desired position to potential customers.

These common themes reinforce the notion of the convergence of marketing, operations, and human resource management in the development and implementation of a position in a service firm. With the help of several well-known service providers, we next take a look at important steps in carrying out a broad positioning program.

IDENTIFYING POSITIONING OPPORTUNITIES

For the past two decades, marketing scholars and managers have been developing the concept and practice of positioning. Basically, it involves: (1) measuring customer needs, (2) grouping customers with similar needs into segments, (3) "mapping" such segments according to needs as well as their attractiveness, (4) estimating the extent to which competitors are able or willing to meet such needs, and (5) on the basis of this information and appraisal, identifying "niches," opportunities for the design and delivery of products or services better able than the competition to meet important customer needs.

To illustrate this process, let's turn to the market for home loans. Traditionally, research has suggested that it consisted of a number of segments, roughly corresponding to important life-cycle stages as well as major motives for borrowing. For the sake of discussion, consider several of these segments, not necessarily the most important.

The first of these segments for years was populated by the newly married couple with limited assets or income, seeking to purchase their first home. Primary needs of this segment are the availability of financing within the capacity of the couple to meet monthly payments of principle and interest.

Price, the rate of interest, is important only to the extent that it does not raise the total monthly cost of the loan over a maximum budgeted amount. By stretching loan payments over a longer period of time, lower monthly loan payments often are achieved at the cost of higher total interest payments over the life of a loan. The design and sheer availability of financing is much more important than price (interest rates) to members of this segment. We'll call this our nest-forming or "young nester" segment. As the age of "baby boomers" has advanced through the nesting stage, this segment's growth has leveled off somewhat.

With the arrival of family additions or the departure of grown children, residential needs of families change, leading to the decision to sell existing residences and purchase other ones. This segment of second-time or third-time residential buyers tends to be older, more knowledgeable about financing alternatives, and in possession of greater equity or other financial means than members of our first segment. As a result, its members often seek larger loans for larger homes (if the nest is being expanded significantly) in more expensive locations. Because both their credit rating and financing knowledge is likely to be higher than in their youth, members of this segment may be more sensitive to interest rates, shopping among two or more financial institutions rather than accepting the terms of the first one willing to loan them money. This segment, which we'll call "birdhouse builders," probably is as interested in price as it is in other terms of the loan, such as the length of period for repayment. (In fact, it may desire shorter repayment periods to minimize total outlays for interest or coincide with long-term retirement goals). This segment has shown steady, if not spectacular growth, in the United States.

A third group of borrowers may seek to finance a home not primarily because they need the money but instead because interest charges, at least in markets such as the United States, are deductible for income tax purposes. They too may tend to be more mature. And because of their motive for borrowing, they may have limited sensitivity to the rate of interest they pay as opposed to other loan provisions which, for example, may allow them to pay off the loan in advance without penalty with a change in the income tax law. We'll call this segment "tax minimizers." Its growth has slowed somewhat in the United States with the recent reduction of tax rates and hence interest deduction benefits for upper-income groups.

These three market segments can be found on the map shown in Figure 4–3. By arraying the market segments along the dimensions of "design vs. price sensitivity" and "growth in segment size," some idea of the relative attractiveness of each can be obtained. This is the first step in identifying a potential niche or positioning opportunity.

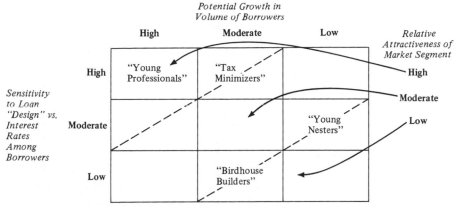

FIGURE 4–3 One View of the Relative Attractiveness of Several Market Segments for Home Financing.
SOURCE: Authors' conclusions, based on industry research.

Traditionally, borrowers in all of these segments have endured a lengthy, inconvenient process that involves a great deal of time and some risk. Often it involves finding the desired home, perhaps placing a winning bid for it, making a deposit subject to the approval for financing, completing the application for a loan, having credit references checked and financial capacity verified, having the property value appraised, possibly being refused by one or more lenders (banks, savings and loan institutions, or others) for all or some of the amount requested, and starting the financing or even the home-buying process over again. The process typically has taken weeks even after the selection of the property to be bought. Financial institutions eventually have responded to all financing needs of home buyers except timeliness and convenience. The home loan often has been regarded by managers of such institutions as a favor or privilege bestowed on a fortunate borrower who is expected to do a great deal of legwork and wait respectable periods of time while lenders carry out all manner of efforts to minimize their loan risks. The home lending industry has done a remarkable job of managing customers' expectations for timeliness and convenience down to the level of service that lenders have been willing to provide. All the while, they have failed to meet borrowers' real needs for these things. Ironically, members of the segment least needing timeliness, the "tax minimizers," probably receive the best service on this dimension because they have the best credit ratings and the least need for money with which to purchase a home.

The competitive positioning map in Figure 4–4 shows our market segments, arrayed in terms of the degree of attractiveness identified in Figure

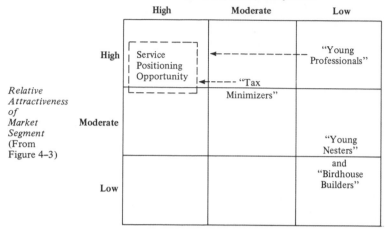

FIGURE 4–4 One View of the Competitive Market Opportunity Among Several Market Segments for Home Financing Designed to Meet Needs for Timeliness and Convenience
SOURCE: Authors' conclusions, based on industry research.

4–3, in relation to the degree to which their needs for timeliness and convenience are met by existing financial institutions. It suggests, however, a real opportunity for a financial institution willing to meet customers' needs for timeliness and convenience in home financing. This opportunity may be fueled by the growth of a new market segment with different expectations about service timeliness and convenience and a general trend toward immediate response in service delivery in our post-industrial society. Enter the rapidly growing segment of the "young professionals."

One product of the post-Vietnam era in the United States was rapid change in the life-styles of people in their twenties, leading to later marriage and child rearing, more emphasis on graduate professional study, and a stronger career orientation for a growing group of young people with good incomes, few family responsibilities, and little leisure time. In large numbers, this group has turned to condominium ownership as a form of investment as well as one of the few "roots" in an otherwise rootless professional life. Members of this segment were reared in an age of instant gratification, can command financing, have become used to demanding and paying for good services, and have little time to deal with the seemingly endless steps involved in locating and financing a residence. Clearly this is an attractive segment (as suggested in Figure 4–3) whose needs are not being met by the financial establishment (as indicated in Figure 4–4). It represents a real opportunity for a breakthrough service, one recognized early on by Robert D. Horner, chairman of Citicorp Mortgage Corporation.

DESIGNING AND POSITIONING THE BREAKTHROUGH SERVICE[12]

Horner's response was to encourage the development of what has been called McMortgage, the Jiffy Loan, Fast-Money, and the Fifteen-Minute Mortgage. According to Horner, "There's no reason why in this computerized society, you shouldn't be able to walk into an office, apply for and receive a legally binding home-loan commitment in 15 minutes."[13] And he means walk into an office sight unseen and walk out with a loan commitment for up to $500,000, 15 minutes later. That's the objective that he set for his organization. As Horner put it: "Given the speed Americans now expect and receive in their dealings with everything from food to lubrication, an instant commitment should be the performance standard mortgage lenders aspire to attain."[14]

This clearly required "myth breaking" initiatives, the design of services that change the way customers do business, and the development of a strategic service vision around a dramatic premise, the instant home loan. The stage was set for the development and positioning of a breakthrough service. Horner's staff at Citicorp Mortgage Corporation went to work on the Ps of service positioning.

The *procurer* or target market would be the time-conscious borrower willing to pay a premium for a fast loan commitment. The *product* would be a commitment identical to one now requiring an average waiting period of 30 days. The *process* would require: (1) on-line computer networks connecting Citibank with its loan issuing offices and major credit-check bureaus, allowing a thorough screening of an applicant's credit references in minutes, and (2) a computer-driven loan application appraiser, utilizing artificial intelligence as the underwriter based on a computer analysis of personal information submitted by an applicant. This was combined with the practice of overnight property appraisals for those properties not already appraised at the time of application, with the immediate loan commitment to be adjusted downward only in the event of an unexpectedly low appraisal.

Horner's organization set out to develop all of these things. As for *plant* and *provider,* it was decided to divorce both from the typical lender. As a result, Citicorp Mortgage was the first to design and market a 15-minute mortgage commitment through real estate brokers' and builders' offices. Immediately after completing a bid for a home and a purchase contract, a loan applicant can get a mortgage commitment on the spot. Training for providers, brokers' employees, involves methods for gaining access to and administering the computer-driven loan appraisal programs as well as channels for referring those who "flunk" the application process to special Citicorp Mortgage counselors to see if special financing can be arranged. Initial reactions from brokers able to break the financing bottleneck and provide a complete service have been very positive; both their jobs and their control over the success of the process have been expanded. The service eventually will be offered to all 4,000 participating real estate brokerages and builders affiliated with Citicorp's "Mortgage Power" program.

If further certification of Citicorp Mortgage's accomplishments as a breakthrough service designer is needed, it is provided by the fact that competitors are rushing to develop their own versions of the 15-minute mortgage commitment. Given the coordination among the positioning "Ps" that it requires, it may not be quite as easy to emulate as it might appear on the surface. It serves to illustrate the guidelines for truly creative service development and positioning. And it suggests a wide range of possibilities worth exploring at greater length, many of which can be emulated only with great difficulty.

COMMUNICATING THE DESIRED POSITION

Only after the target market segment has been identified and the service concept, operating strategy, and service delivery system (identified by the "Ps" of service positioning in Figure 4–2) put in place is it time to communicate the position to a potential customer. American Airlines illustrates this principle.

American consistently has targeted the business traveler. Among the most important results desired by these clients is on-time performance. So American's management in recent years consistently has made an effort to achieve such results by reorganizing boarding procedures (a frequent cause of late departures contributing to late arrivals), revamping unscheduled repair procedures, and adjusting schedules to reflect more realistic operating times. All of these efforts have given airline personnel a better chance of performing on-time service successfully, a source of high morale. Only after making sure that all of this was in place and working, as reflected in industry on-time performance statistics, did American set out to communicate its results-oriented position to business travelers through an advertising program proclaiming it the "On-Time Machine." Little wonder that this dominated its rival United Airlines' recent advertising campaign in the minds of business travelers, a campaign suggesting that United represented "Clout."

COMPETITIVE ADVANTAGE
THROUGH CONTRARY POSITIONING

Citicorp Mortgage could have continued to emulate its competition, adhering to accepted mortgage lending industry practice and relying on the good name of its parent company to attract business to its doors. But emulation as a strategy restricts alternatives and the range of opportunity available to a competitor. It often requires "brute force" efforts to bring more money or more people to bear on the task of supplying largely undifferentiated services, taking us back to the pizza restaurant syndrome. This is positioning by management abdication, given the wide range of possibilities for differentiation available in every service industry.

As an alternative, the company's management could have decided to limit itself to a marketing ploy to establish a distinctive position in the minds of its potential customer. This is in part what Robert Townsend did when he launched Avis's "We're only number 2 . . . we try harder" campaign against rental auto industry leader Hertz, shrewdly using it both to give the firm positive recognition in the minds of consumers and as a marketing device within the organization to motivate Avis employees.[15] But breakthrough service positioning is much more than a marketing ploy, especially one with more fanfare than substance. The recent acquisition of Avis by its employees, with emphasis on monthly employee-management sessions producing innovations and other improvements in performance that has tripled the value of a worker's share in the company in its first two years, gives Avis a much better chance of overtaking rival Hertz than any previous effort to market the company and its services to customers and employees through an advertising campaign and decorative buttons.[16] And it is just such a broadly based positioning effort that Citibank Mortgage elected to pursue.

Positioning opportunity may arise out of outmoded industry practice, as Citicorp Mortgage Corporation concluded. This is especially true when prevailing practice fails to reflect change in social and economic behavior of customer segments. Changing laws, for example when entire industries are deregulated, may provide opportunity for competitive advantage. At other times, it may be the development of a superior technology, such as that for one-hour photo processing. This all makes positioning a bit like shooting at a moving target (one or more market segments) with a less-than-perfect gunsight while being jostled by several competitors trying to hit the same target.

One firm's positioning success may suggest competitive alternatives. For example, the success of McDonald's operating strategy is inarguable. And yet it has provided opportunities for competitors to fashion effective business strategies through contrary positioning. They have involved efforts to distance themselves from McDonald's by playing their offerings off against those of their major, highly focused competitor.

CONTRARY POSITIONING

Burger King for years has advised people you can "Have It Your Way," a conscious effort to provide an alternative to McDonald's mass-produced, one-quality hamburger to more discriminating diners wishing to add their own favorite condiments to a sandwich with meat that is grilled rather than fried. The inability of Burger King's management in recent years to effectively communicate this basic strategy does little to dim the brilliance of the concept, especially in view of the fact that the effectiveness with which McDonald's management carried out it strategy left few major openings for competitors.

Wal-Mart Stores, Inc., has developed a science of locating its stores close to smaller- and middle-sized markets largely populated by consumers with moderate incomes seeking good value in their purchases, markets that one Wal-Mart store can dominate. Its management knows precisely where it does not want to operate stores and, until recently has studiously avoided the large metropolitan areas populated by K Mart, Sears, and other of its major competitors.

The contrary position adopted by other firms at times has flown in the face of generally held beliefs, industry practices, and unwritten codes of business behavior. Breakthrough positions have violated customs, completely restructuring industries in the process. We're told by those who have achieved them that they often result from an informal, inferential, largely undocumented process characterized by the following questions:

1. What do members of various customer segments want?
2. To what extent is this conditioned by what they have gotten?
3. To what extent can prospective customers identify what they want beyond the boundaries of what they have gotten?
4. In what ways have traditionally expressed customer needs been addressed?
5. How are the typical building blocks of service concept, operating strategy, and service delivery system used for establishing competitive position in an industry?
6. What are the "laws" of the industry, associated with generally ac-

cepted problems, constraints, and competitive practice, often resulting in an unstated, but effective, conspiracy against change?

7. What are nontraditional, counterintuitive, ways of addressing realized or unrealized customer needs?
8. Do they leverage value over cost? For whom?
9. How easy are nontraditional, "law-breaking" positions or methods
   of achieving them to emulate or defend?
10. In view of this, how do we best break the "law" or existing industry
    "conspiracy"? Is it worthwhile to do? How do we find out?

PROBING CUSTOMERS' "OUTRAGEOUS THOUGHTS"

In identifying needs and ways of meeting them, customers have difficulty
thinking beyond the range of their previous experiences. Had entrepreneurs
listened to customer reactions to descriptions of heretofore unknown product
or service concepts, we probably would not have access to xerography,
facsimile transmission, or cellular telephone service today.

Upon being prompted to think beyond the range of previous experience,
customers are notably unreliable in estimating reasonable prices or the degree to which they would use a hitherto unavailable product or service.

Shortly after the deregulation of the passenger airline industry, one of us
was involved in a project to explore the feasibility of a new super-first-class
service, one that was to be the first of its kind. The service envisioned was
one that would be performed in commercial jets reappointed with roughly
one-fourth of the usual number of seats configured in a variety of ways to
facilitate in-flight meetings and provide privacy; serve the finest food; provide in-flight secretarial, communication, and computing services; and facilitate security at check-in. But when asked what they desired from such a
service before being apprised of the complete service concept, most executives returned to the important and age-old needs of convenient departure
times and on-time service. There was significantly less enthusiasm for en-
gaging in lengthy discussions about what else a superior service should
provide, although clearly the status conferred by the opportunity to utilize
such a service appealed to a subsegment of those interviewed.

It was necessary to assess additional questions about how much respondents would be willing to pay for such service and whether corporations
would be willing to guarantee to pay for seats on every flight, in essence
handling their own reservation process for frequently traveling employees.
For this purpose, sketches of the plane, descriptions of the system, and
alternative prices were displayed as part of a concept test. Prices were

quoted in multiples of first-class rates. Few respondents indicated an enthusiasm for paying more than then-current first-class rates. But the way in which they replied in focus group interview responses to the question suggested a lack of conviction for any particular fare level. Further, most could not translate their companies' policies on travel into a likely response to the guaranteed-space concept.

The entrepreneur sponsoring the study finally concluded that the only way to test his idea was to implement it, something regarded as too costly at the time (although implemented later by others). The experience suggests that prospective customers often are able to define only important and somewhat traditional dimensions desired in a new service, an observation reinforced by the experience of Christopher Lovelock and others involved in researching markets for services.[17] It's up to an entrepreneur to take it from there in thinking like a prospective customer.

Fortunately, some services do not require a large investment for a market test. Even capital equipment can be leased. But others, especially those requiring the construction of a network (for transportation, communication, or transactions), often require a sizable investment, a great deal of time for development, and a strong stomach for risk.

"LAW-BREAKING" OPERATING STRATEGIES

Every industry has its unarguable "laws." They describe things as they have always been. Examples of these in the electric utility industry are: (1) Electric utility companies naturally have high fixed costs stemming from large capital investments in plant and wiring, and (2) because of their high fixed costs, electric utility companies must seek economies of scale through larger plants and networks. These may have held true for many years, but innovative methods of power generation, the ability to use other companies' lines for distribution, and improved technologies to limit loss in the long-distance transmission of power have opened the industry to new competition. And these innovations have raised serious doubts about traditional operating strategies. It is no longer necessary to own an entire network, thus reducing the fixed-cost element of the business. This in turn has brought into question the generally accepted "bigger is better" thesis. It suggests too that the premises for regulating monopoly service providers to protect customers no longer exist to the same degree and require reexamination.[18]

In other industries, conventional practice takes on the dimensions of an informal and unspoken conspiracy. For example, why is airline food so bad, we ask? It has to represent an opportunity for contrary positioning. Explanations for this common traveler's plight are that: (1) airline passengers don't rate food service as an important factor influencing their choice of an airline, (2) airline managements thus conclude that they would drop food service if they could get away with it and that they should hold such costs to a bare minimum, (3) flight kitchens, whose managers maintain that they could produce excellent, tasty meals, cite the fact that airlines call the shots, designing aircraft food handling equipment primarily for economy and ease of use rather than quality of food and squeezing meal costs to a minimum, and (4) airline managements, not wishing to stir up passenger complaints that can't be satisfied anyway, rarely survey passengers about food. In spite of the fact that in-flight food and service are rated more importantly by some travelers (especially those traveling frequently, over longer distances, and more likely to be paying full fare) than others, the quiet conspiracy against the ultimate consumers, the passengers, continues.[19]

Experiences from other service industries suggest that the conspiracy eventually will be broken by a combination of an airline deciding to differentiate itself to frequent travelers primarily in terms of in-flight services, a cooperative effort by the airline and its catering firm to redesign the process by which high-quality meals are developed, prepared, and processed both on the ground and in the air, and a new food technology allowing for the improved preparation of a wider range of foods and meals that look and taste more like those served in three-star restaurants.

Competing firms in one service after another have shattered commonly held beliefs about basic ways of running businesses in their respective industries. No one factor accounts for the success of any one of these breakthrough companies. Each often distances itself from the competition in its industry in several of the ways shown in Figure 4–5, grouped by the "Ps" of service positioning. This is understood implicitly by pioneers who have contradicted generally accepted concepts of designing and delivering services in such well-known firms as Club Med, Carrefour, and Scandinavian Airlines System (SAS), as well as in lesser-known companies such as Bonneville Pacific and Guardian Savings & Loan.

Take Club Med, for example.[20] It extended the concept of the packaged vacation to the ultimate degree, creating a number of all-inclusive destination resorts in out-of-the-way locations around the world in which the primary objective, at least initially, was to offer a carefree vacation experience for self-selected, single, young-at-heart adults seeking a place where they could forget the "real world." It achieved this by developing a standardized general approach to the operation of its resorts, customized by the "high-touch" interaction with the GOs (gentils organisateurs) on the staff of each of Club Med's vacation "villages," and the large menu of activities at each

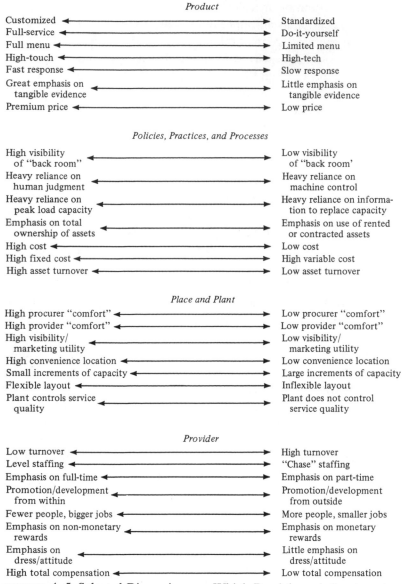

FIGURE 4–5 Selected Dimensions on Which Breakthrough Services Are Positioned in Relation to Customers and Competitors

resort from which the GMs (*gentils membres*) or guests can take a "do-it-yourself" approach to customizing each day. This *product* requires ample capacity of various types of facilities such as tennis courts to accommodate the whims of guests, an important element of its *policies and practices*. By involving guests in creating their own experiences, in part just by interacting with each other, an important *policy,* Club Med is able to offer vacations at relatively low cost and price. For example, even though it caters to singles, Club Med emphasizes double accommodations in its villages and takes responsibility for pairing up singles of the same sex as roommates. Thus it fills a higher proportion of its beds than other resort hotel operators, some of whom may have higher room occupancy. This is sold as part of the *product,* although it is a critical element of the *process* that leverages value over cost and influences the design of the *plant* as well.

Product design at Club Med involves differentiation from its competitors (who since have emulated it) in emphasizing physical evidence of a carefree vacation in a world of plenty. Guests are asked to adhere to Club Med *policies* and check all valuables, watches, and other artifacts of the care-laden world upon entering a village. Money not placed in safekeeping is used to purchase beads that can be worn around the neck and used to purchase drinks and other items not included in the package. Food and other items included in the package are provided without limit, around the clock, and in a way that creates the appearance of great profusion. It is intended for a clientele that in part equates quality with quantity.

Clearly this approach to *product* and *process* requires *providers* that are able to interact with guests, help organize activities in a highly responsive way, often depending upon weather or special holidays, and both staff and manage the village "back-room" activities to a degree unheard of in other resort hotels and often in the full view of guests. They must be, sometimes simultaneously, social directors, entertainers, waiters, and housekeepers, able to put in 18-hour days on a regular basis. Both attitude and stamina are critical. Compensation largely is in nonmonetary rewards such as room, board, and life-style. Given the intense pressures of the job, Club Med must be able to accommodate through its recruiting and training a relatively high level of staff turnover.

The high-touch philosophy and ad hoc social "management" of a Club Med village requires a *plant* with a flexible layout but one that helps, through its athletic and kitchen facilities, control service quality.

Club Med brings to bear many of the elements shown in Figure 4–5 in a service that represented in its early days a distinct departure from traditional competitors offering either tours or destination resorts where guests were required to handle their own money and organize their own vacation activities.

Carrefour's approach to food retailing continues to break many rules of the industry.[21] In fact, it may not be a food retailer. Its *product* is a total one-stop shopping experience. It does retail food, but in such large quantities at low cost and price that it has broken new grounds in that industry. It *processes* many of its items in pallet-load as opposed to case quantities, getting the lowest purchase price and handling costs. It was one of the first retailers of its kind to devote more space to nonfood than food items. And it planned an unheard-of amount of space in its stores for services to enhance its one-stop shopping *product,* many of them operated by lessees at rents that contribute handsomely to Carrefour's overall profit.

This requires the construction of ample *plant* space, in the form of huge stores ranging up to the size of six (American) football fields under one roof, with a heavy reliance on high-tech methods of handling particularly its food products. Normally food retailing, especially in facilities this large, would be highly capital intensive. But initially, Carrefour financed nearly all of its needs for facilities and inventories by taking advantage of the liberal 90-day trade credit typically made available by suppliers to its less efficient, smaller competitors in France, selling its products in a much shorter period of time and using the leftover funds to reduce its investment and achieve extremely high asset turnover (sales divided by assets) rates for its industry.

As you might imagine, there are fewer but larger jobs in a Carrefour than in a typical supermarket, allowing the company to compete for the best *providers* with ample compensation and benefit packages.

Scandinavian Airlines System (SAS), unlike other airlines, is seeking to create a total global travel service for its frequent business travelers.[22] This *product* will allow a traveler to check bags through from a hotel room in Stockholm to one in New York with all intervening services of hotel, limousine, rental auto, food, and air transport supplied by SAS or one of its affiliates linked by a common database and network for which the *processes* and *plant* are being assembled and tested. This requires also the development of a first-rate training center to prepare *providers* to staff the integrated service.

It's not necessary to be big, well-known, or global to pursue precedent-setting positioning, as Bonneville Pacific and Guardian Savings & Loan remind us. Bonneville Pacific builds power plants and sells electricity to utilities that elect to buy power rather than produce it themselves. This raises the question of how this Salt Lake City-based company can make money selling power to a utility that should have a lower cost structure, given its ability to raise funds for construction at relatively low costs for capital. But according to chairman Raymond Hixon, "We can build new power plants cheaper than the utilities can and make more money and still provide better rates than they're getting now."[23]

Bonneville Pacific does it by building smaller hydroelectric, geothermal, or gas-fired cogeneration plants than other utilities have thought most "efficient." But this enables the company to complete projects faster, without attracting environmental concerns directed to large nuclear projects. The resulting capacity utilization is higher as power sources are developed in increments that more closely reflect customer demand. The result is a lower-cost *product,* produced with a *process* involving much higher or faster asset turnover than other firms in the industry, resulting from a better use of available capacity in a *plant* which is expanded with smaller increments of capacity. For utilities buying from Bonneville Pacific, the usually high fixed costs associated with large investments by other utilities are avoided entirely.

Guardian Savings & Loan Association by 1987 achieved the position of the most profitable large savings and loan institution in the United States, realizing a return roughly seven times greater than the average of the other 99 of the largest 100 in this ailing industry.[24] Of all places, it is located in what has been a disaster area for savings and loan institutions, Texas. It has achieved this enviable record through contrary positioning.

While its competitors expanded *product* line, Guardian reduced its "menu" to accepting deposits, offering money market funds, and selling certificates of deposit. Period. Its competitors used their depositors' money to make real estate loans locally at significantly higher interest rates than could be achieved elsewhere. Guardian instead mostly purchased Ginnie Maes, the residential mortgage pools guaranteed by the U.S. government, receiving lower rates of interest than its regional competitors. In addition, Robert and Jeffry Parker, co-owners of Guardian, hedged even these investments to provide further protection against interest rate swings. When the bottom dropped out of the Texas real estate market, Guardian's investments were nationally diversified and protected. What home mortgages Guardian does offer in the local area are fixed rate at a time when Guardian's competitors all offer only mortgages whose interest rates vary with the prime rate and other indicators of the cost of money. Competitors claim this provides them with a hedge against inflation. But Guardian's owners feel that when the rates on variable rate mortgages go up, they create costly foreclosures. As Jeff Parker puts it, "Besides, ARMs (adjustable rate mortgages) are very complicated and customers are always calling with questions. Someone has to be paid to take those calls."[25]

Cost control thus also differentiates the Parkers from many of their more flamboyant competitors. Guardian offers no checking services, so the few people who come to its branches are there to deposit and withdraw money. The company does not open accounts by mail, insuring a more loyal local clientele. Further, Jeff Parker claims that when checking services were offered, "They were 1% of the deposits but 80% of the transactions we processed.''[26] Similarly, sales of traveler's checks and credit card advances are regarded as expensive, and individual retirement accounts (IRAs) too complex to explain. All are taboo at Guardian. Advertising is limited to newspaper ads and large signs on the branches.

Cost control is reflected in *process, plant,* and *providers* as well. In 1988, Guardian had only 210 employees, no expensive-to-operate automated teller machines (ATMs), and no evening and weekend open hours. Its owners claim that the "Mom and Pop savers" it targets aren't attracted to ATMs anyway. Many of its 35 branches are staffed with just two people because of the simplified nature of transactions, the limited foot traffic in the branch, the limited opening hours, and the fact that transaction processing is handled by a central computing system in a Houston headquarters facility that isn't a branch and therefore doesn't even have a Guardian sign on it.

Guardian Savings & Loan, Bonneville Pacific, Club Med, Carrefour, SAS, and Citicorp Mortgage illustrate contrary positioning with a vengeance. It has paid off handsomely for all of them.

CONSCIOUS POSITIONING OF EACH STEP IN A PROCESS

Lynn Shostack, a consultant and former service executive, has suggested carrying positioning ultimately to each step in the process of delivering a service.[27] She suggests centering the effort around decisions to select one of our strategic directions at each step. These directions involve more or less of what she calls divergence, the degree of uniformity in the service offered, and complexity, the number of steps designed into the production and delivery of the service. Figure 4–6 illustrates the application of this approach to producing and delivering a restaurant meal. It requires flow-charting the service, identifying the traditional or current approach to each step, designing alternatives of lower not higher divergence and complexity, and deciding which practices to follow at each step of the process. As Figure 4–6 suggests, the first step in the process of producing and delivering a restaurant meal, matching customers to tables, could range from a low-complexity/divergence alternative of a no-reservation policy all the way to a high-complexity/divergence alternative policy of allowing customers to select tables, with potentially higher costs of labor imbalances and low capacity utilization.

It is important to insure that practices developed at each step are internally consistent and convey a clear "message" to prospective customers about the amount of complexity and divergence they can expect in the service product and the way it is to be delivered, as well as differences from compet-

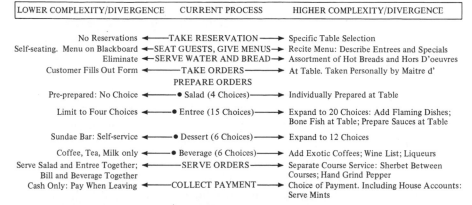

FIGURE 4–6 Structural Alternatives in Positioning a Restaurant Service
SOURCE: G. Lynn Shostack, "Service Positioning Through Structural Change," *Journal of Marketing*, January 1987, pp. 34–43, at p. 41. Reprinted from *Journal of Marketing*, published by the American Marketing Association.

ing firms. For most services, the same approach would be required for "back of the house" process steps.

EASE OF EMULATION BY COMPETITORS

The value of a positioning strategy is enhanced to the degree that it is one that competitors find difficult to emulate. Such difficulties may arise because of inadequate funds, inadequate technology, the lack of a costly-to-build network, a competitor's strong customer franchise, regulatory barriers, or the absence of human resources or required management attitudes. Consider our previous examples.

Club Med achieved a significant head start on its competition in acquiring resort sites, financing them, and building a network of locations and a franchise targeted toward young, single vacationers. It did not rely on advanced technology or regulations that might have constrained its competition. It did benefit from the reluctance of traditional hotel operators to take seriously Club Med's targeted market segment and to design and operate resorts in what may have been regarded as a "counterculture" manner. And it understood the importance of the careful selection, development, and motivation of a dedicated staff and managerial group.

Carrefour instead centered its strategy around low-cost financing, the technology of building design, and low-cost operating methods. It benefited as well from the fact that the complaints of small local shopkeepers in

France to its deathly competition produced ordinances forbidding *another* hypermarché (super supermarket) from locating in the same community, thus unwittingly protecting Carrefour.

At SAS, Bonneville Pacific, Guardian Savings & Loan, and Citicorp Mortgage, competitors have access to comparable financing and technology. SAS and Guardian have a certain degree of regulatory protection in their home markets. And of course SAS has its network and customer franchise. Deterrents to emulation that all of these organizations hold in common are their human resources and especially management attitudes. Most important of all, of course, are the ways they have carefully pieced together a focused, internally consistent strategic service vision and positioned it in relation to competitors and customers. This has produced the final "P," profit.

Profit results from high quality and productivity. It is to these that we devote our attention next.

5

Determining the True Costs and Benefits of Service Quality

If there is a moment at which service managers most often are moved to act in seriously seeking service breakthroughs, it's the moment at which they first realize the true cost of poor service. We have been told by several that it was a watershed point in their companies' turnarounds. And we have in mind major companies in their respective industries.

This is a dramatic example of the familiar saying, "What gets measured is what gets managed." Measuring the true cost of poor service can be a dramatic call to management action. Consider an example based on estimates provided by the management of Club Med, the world's leading all-inclusive resort operator.[1]

In 1986 Club Med realized $18 million in net income from the $337 million in revenues it earned that year in its North American operations. That same year, it attracted roughly 200,000 new customers (*gentils membres*, or GMs) to its resorts. Its marketing research indicated that 80% of these new GMs were enthusiastic about their experience; 20% were not. Of the satisfied GMs, it was estimated, based on previous research, that 30% would return to a Club Med resort and that these "loyal" customers would vacation at Club Med an average of four times. The average contribution from each visit was estimated at about $1,000, making each loyal GM worth about $4,000 in a "lifetime" contribution stream to Club Med. Based on these estimates, management concluded that the stream of contribution over the years that it could expect from the "class of 1986" of new GMs in its North American operation was about $192 million, assuming it could maintain its guests' perceptions of Club Med quality.

Then a sobering thought struck the company's management. What if a lapse in the quality of service resulted in the proportion of satisfied customers dropping just one percentage point, from 80% to 79%, and the visits by "loyal" GMs dropping just from 4.0 to 3.5 times? It didn't take higher mathematics to calculate that this represented a potential pre-tax loss of contribution of $26.1 million, roughly equivalent to its after-tax net income in 1986.[2]

This little horror story contains several messages. The first of course concerns the high cost of quality. The second, which is just as important, is that unlike most companies we know, Club Med has at least taken the trouble to determine the potential impact of deteriorating quality on its profit performance. But perhaps the most chilling of all is the realization that this story documents only one of the many possible costs of poor service.

THE COSTS OF POOR SERVICE QUALITY

The first step in cost measurement is the preparation of the itemized bill, such as the one shown in Figure 5–1. It includes both internal and external costs of failure, as well as those that are verifiable and nonverifiable.

INTERNAL FAILURE COSTS

Internal failure costs are the costs of correcting defects uncovered by the producer before they reach the customer. In services with a back-office function, such as insurance companies and banks, internal failure costs result from errors like improperly coded applications. A secretary who has to reschedule a meeting for several managers, because one of the managers forgot about another appointment, incurs significant internal failure costs in the time wasted in scheduling another meeting room and coordinating schedules among meeting participants. Frustration on the job leads to labor turnover.

Internal service failure has secondary effects that are very costly, if not always visible. Increased service employee turnover is an example. Immediately visible and measurable costs of high employee turnover include recruitment and training costs. Less visible, but important associated costs can include the quality of recruiting and recruits, reduced productivity, and even a loss of corporate culture.

For example, high turnover puts extra demand on recruiting efforts. As a

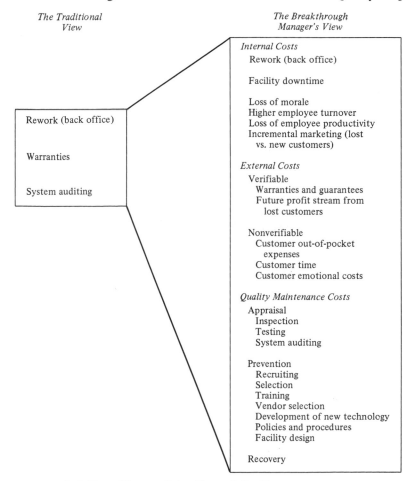

*The Traditional
View*

*The Breakthrough
Manager's View*

Rework (back office)

Warranties

System auditing

Internal Costs
  Rework (back office)

  Facility downtime

  Loss of morale
  Higher employee turnover
  Loss of employee productivity
  Incremental marketing (lost
    vs. new customers)

External Costs
  Verifiable
    Warranties and guarantees
    Future profit stream from
      lost customers

  Nonverifiable
    Customer out-of-pocket
      expenses
    Customer time
    Customer emotional costs

Quality Maintenance Costs
  Appraisal
    Inspection
    Testing
    System auditing

  Prevention
    Recruiting
    Selection
    Training
    Vendor selection
    Development of new technology
    Policies and procedures
    Facility design

  Recovery

FIGURE 5–1 Two Views of the Cost of Quality

result, recruitment becomes a frenzied task, leading to a drop in average quality per recruit and greater variability in the quality of recruits.

New employees require time to learn company policies and procedures, adversely affecting company productivity. The attention and time required to train new recruits places an extra burden on experienced staff. The departure and arrival of new employees tend to disrupt jobs that require a coordinated team approach, and a high rate of employee turnover leads to a decreased proportion of ''old timers'' who pass along essential elements of culture.

The high cost of employee turnover is especially evident once the customer becomes part of the service process. Short-term costs can include a sense of loss in customers who developed relationships with former employees. Customer dissatisfaction can also result from ''spot'' staff shortages that impair service delivery. Long-term costs of employee turnover include negative word of mouth, spread by disgruntled ex-employees and dissatisfied customers, both of which unfavorably influence potential customers. These are generally reflected in what we choose to call external failure costs.

EXTERNAL FAILURE COSTS

External failure costs accrue from errors experienced by customers. For example, a coding error that should be caught (or, better, prevented from happening) by clerical personnel results in an external error discovered by the customer who receives an incorrect bank statement. Some tend to be more verifiable than others.

Verifiable Failure Costs. Verifiable failure costs are incurred when a defect that is experienced by a customer and brought to the server's attention results in a cost of some type. The standard product warranty, for example, which covers defects in workmanship or material for a limited period of time or use, is intended to cover the costs of external verifiable errors. In services, airline passengers who are bumped from their flights as a result of an error in overbooking are often compensated with free airline tickets, thus creating a verifiable cost of failure. Because of service intangibility, such verifiable costs tend to be much lower in services than is the case with tangible goods. For example, what does the customer who sees a bad play have to take back?

Sales representatives for a range of service companies have told us that it requires three to five times more effort, often over a period of years, to regain a customer lost because of poor service than to induce a new customer to try the service. There are good reasons to lose a customer (including, for example, the conscious refusal to lower a price to meet a competitor with inferior service). But poor service, often accounting for 20% to 30% of lost customers, is not one of them.

When a customer is lost because of poor service, a decision has to be made whether to allocate effort to regain that customer or to attract several new customers to a service. Too often, this decision does not take into account the secondary benefits, such as reduced bad will and negative word-of-mouth advertising as well as improved server morale, resulting from regaining a formerly dissatisfied customer.

Nonverifiable Failure Costs. Of much greater importance are nonverifiable external service failure costs. These are the difficult-to-measure, "hidden" costs of customer dissatisfaction that occur which are not reported to the producer. Nonverifiable failure costs include customer out-of-pocket costs as well as the cost of time and aggravation. So-called casualty insurance that typically insures only against the verifiable costs of lost property by our reckoning barely qualifies to be called insurance. In most minor losses, the costs of money, time, and aggravation spent in collecting the insurance often outweigh the explicit value of the collected claim. When this includes, in addition, the possible abuse from rude claims agents, it adds insult to hard-to-measure injury.

COST OF QUALITY = BENEFITS OF GOOD QUALITY

The bill for poor service, as suggested in Figure 5–1, can be high for both servers and customers. On a more positive note, however, this really documents the benefits of good quality. And it may provide useful guidelines about how much to spend for maintaining good service or correcting defects and how to spend it. It suggests too the tremendous leverage that can be obtained from effective spending to prevent or correct service failures.

THE COSTS OF MAINTAINING GOOD QUALITY

Outstanding service providers spend heavily for quality appraisal, prevention, and service recovery.

APPRAISAL COSTS

Appraisal costs, usually thought of in the manufacturing setting as the costs of inspecting for errors at various stages of the production process, have several components, including inspection, testing, and system auditing.

Inspection. In service operations where the degree of customer contact is low and data, not customers, are being processed (such as in back-office "paper factories"), the inspection process is similar to that found in traditional manufacturing settings. Work is processed in stages, whether manually or eléctronically, and inspection methods often are applied. First Chicago Corporation, for example, at its First National Bank of Chicago subsidiary, measures hundreds of accounting and clerical activities, using statistical process controls.[3] In architectural firms, reports are often subjected to review by one or more peers before they are released to clients. Even in services that involve relatively high levels of customer contact, inspection of the facility or equipment is normally performed before the customer enters "the service factory."

For example, a restaurant maître d' will visually inspect table settings before opening the restaurant to customers.

Once a customer becomes involved in the production process, the situation in many services, inspection is of limited value. In most cases, an error observed by an inspector is an error experienced by a customer. Nor can all potential problem causes be inspected in advance. For example, resorts have no way of "pre-inspecting" the weather to assure guests of a rain-free vacation.

Testing. Simultaneity of service production and consumption also make testing, the second type of quality-appraisal activity, problematic. How does one "test drive" the product of a baseball game before the game begins? The technical component of many services can often be tested, however. Roller coaster rides at a state fair, for example, can be tested before the public is allowed to ride. Of course, testing roller coaster equipment is not the same thing as testing the experience of a roller coaster ride. Only the customer is able to judge the experience of the ride and decide whether it is satisfactory.

Auditing. System auditing is invaluable to service managers for detecting and preventing potential errors. Pilots perform a systems check on their aircraft before each flight. "Mystery shoppers" are often used to check the system capability of a retail store. Sylvio de Bortoli, a Club Med *chef de village* (resort manager) whose guest satisfaction ratings were consistently the highest among those at Club Med, mastered the technique of system audit. In each village he managed, he developed a patterned walking tour route that kept him up-to-date regarding all aspects of the capability of the "village system" to produce high-quality service.

PREVENTION COSTS

These costs are associated with efforts to keep errors from occurring. At Club Med, Sylvio de Bortoli not only audits effectively but is an excellent example of a service manager who specializes in error prevention. In the Club Med system, new teams of employees (called *gentils organizateurs* or GOs) are assembled to staff the villages (all-inclusive resorts) every six months, a practice referred to as "rotation." Most village chiefs accept, with a little haggling, the list of GOs assigned to them by the corporate personnel office. Not de Bortoli. When we observed him, he spent a great deal of effort attempting to influence corporate's assignment decisions. For example, while other village chiefs hated to leave their villages, knowing that they would be needed to handle the frequent and often serious problems that cropped up, de Bortoli journeyed to Paris headquarters every six months to assemble and submit to personnel his list of "preferred job candidates" for his next team. He pored over the company's personnel files, and called over village chiefs to obtain more information about GOs who looked promising. By taking the time and trouble to handpick GOs, de Bortoli was doing more than assembling a group of individuals with good potential for interacting well with guests. Acutely aware of the importance of having team members who could interact well with each other, he was also minimizing the potential for having GOs on his team who created problems among team members. This is defect detection at its best, and is particularly important in services where quality cannot be "controlled in" through inspection and statistical process control.

A similar focus on error prevention is demonstrated by an international security guard company in an industry often characterized by low wages, bad hours, poor employee morale, and high turnover. The industry is plagued by "no posts," security guards who don't show up to staff their posts. One company has one division, which it acquired, that has absolute dominance in its regional market. Unlike its competitors, this organization devotes extraordinary resources to error prevention through sophisticated hiring, training, and employee-retention policies and practices. They have created a "high-commitment" environment in which security guards feel an exceptionally strong sense of pride and responsibility. They are made to feel like members of an elite team, and they respond accordingly. Through this approach and many other forms of defect prevention, the company has set the industry quality standards.

RECOVERY COSTS

Recovery costs result from efforts to compensate for service quality lapses prior to the end of a service encounter and prior to the loss of a customer. Because service recovery, one important device for achieving total customer satisfaction, is addressed in some detail in Chapter 6, we'll limit our comment here to the observation that the size of the "bill" shown in Figure 5–1 for most services places a high premium on service recovery. The "merely good" service providers spend far too little on it.

MEASURING THE COSTS OF POOR SERVICE QUALITY

Understanding the true cost of poor quality leads directly to a recognition of the value of quality maintenance and improvement. It suggests how much should be invested in quality improvement activities.

PROBLEMS OF MEASUREMENT

The problem of inadequate quality cost measurement is endemic to all industries, but it is particularly troublesome for service firms. Reasons include: (1) service intangibility, (2) the lack of error data, (3) the expense of installing quality-cost measurement systems, (4) the incompatibility of cost-of-quality measurement with existing organizational culture, and (5) the design of traditional accounting systems.

Service Intangibility. The intangibility of services makes measuring quality-related outputs problematic. For example, how is a consulting firm to determine whether its consulting service is error-free or defective? It is difficult (if not impossible) to measure whether the advice "conforms to spec." Further, if poor advice could be identified, how does one calculate the cost of poor advice?

Lack of Error Data. Unlike tangible products, services cannot be returned. Consequently, service firms often have little evidence of service failure. How can the cost of errors be determined when their occurrence is unknown? The problem is compounded by the typical situation in which internal systems are lacking for customers to register complaints about quality problems. As a result, systems that create an incentive for customers to complain are crucial to getting a grasp on the cost of poor quality.

Resources Required to Install a Quality-Cost Measurement System. Developing an error-identification and costing system demands management time and financial resources. Because managers are generally not knowledgeable about what poor quality is costing their companies, quality-cost systems are rarely on the list of high-priority items.

Incompatibility of Cost-of-Quality Measurement With Organization Culture. A systematic approach to measuring quality costs may be at odds with an organizational culture that is rooted in creativity and experimentation, an advertising agency, for example. In fact, an approach that emphasizes error identification, root-cause analysis, and cause elimination could indeed stifle creativity. For example, a software development company would be unwise to develop a quality measurement system that recognizes as wasted time periods when programmers engage in informal bull sessions because these sessions often lead to conceptual breakthroughs. The potential for choking creativity and spontaneity must be considered when an organization's management thinks about measuring quality costs.

An interesting reverse example of the tension between creativity and formal measurement of quality costs involves a well-known consulting firm that teaches quality concepts to executives. In short executive education programs, attendees' primary interest is usually how the course content relates to their organizations; they want the course material customized to their needs. Consequently, the need for creativity and spontaneity in the classroom is high. Unfortunately, the firm takes a rigid manufacturing-based approach to quality, taking the view that quality is achieved by driving all variations out of the system. Specifically, its leadership considers any deviation from prescribed lesson plans to be costly service failures, which means that class content is exactly the same from one class to the next, the opposite of what its customers need. Its philosophy of service standardization is literally driving failure costs up. More than one disgruntled executive has commented that they wish they could have heard less quality dogma, instead of focusing on applying the classroom concepts to their organizations.

Design of Traditional Accounting Systems. Traditionally, accounting systems are designed to capture revenue and expense data by activity, function, and resource. Benefits and costs of quality do not fit these kinds of classifications, requiring that measurement efforts, whether periodic or continuous, be conducted outside the traditional accounting process. Internal accountants can be helpful, but they must be willing to approach the task creatively and with a broad mind.

METHODS OF MEASUREMENT

A full understanding of the benefits and costs of service quality requires information, however appropriate, about what actually happened in a service encounter (as objective as possible), how employees and customers felt after experiencing these events, subsequent actions on the part of employees (for example, staying on the job) or customers (for example, repeating their purchases), and costs incurred by both servers and customers both to prevent and correct poor service. Few organizations collect all of these types of information. How is each obtained?

Service Events. In some services, direct observation of service encounters is possible. Supervisors of bank tellers, for example, have the opportunity to collect information about the quality of service being delivered in relation to company standards. Other forms of observation are more discreet. Gambling casino dealers are regularly observed from control ports built into casino ceilings. Telephone complaint processing personnel may have their calls monitored by personnel using listening devices. This often is done with the full knowledge of personnel being monitored, thus reducing ethical questions about such methods.

Firms desiring more objective information rely on "mystery shoppers," individuals assigned the task of posing as customers to collect information concerning their actual experiences. Younkers, a midwestern department store chain, carries out 12,000 mystery shoppings a year in support of its Satisfaction Plus quality and productivity effort. The practice has become so widely accepted that fledgling firms are being organized to specialize in mystery shopping and reporting.[4]

Service Perceptions. Facts are useful, but they take a back seat to customers' perceptions in measuring the benefits and costs of service quality. Together, facts and perceptions can be used to calibrate service quality at a level keyed to what customers find acceptable, whether the objective is to exceed this level by a little or a lot. A good example of this type of effort is American Airlines' actual observation of the time spent in waiting by its customers for ticket purchases, coupled with questionnaire data about whether these same customers thought the waiting time they experienced was reasonable.

Fairfield Inn's Scorecard system which obtains information electronically from hotel patrons at check-out time about room cleanliness and courteousness of the service they experience suggests another way of collecting such data.

Subsequent Customer Actions. It is difficult to monitor customer behavior as the result of good or poor service and perhaps even more daunting to establish case-and-effect relationships explaining such behavior. But through efforts to track customer usage and systematically interview customers when service usage patterns have declined, it is possible to establish estimates of costs of poor service. This may be most feasible for the supplier of an industrial service involving frequent service purchase. Consider the experience of one major trucking company with which we are familiar.

This national motor carrier provides freight service to an estimated 80,000 largely industrial and commercial customers served by roughly 800 sales representatives working out of nearly as many freight terminals on the company's route network. It has classed the volume of usage of its customers into five categories, depending on the amount of revenue each produces. Customers whose accounts drop in volume from one category to a smaller one are noted on an exception report to terminal managers, to whom sales representatives report. While it is a matter of local judgment, the more diligent of the terminal managers ask their sales representatives to determine the cause for declining business. The validity of information from these "diagnostic" interviews varies with the ability of the interviewer to elicit real reasons for declining customer usage. But the pooling of information from six such sets of interviews for a recent year yielded highly useful information.

The six sales representatives, collectively selling to about 600 customer accounts, had 90 customers whose declining usage of the firm's trucking services had dropped them from one volume category to a smaller one. The average decline in revenue which this represented was about $35,000 per customer per year, on which the company earned contribution over direct costs of about $7,000. Based on conversations with these customers, it was learned that 80% of them had bought less service because they could get a better price from competitors, the volume of their business overall had declined, or the pattern of their shipments had shifted to cities served by other trucking companies. This left 20%, or 18 customers, whose decisions to cut back usage resulted from service failures such as missed packages or deliveries, excessive damage, inadequate shipment tracing, poor information, or rude service employees. With this information, a dollar value could be attached to each cause of poor service to be used as the basis for budgeting corrective action.

Perhaps more important, when extrapolated to all customers and sales territories, the finding suggested that the company's annual loss of business due to service failure involved 2,400 customers, $84 million in revenue, and $16.8 million in lost contribution, a sum sufficient to fund several extensive corrective initiatives. This did not include costs incurred by customers in correcting service failures, locating new suppliers, and establishing new shipping practices and relationships.

Appraisal, Prevention, and Recovery. The measurement of these costs is subject to a great deal of judgment and some debate.

In appraisal, the cost of a "mystery shopper" audit program, for example, can be measured quite explicitly. But efforts to inspect test services often are carried out as part of the job of supervision or delivery and can only be assessed through individual estimates of time required to satisfy company procedures or otherwise carry out these activities at each operating location.

Prevention costs often are dismissed as those that are part of any manager's responsibility in managing a service, therefore assignable to a special category only at the risk of double counting. Nevertheless, they can be pinpointed by examining the differences in practice between successful and unsuccessful managers, as exemplified earlier by Sylvio de Bortoli at Club Med. The point is not so much to precisely measure such costs, but to budget expenditures to help less successful managers to emulate those who are most successful in preventing service failure, something that can only be done as a result of systematic observations of behavior differences. This may involve, as in the case of Club Med, increased training in the preselection of village staff members or additional travel funds to be spent in the selection process.

Recovery costs often are associated with money spent to correct service errors. Unfortunately, they too rarely involve estimates associated with servers' and customers' time spent in the recovery process, some of it spent in a determination of suitable settlements. A growing number of service organizations have concluded that it is worth it to increase the budget for explicit settlements in order to save employee time for other work as well as reduce customer aggravation.

THE RELATIONSHIP BETWEEN COSTS AND SERVICE QUALITY

There is a wide difference in attitudes among breakthrough service managers and their competitors on the results to be obtained from expenditures of time and money to produce service quality. It is explained by the differing assumptions with which each approaches the task.

The "merely good" service managers with whom we have talked speak of "optimal" service levels, those at which further expenditures for good service do not produce commensurate results in terms of lower costs of failure. Their view of the problem is the traditional one involving "trade-offs," as portrayed in Figure 5–2.

This conventional theory holds that error-prevention costs increase as the level of quality improves. The higher a firm aims in terms of quality, so goes the argument, the more it will spend on such prevention activities as training

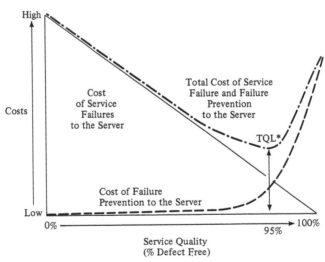

*TQL = Target quality level, the point at which the total costs of service failure and failure prevention are minimized.

FIGURE 5–2 The Traditional View of the Trade-Off Between Costs of Prevention and Service Failures

and investment in capital equipment. Moreover, prevention costs are assumed to increase exponentially to achieve incremental quality gains, reaching astronomical proportions as the percentage of defect-free output approaches 100 percent. This theory, which is accepted by such production experts as Armand Feigenbaum[5] and Joseph Juran,[6] grows out of the assumption that it is extremely expensive to eliminate the last possible error from a system. As a result, managers have been encouraged to accept the idea that there is a "target quality level" (TQL) of less than 100% quality, as shown in Figure 5–2, beyond which prevention costs exceed the incremental reductions they make in failure costs.

Breakthrough service managers don't see it this way. First of all, they measure the costs of service recovery and see them decline along with costs of service failure (including external customer-related costs referred to in Figure 5–1) as quality improves. Second, they don't accept the traditional notion that costs of appraisal and prevention rise geometrically to infinity as the 100% service level is approached, a notion supported by our observations of quality-improvement efforts in service companies. And third, the fact that they understand the high cost of poor quality, not only in terms of lost customers (and customer-incurred costs) but poor employee satisfaction and morale, means that they place a higher value on service perfection than their counterparts in "merely good" service firms. These differences in views, summarized in diagrammatic form in Figure 5–3, lead to the conclusion that a "target quality level" (TQL) of 100% quality is the goal that should be sought. This is dangerous thinking. But the danger in it is for competitors.

ENLISTING CUSTOMERS IN THE COST MEASUREMENT PROCESS

Just as breakthrough service providers may enlist customers in service delivery, they have also involved them effectively in the measurement of the cost of service failures. Just how this is done is a topic to which we turn next.

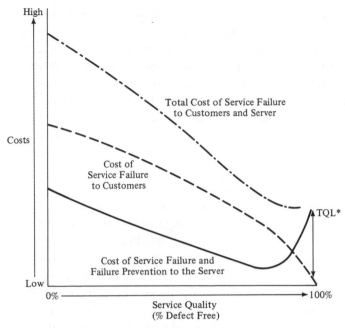

*TQL = Target quality level, the point at which the total costs
of service failure and failure prevention are minimized.

FIGURE 5–3 The Breakthrough View of Relationships
Between Costs of Prevention and Service Failures

6

Developing Devices for Achieving Total Customer Satisfaction

The Henry Ford Community College (HFCC) in Detroit has taken a bold step to anticipate and discourage possible service failure. It guarantees its education. As part of its two-year program to prepare students either for upper-level college education or a job, HFCC offers to provide full refunds of tuition for course credits not accepted at other schools to which students might transfer from its two-year program of study. Further, it offers up to 16 custom-designed semester hours of retraining free if a graduate is judged by an employer to be lacking in skills needed for an entry-level job.[1]

Other organizations go even further. L. L. Bean, the Freeport, Maine, retailer store and mail-order house, offers "100% satisfaction in every way . . ." An L. L. Bean customer can return a product at any time and get a refund replacement, credit, or a refund. If a customer returns a pair of L. L. Bean boots after ten years, the company will replace them with new boots, no questions asked. This company has guaranteed satisfaction since the day in 1912 when Leon Leonwood Bean first mailed out his circulars with the notice shown in Figure 6–1. Dissatisfaction with a Manpower, Inc. temporary worker results in an immediate credit to a client's bill. If invoking the guarantee requires written correspondence, the company even refunds the client's cost of postage.

Bain & Company, one of the leading management consulting organizations that emphasizes long-term relationships with clients and assistance to them in implementing suggestions made by Bain consultants, has on occasion offered to forgo its fee if it is unable to live up to promises made to a

NOTICE

I do not consider a sale complete until goods are worn out and customer still satisfied.

We will thank anyone to return goods that are not perfectly satisfactory.

Should the person reading this notice know of anyone who is not satisfied with our goods, I will consider it a favor to be notified.

Above all things we wish to avoid having a dissatisfied customer.

Reprinted from an L.L. Bean 1912 circular.

FIGURE 6–1 Notice from a 1912 L. L. Bean Circular
SOURCE: L. L. Bean, Inc.

client. According to the CEO of one of its clients, Cablic, a $500 million electronic cable company, "We get very, very high return, but if they fall short of performance, they don't get paid. Period."[2]

Buoyed by the knowledge of what good service is truly worth, these organizations are characteristic of a small number that seek outstanding, not just good, results from their customers. They seek total, not just partial, customer satisfaction. This does not mean that they always deliver perfect service, however diligently they might strive for it. It does mean that each must understand what is important to customers, assess accurately its capabilities for delivering what is important, establish clear standards for service performance, develop effective measures and incentives, and devote attention to how best to recover from service failures in order to preserve customer loyalty.

One important vehicle for both communicating and delivering on a service promise is the service guarantee. Our first reaction on encountering such guarantees in several firms was that they were gimmicks. And if viewed only as marketing ploys, they probably are. But service guarantees in the hands of breakthrough service organizations are much more, providing a tangible organizing device for achieving total customer satisfaction, the highest form of service quality.

THE SERVICE GUARANTEE[3]

Outstanding service firms differentiate themselves on the basis of quality dimensions that are important to their customers and then either explicitly or implicitly guarantee results. The guarantee itself can convey a powerful marketing message. Perhaps even more important, a well-crafted service guarantee forces a company to produce high quality because anything less will induce its customers to invoke the guarantee, which can be expensive. Hence, the guarantee can be thought of as a tool both to obtain information about quality and force an organization to "hold its (collective) feet to the fire" regarding service quality.

It is one thing to guarantee a camera, which can be inspected before a customer sets eyes on it and which can be returned to the factory for repairs. But how can you pre-inspect a car tune-up or send an unsuccessful legal argument or bad haircut back for repair? Obviously you can't.

That doesn't mean customer satisfaction can't be guaranteed. For example, most pest control services claim they they will reduce pests to "acceptable levels." But "Bugs" Burger Bug Killers (BBBK), a Miami-based pest-extermination company, promises to eliminate them entirely. Its service guarantee to hotel and restaurant clients promises:

1. You don't owe one penny until all pests on your premises have been eradicated.
2. If you are ever dissatisfied with BBBK's service, you will receive a refund for up to 12 months of the company's services—plus fees for another exterminator of your choice for the next year.
3. If a guest spots a pest on your premises, BBBK will pay for the guest's meal or room, send a letter of apology, and pay for a future meal or stay.
4. If your facility is closed down due to the presence of roaches or rodents, BBBK will pay any fines, as well as all lost profits, plus $5,000.[4]

In short, Al Burger, CEO of BBBK, says, "If we don't satisfy you 100%, we don't take your money." It is a tangible expression of Al Burger's belief that "If the work isn't perfect, you shouldn't get paid."[5]

The result? BBBK, which operates throughout the United States, charges up to six times more than its competitors and yet has a disproportionately high market share of clients with severe pest problems in its operating areas. Its service quality is so good that the company rarely needs to follow through on its guarantee. In 1986, for example, it paid out only $120,000 on sales of $33 million, just enough to prove that its promises weren't empty ones.

In contrast to many existing service guarantees, BBBK's contains most of the elements of an outstanding one. These are that it is: (1) unconditional, (2) focused on customer needs, (3) a clear standard for service delivery performance, (4) easy to understand and communicate, (5) meaningful, both in ways important to a customer and in terms of a significant penalty or payout, (6) easy to invoke, (7) credible, and (8) a declaration of trust in both customers and employees.

UNCONDITIONAL IN CHARACTER

An unconditional guarantee is just what is says. No "ifs," "ands," or "buts." Lands' End, the highly successful mail-order retailer, tells its potential customers:

> We accept any return, for any reason, at any time. Our products are guaranteed. No fine print. No arguments. We mean exactly what we say: "GUARANTEED. PERIOD."[6]

Is this naive? An invitation to financial disaster? No. At Lands' End it is the cornerstone of an effective service delivery system, marketing program, and human resource strategy all wrapped up in one statement.

Clearly, it offers customers important assurances about risks generally associated with mail-order merchandise bought on a sight-unseen basis. And it puts the power to invoke the guarantee in the customer's hands. The service is good only if the customer perceives it to be good.

More important, its effectiveness is undiminished by conditions. This means that there are no problems in interpreting the guarantee, either for customers or Lands' End's employees. No time is wasted in long phone calls or consultations with supervisors. And perhaps most important of all, the guarantee communicates an important message to Lands' End's employees about what is expected of them and the nature of the company they work for.

Mitchell Fromstein, CEO of Manpower, Inc., says:

> At one point, we wondered what the marketing impact would be if we dropped our guarantee. We figured our accounts were well aware of the guarantee and that it might not have much marketing power anymore. Our employees' reaction was fierce—and it had a lot less to do with marketing than with the pride they take in their work. They said, "The guarantee is proof we're a great company. We're willing to tell our customers that if they don't like our service for any reason, it's our fault, not theirs, and we'll make it right." I realized then that the guarantee is far more than a simple piece of paper that puts customers at ease. It really sets the tone, externally and, perhaps more important, internally, for our commitment to our customers and workers.[7]

FOCUSED ON CUSTOMER NEEDS

Knowing what customers want is the *sine qua non* in any effort to structure a service guarantee. A company has to identify both the importance which customers attach to each element of a service and their expectations for each. Lacking this knowledge, a company that wants to guarantee its service may very well guarantee the wrong things.

Obvious, you say? Consider this example. As one of the elements of a recent guarantee, Lufthansa Airlines promised that: ". . . if you have a confirmed reservation in first or business class on a transatlantic flight, you're guaranteed seating in that class."[8] Presumably, the purpose of a reservation system is to eliminate the need for a guarantee of a seat in the class in which it is reserved. Worse yet, when asked to explain what the guarantee meant, a Lufthansa representative responded, "I don't know. It does sound strange, doesn't it?"[9]

Repeated surveys of visitors to its hotel restaurants by the Marriott Corporation have indicated that customers expect courteous, timely service and food that looks and tastes good. And it has followed through with a guarantee that reflects both these needs and provides standards for performance.

A CLEAR STANDARD FOR PERFORMANCE

A recent visitor to Allie's Restaurant in the Bethesda, Maryland, Marriott Hotel would have found the following guarantee on the front of the menu:

. . . If we do not fulfill any one of the following, we will gladly pay for your dinner. Just tell us what went wrong. Our only goal in this is to keep you coming back again and again and again.

Guarantee

1. Our service staff will be friendly and courteous evidenced by their smiles and cheerful attitudes.
2. Your entree will arrive no longer than 20 minutes after you place your order.
3. We guarantee our food will look good and taste great . . .[10]

This guarantee includes a clear, objective standard (no more than a 20-minute wait after the order). Other customer needs for which absolute standards are impossible are nevertheless addressed as well. Together, they convey a strong message to Marriott employees about what is expected of them.

EASY TO UNDERSTAND AND COMMUNICATE

Domino's Pizza, as almost all college students in the United States know and can recite, promises 30-minute delivery or $3 off the price of the pizza. The message is short and memorable and the standard clear. The guarantee contains few of the conditions (only one, 30-minute delivery) that diminish the clarity and memorability of otherwise good service guarantees.

MEANINGFUL TO THE CUSTOMER AND THE PROVIDER

A meaningful guarantee gives customers the incentive to invoke the guarantee by calling for a substantial payout if the promise is not fulfilled. The type of payout and its magnitude depend on factors such as the cost of the service, the seriousness of the failure, and customers' perceptions of what's fair. The adage "Let the punishment fit the crime" is an appropriate yardstick. At one point, Domino's Pizza (which is based in Ann Arbor, Michigan, but operates nationwide) promised "delivery within 30 minutes or the pizza is free." Management found that many customers considered this too generous; they felt uncomfortable accepting free pizza for a mere 3- or 4-minute delay. Consequently, Domino's adjusted its guarantee to "deliver within 30 minutes or $3 off," and customers appeared to consider this commitment more reasonable.

On the other hand, Al Burger at "Bugs" Burger Bug Killers believes that the penalty associated with a failure to meet a service guarantee should be significant enough to provoke preventive and corrective behavior by the provider. He puts it a little more dramatically:

> It's unethical to . . . do work without a guarantee that can put you out of business. . . . If your company is unwilling to come up with a guarantee that will protect the consumer against defects, you're working for a second-rate company.[11]

EASY TO INVOKE

Too often, service organizations regard complaints as an annoyance. Enlightened service providers regard complaints as "golden nuggets" of information, the very foundation for service improvement, and a guarantee as a device for panning the gold. They encourage unhappy customers to invoke the guarantee rather than discourage them from doing so. Usually this means providing alternatives to written complaints and documentation that discourage many annoyed customers from going to the trouble to complain. Consider the following examples:

Traveler's Advantage, a division of CUC International, has in principle a great idea: to guarantee the lowest price on the accommodations it books. But to invoke the guarantee, customers must prove the lower competing price by booking with another agency. That's unpleasant work. By contrast, Cititravel, a subsidiary of Citicorp, guarantees the lowest price on the accomodations it books. A customer who knows of a lower price can call a toll-free number and speak with an agent, as one of us did. The agent told him that if he didn't have proof of the lower fare, she'd check competing airfares on her computer screen. If the lower fare was there, he would get that price. If not, she would call the competing airline. If the price was confirmed, she said, "We'll refund your money so fast, you won't believe it—because we want you to be our customer."[12]

Poor service typically puts customers "out-of-pocket" for unexpected expenses and inconvenience. To prolong the settlement period through complicated or slow collection procedures adds insult to injury. That's why, for example, dissatisfaction with a Manpower, Inc., temporary worker results in an immediate credit to a client's bill. Or why American Airlines ground personnel are empowered to pay cash-on-the-spot for complaints related to damaged baggage, even though the airline does not publish a guarantee for settling such claims.

Enlightened service providers understand that once poor service has been delivered, easy and quick settlement is cost effective for both the customer and the supplying firm. Further, it minimizes an unpleasant task for frontline employees.

CREDIBLE

Credibility in a service guarantee has two faces. First, the guarantee itself must be structured so that potential customers will believe it. Guarantees like "Lose 60 pounds in six weeks or your money back" tend to be dismissed by sophisticated weight watchers.

On the other hand, guarantees can offer credibility to those who offer them. On the surface, the BBBK guarantee, "no pests," sounds unbelievable, especially in an industry with a reputation for poor quality. But Al Burger's guarantee contains an extraordinary payout that covers all aspects of customers' costs, including rework, lost profit, and aggravation. The magnitude and scope of the payout conveys the message that Burger means what he says.

In a similar vein, the guarantee described earlier that is offered by the Henry Ford Community College has helped that institution build credibility several ways. It has had the clear effect of lowering the perceived risk of students who are concerned about the transferability of credits or the relevance of their studies to a specific job. And it has provided reassurance to state legislators, who are responsible for state aid and are sensitive to whether students who are trained in occupational programs become successfully employed.

A DECLARATION OF TRUST

How a guarantee is expressed can be as important as its content. A good guarantee communicates trust as well as the company's ability to deliver on its promises with no equivocation. The following guarantee offered by Virgin Atlantic Airways does this with a bit of humorous candor:[3]

> Experience a round-trip flight on Virgin between April 1 and April 30. Then, if you believe you've had a more accommodating flight to London in any other business class, we'll gladly refund the return portion of your ticket. (Well, maybe not gladly, but certainly with a smile on our face.)[13]

Good guarantees are evocative, reassuring. The best pry open the heart as well as the pocketbook. And they communicate an attitude of trust in both customers and employees. For example, Smith and Hawkins, a mail-order catalog retailer, tells its potential customers:[4]

> Our guarantee is simple. If you are not satisfied with any product at any time, for any reason, or no reason, we will either replace the product or refund the full purchase price. No quibbles, no hassles. We trust you. You have confidence in our products, and this guarantee has been our promise of quality since the day we began in business.[14]

THE GUARANTEE AS A SOURCE OF
MARKETING AND OPERATING LEVERAGE

A guarantee has been found to be a powerful management tool for service organizations. It provides marketing leverage by encouraging the entire organization to focus on customers' definitions of good service, not on executives' assumptions about what good service is. These can then be communicated with maximum impact through the guarantee to customers. Second, it provokes an evaluation of a firm's entire service delivery system for possible failure points. Third, it generates reliable data (through payouts) about those failure points, the first step in corrective action. But perhaps most important of all, it invariably injects a sense of urgency into all of these activities. The end result, of course, is unshakable customer loyalty.

MARKETING LEVERAGE

The odds of gaining significant marketing impact from a service guarantee are higher when: (1) the price of the service itself is high, (2) the customer's ego is on the line (for example, when getting a haircut), (3) the negative consequences of service failure are high, (4) the industry has a bad image for service quality (as, for example, many repair or pest-control services), (5) the customer's expertise with, and self-confidence in, buying the service is low, (6) the company depends on frequent customer repurchases, and (7) the company's business is affected deeply by word of mouth (as is often the case with professional services, restaurants, and resorts, for example).

The very act of preparing a guarantee requires a careful appraisal of customer needs. At Henry Ford Community College, for example, this required the assembly of information from both of its major constituencies, students and state legislators. The decision to develop a guarantee thus provides an excuse for what may be a much-needed market appraisal.

Because many guarantees offer a cost-free replacement of defective service experiences, they represent an opportunity for a service company to preserve a valued relationship. In and of themselves, they provide a second chance for a firm to maintain customer loyalty through effective service recovery, a matter we will turn to in some detail later.

OPERATING LEVERAGE

Committing to total customer satisfaction has helped force organizations to provide it. It has enabled managers to get control over their organization through a device that both generates information about service failure and provides an incentive to act on it. It may have its greatest value where the costs and causes of failure are unknown to personnel, including management, and where quality in general is difficult to control.

Making Costs Explicit. Costs associated with poor education are hard to measure. That's why the service guarantee offered by Henry Ford Community College attempts to do just that, put a dollar figure on the failure of an educational service. It may not reflect all such costs. But it is a step. And the resulting impact on a hard-to-manage process is interesting. The school's president, Stuart Bundy, maintains that one of the primary benefits of the guarantee is that teachers feel pressured to put together their courses with greater care and do a better job of class preparation.[15]

The shock value of a guarantee to a company's associates may be great. This is especially true if an effort is made to reflect total cost penalties from poor service in the guarantee itself, as has been done at "Bugs" Burger Bug Killers. Knowing that the explicit cost of service failure is not trivial provides a spur to determining the cause of the failure. Coupled with a program to charge such costs to the budget of an operating unit and take them into account in determining management compensation, it can offer a compelling reason to reevaluate the service delivery system.

Reevaluating the Service Delivery System. In developing a guarantee, managers must ask questions like: What failure points exist in the system? If failure points can be identified, can their origins be traced and overcome? A company that wants to promise timely service delivery, for example, must first understand its operation's capability and the factors limiting that capability. Many service executives, lacking understanding of such basic issues as system throughput time, capacity, and process flow, tend to blame employees, customers, or anything but the service delivery process.

Even if employees are a problem, management can do several things to "fix" the organization so that it can support a guarantee. For example, the pest-control industry has historically suffered from unmotivated personnel and high turnover. Al Burger overcame the status quo by offering higher-than-average pay (attracting a higher caliber of job candidates), using a vigorous screening program (making those hired feel like members of a select group), training all workers for six months, and keeping them motivated by giving them a great deal of autonomy and lots of recognition.

At the same time that it provides a motive for reevaluating the service delivery system and even the operating strategy, a service guarantee can provide information about critical failure points of importance in fixing the system.

Injecting a Sense of Urgency. A service guarantee is an unsurpassed spur to action. It releases energy by making the hemorrhaging from poor service visible. And energy, sheer hustle, is as important as a strategic plan in today's rapidly changing market conditions. As Amar Bhide has put it:

The competitive scriptures almost systematically ignore the importance of hustle and energy. While they preach strategic planning, competitive strategy, and competitive advantage, they overlook the record of a surprisingly large number of very successful companies that vigorously practice a different religion. These companies don't have long-term strategic plans with an obsessive preoccupation on rivalry. They concentrate on operating details and doing things well. Hustle is their style and their strategy. They move fast, and they get it right.[16]

Service guarantees impart a sense of energy by clearly focusing employee efforts on a single goal (customer satisfaction) and exacting a penalty when a service error occurs. This sense of urgency can be destructive, however, if it produces a fear of failure on the part of employees. It requires that the internal uses to which a guarantee is put be positive. This means rewards for excellent performance and further training in cases of poor performance.

MANAGEMENT CONCERNS

Why don't we see more service guarantees if they can produce so many benefits? In large part, this is because of perceived risks that managers are unwilling to expose themselves to. These include the possibility that service is influenced too greatly by uncontrollable factors, that customers will cheat in claiming service failure, and that resulting program costs will be too high.

Uncontrollable Factors. How many variables are truly beyond management's control? Not the work force. Not equipment problems. Not vendor quality. And even businesses subject to "acts of God" (like weather) can control a great deal of their service quality.

BBBK confronted this objection directly. By asking, "What obstacles stand in the way of our guaranteeing pest elimination?" Al Burger discovered that clients' poor cleaning and storage practices were one such obstacle. So the company requires customers to maintain sanitary practices and in some cases even make physical changes to their property, such as putting in walls. By influencing customer behavior, as we saw earlier at ServiceMaster and the Hartford Steam Boiler Inspection and Insurance Company, BBBK could guarantee the outcome.

A sports franchise may have as much difficulty fulfilling its customers' expectations as any service. How can you possibly guarantee a win? And yet Bob and Mindy Rich, owners of one of the most successful minor league baseball franchises, the Buffalo Bisons, have set out to implicitly assure their customers that they will have a good experience when they come to the ballpark. The service is delivered through such things as the Rich's own well-designed player development program, clean restrooms, and outstanding ballpark food, served in a Food Court outside the stadium, by costume-clad vendors in the ballpark, and in a 300-seat restaurant overlooking the field. According to Bob Rich:

> Our theory is that we're in a sport where we know we're going to lose roughly half our games. So what we're trying to do is control the things we can control. When people come to the park, they have a good family experience.[17]

The Rich's team in 1988 drew nearly 1.2 million fans to games in a stadium that seats only 19,500 in a city with a population of about 325,000 and shrinking, and by losing, like nearly all professional baseball teams, about half its games. So much for the inability to manage the uncontrollable factors.

Customer Cheating. Fear of customer cheating is another big hurdle for many service managers considering offering guarantees. But experience teaches a different lesson: What inevitable cheaters cost a company most often amounts to very little compared to the benefits derived from a strong guarantee.

For example, when Domino's Pizza first offered its "delivery within 30 minutes or the pizza is free" guarantee, some college students telephoned orders from hard-to-find locations. The result was free pizza for the students and lost revenue for Domino's. But Phil Bressler, an early Domino's franchisee, takes the view that the revenue lost was an investment in the future. As he says, "They'll be Domino's customers for life, those kids." Further, Bressler argues that customers cheat only when they feel cheated:

> If we charge $8 for a pizza, our customers expect $8 worth of product and service. If we started giving them $7.50 worth of product and service, then they'd start looking for ways to get back that extra 50 cents. Companies create the incentive to cheat, in almost all cases, by cutting costs and not providing value.

Cost Burdens. Managers are likely to worry about the costs of a service guarantee program, but for the wrong reasons. Such a program does cost money, particularly during the start-up phase. How much probably depends on the seriousness of a company's quality weaknesses, the nature of its current relations with employees and customers, and the nature of the business and its competitive dynamics. But even though a guarantee may require an up-front investment, badly performed services also incur costs. These are primarily the costs of failure, which come in many forms, mostly unmeasured, such as the cost of lost business from disgruntled consumers. In a service guarantee program, the costs of mopping up after failures are spent instead on preventing failures, with a resulting positive impact on revenues as well.

GUARANTEE DESIGN ISSUES

Firms contemplating the implementation of a service guarantee must decide whether it should be explicit or implicit, specific or total in coverage, and conditional or unconditional.

EXPLICIT VERSUS IMPLICIT GUARANTEES

Explicit service guarantees have the advantage of both serving as a marketing tool and encouraging customers to supply information about a service to its provider. But some excellent service companies do not offer written guarantees. The Seattle-based Nordstrom department store chain and the Toronto-based Four Seasons Hotels, for example, have "implicit" guarantees that permit complete discretion in meeting customer needs. At each company, the corporate policy that drives employees is, "Do whatever it takes to satisfy the customer." While perhaps lacking the public relations value of a strongly worded explicit guarantee, an implicit guarantee has an advantage from the standpoint that it does not place limits on the compensation given to dissatisfied customers. An implicit guarantee might also be more consonant with the image a company is trying to project. A management consulting firm that feels a publicly stated guarantee might cheapen its image, for example, could choose to offer an implicit guarantee or to guarantee its work on a client-by-client basis.

Companies realize the benefit of implicit guarantees through positive word-of-mouth advertising and "folklore." Folklore includes acts of exceptional service, such as driving a customer to the airport (at Nordstrom) or finding alternate accommodations for guests who are "bumped" due to overbooking, paying the bill at the other hotel, and providing them with limousine service (at Four Seasons).

CONDITIONAL VERSUS UNCONDITIONAL GUARANTEES

Most guarantees require customers to complete certain actions to qualify for the guarantee. Before agreeing to eliminate pests, for example, "Bugs" Burger requires customers to agree in writing to a thorough preparation of their premises for monthly servicing, one which eradicates the breeding places of pests and makes the guarantee easier to live up to. Such guarantees need to be worded very carefully so that the customer is aware of what is expected. In general, the greater the complexity or number of conditions, the harder a guarantee may be to administer and the less marketing and operating impact it may have. That may explain why Nordstrom, for example, has attached no conditions to its implicit guarantee that customers may return merchandise with no questions asked, whether or not they have a receipt showing that it was purchased from Nordstrom. This kind of guarantee raises few questions and requires little time to administer, insuring outstanding customer service and making available a maximum proportion of salespersons' time for selling.

SPECIFIC VERSUS TOTAL GUARANTEE

Federal Express stands for "absolutely, positively by 10:30 A.M.," not sometime tomorrow, probably. Its specific money-back guarantee is measurable to some objective standard set by Federal Express. In contrast, the standard for an unconditional guarantee is absolute customer satisfaction, as perceived by the customer.

Specific guarantees are useful in conveying an important, memorable marketing message and in giving customers a precise idea of what to expect when it is important, for example in package delivery. They are also useful in limiting a firm's liability when the outcome of the service is not immediately known. For example, an investment broker may choose to guarantee a minimum rate of return rather than unconditional satisfaction to protect against changing economic conditions.

Total guarantees are most appropriate when customer satisfaction is derived both from results provided by the service and the way it is delivered, most often in consumer services. They draw attention away from specific elements of performance, such as late airline arrivals, over which a company may not have full control. And perhaps most important, they offer an opportunity to the server to overcome a service failure with outstanding service recovery. In fact, it is attention to effective service recovery that makes explicit, unconditional, total guarantees feasible in many cases.

SERVICE RECOVERY[19]

A group bound for the Club Med resort in Cancun had a nightmarish charter flight from New York. The flight was ten hours late, arriving at 2 A.M. Food ran out early on, as did beverages. The landing at Cancun airport was so hard that oxygen masks dropped from above the seats, and luggage tumbled on passengers below. The pilot's comment was: "If you think *that* was rough, wait till you see how I pull up to the gate!" Most of the passengers considered their vacations ruined before they had begun. Indeed, a lawyer upset by the delay in the start of his vacation was having a field day collecting names and addresses for a possible class-action suit.

But the vacationers were fortunate to have Sylvio de Bortoli as the local Club Med Chef de Village. De Bortoli, legendary for his high customer satisfaction ratings, upon learning of the airplane's late arrival, had prepared a special greeting for the new guests. He took half of the staff to the airport, where they personally greeted each person, helped with their bags, listened sympathetically to their tales, and drove them to the Club Med village. When they arrived, the passengers were flabbergasted to find that the other half of the staff had prepared a lavish welcoming banquet, complete with a mariachi band and champagne. Moreover, the staff had rallied the other guests to wait up and greet the newcomers. The 3 A.M. welcome party lasted until sunrise, with guests commenting that it was the most fun they had had since college. The effect? Suffice it to say that the topic of a lawsuit never came up again. Sylvio de Bortoli had pulled off another of his famous service recoveries, more than compensating for a service lapse for which he was not even directly responsible.[20]

This is a memorable example of service recovery in achieving customer satisfaction. Other less spectacular but no less effective approaches to the same problem are being implemented every day. For example, the First National Bank of Chicago pays home mortgage customers $250 if they are dissatisfied with the speed and quality of the bank's loan application process. And First Union National Bank of Charlotte, N.C., sends a dozen roses to customers who have been badly inconvenienced or whose accounts have been "messed up." In some cases, says bank vice president Gail Hoffman, branch managers or bank executives personally deliver the flowers.[21]

Service recovery is one of the most important determinants of service quality and customer loyalty. Customer loyalty has a direct impact on profitability. And yet effective service recovery continues to receive little attention in most firms and in others is shunned like the plague.

WHY EMPHASIZE SERVICE RECOVERY?

We have been told repeatedly that the first "law" of quality is "do it right the first time." If this is accomplished, the result is customer satisfaction.

But while an increasing number of products are being made with highly controllable processes and procedures designed to approach zero defects, many aspects of service are hard (and some impossible) to control.

If all attention and resources are devoted to doing it right the first time, the inevitable result is a lack of attention to what happens when things don't go right. Worse yet, it may lead to an avoidance of any acknowledgement of the possibility of failure, the equivalent of an admission of weakness or a lack of resolve. And yet, by one means or another, customers tell us that both results and how they are achieved are important in a service, and that they are willing to reward handsomely absolute customer satisfaction.

Companies should not underestimate the power of a well-executed recovery. For several years, students in our service management classes have been required to write letters of praise or criticism to companies about a service experience. We have found that nearly two-thirds of the letters, both positive and negative, have been not about the original service experience, but about a recovery experience, actions by servers after either a service failure or customer complaint. The letters of praise are particularly significant. Most of them commended services which had not been performed perfectly, but had involved the correction of one or more problems by responsive personnel.

CRITICAL RECOVERY ENCOUNTER RELATIONSHIPS

Experiences of leading service firms suggest the relationships in the service recovery process shown in Figure 6–2. They pinpoint three "moments of truth" in the encounter at which: (1) the service is performed well or poorly, (2) having performed a service poorly, the server either does or does not elicit a complaint, and (3) having elicited a complaint, the server does or does not achieve effective service recovery. At each of these stages, satisfied or dissatisfied customers may tell other customers, potential customers, service intermediaries, people who generally are consulted for advice on services, other servers, and potential employees of the service organization—a formidable list.

The hierarchy of outcomes, based on research resulting from these encounters, is diagrammed in Figure 6–3. It suggests that while there generally is nothing better than performing a service to a customer's satisfaction at first, there is nothing worse than failing to elicit a response from a dissatisfied customer.

In addition, breakthrough service managers tell us that:

1. A majority of dissatisfied customers don't complain, they just tell other prospective customers, and often. A study by the Technical Assistance

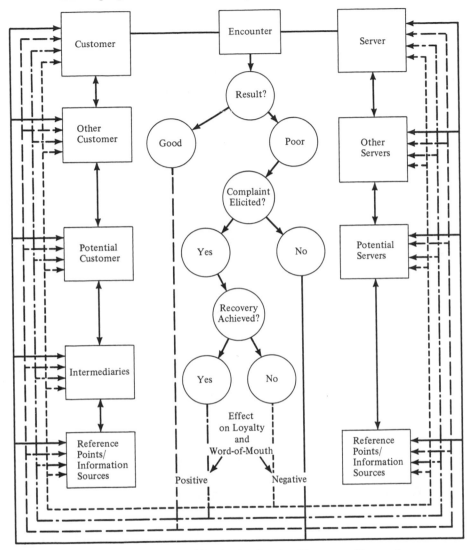

FIGURE 6–2 Important Relationships in the Service Recovery Encounter
SOURCE: Based on relationships reported in Christopher W. L. Hart, James L. Heskett, and W. Earl Sasser, Jr., "The Profitable Art of Service Recovery," *Harvard Business Review*, July–August 1990, pp. 148–156.

Research Programs Institute (TARP) for the U.S. Office of Consumer Affairs found that consumers who felt their complaints had not been satisfactorily resolved typically told nine or ten people about their negative experiences (in contrast to completely satisfied customers who typically told only four or five people about their positive experiences).[22]

2. The resulting negative impact is not limited to prospective customers.

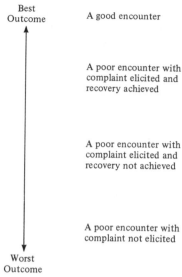

FIGURE 6–3 Hierarchy of
Important Outcomes from the
Service Encounter[a]
[a] Based on a composite of research re-
sults and individual company experi-
ences collected in the preparation of
Christopher W. L. Hart, James L.
Heskett, and W. Earl Sasser, Jr., "The
Profitable Art of Service Recovery,"
Harvard Business Review, July–August
1990, pp. 148–156.

It may also be felt by employees receiving informal complaints and poor
treatment from customers who fall short of filing formal complaints.

3. For this reason, breakthrough service companies try to insure that
dissatisfied customers tell them first.

4. The effective response to service failures and complaints not only has
a high payoff in terms of long-term business, it sends positive signals to both
customers and employees that the service company's policy is to encourage
corrective action and achieve customer satisfaction, enhancing the company
as a place to work in the minds of its employees. This quite likely occurred,
for example, when a Delta Air Lines jet crashed in Dallas in 1985. Delta,
which has a history of excellent service and planning, rushed scores of
employees from its Atlanta headquarters to the scene to be with every family
of the crash victims. The company put aside all budgetary protocol and
spared no expense in its efforts to help people with everything from purchasing new clothing to making funeral arrangements. A cynic might con-

clude that the goal was to reduce claims against Delta, which probably occurred. A point that shouldn't be ignored, however, is that the action made Delta employees feel better about themselves and their company.

BREAKTHROUGH SERVICE RECOVERY EFFORTS

Leading service managers recognize that recovery efforts produce high returns on invested effort. As a result, they go to extraordinary lengths to insure that they elicit customer complaints, analyze points in time or in the delivery process at which the need for recovery is occurring, design appropriate recovery responses, and assign people with appropriate skills to the recovery process.

Eliciting Customer Complaints. Managers either purposely or unwittingly suppress complaints, viewing them as negative marks on short-term performance rather than what one breakthrough service manager has called the "golden nuggets of information" that provide the basis for recovery. As a result, some of the most important information available to a service company is lost. Recognizing this, breakthrough service managers such as British Airways' CEO Colin Marshall try to make it as easy as possible for disgruntled customers to complain, as suggested by this vignette:

> Since taking charge at British Airways four years ago, [Marshall] has tried to give unhappy passengers royal treatment—or at least the chance to complain. In London, disgruntled travelers can tape their grievances as soon as they get off the plane in the airline's new Video Point booths. Customer service managers view the videos and respond to complaints.[23]

Hearing complaints is so important to Robert Masterson, CEO of One Bancorp of Portland, Maine, for example, that he offers customers $1 for every letter they write to him. Over 7,000 people have written to Mr. Masterson, many of them to complain. Mr. Masterson is convinced he is getting his money's worth: "They [the letters] give us an instant kind of feedback on policy decisions. If suddenly we get 10 letters on the same issue, we've got a problem that we better look into."[24]

Toll-free 800 telephone numbers have become the most common method of solving and handling complaints expeditiously. Telephone complaint systems generally are regarded as less expensive as well. For example, "American Express spends five to ten times as much replying to a letter as it does answering a complaint over its toll-free lines."[25]

Evidence suggests that just soliciting and listening to complaints is a better strategy for keeping customers than discouraging complaints. For example, the previously mentioned TARP study for the U.S. Office of Consumer Affairs found that for goods or services over $100 in value, 54% of all customers whose complaints were elicited and resolved purchased again. Of those complaints that were elicited but not resolved, 19% purchased again. But of those whose complaints were not even elicited or heard, only 9% came back.[26]

The return on investment for complaint handling units can be substantial, as suggested in Table 6-1. This may require putting in easy-to-use direct lines of communication between customers and senior management such as British Airways' Video Point booths or J. Willard Marriott's "Will You Let Me Know?" customer questionnaire in each of Marriott's hotel rooms.

Analyzing Service Failure Points. Managers of breakthrough services diagram important service failure points and act proactively to prevent them or plan in advance effective recovery procedures. They recognize that leading indicators of possible service encounter problems and recovery opportunities are: (1) service process steps involving complex scheduling, (2) a complex service process, (3) new service introductions, (4) process steps associated with high employee turnover, (5) inadequate training of front-line employees, and (6) points in the service process at which there is an unusual reliance on suppliers or exposure to other external factors such as weather.

This often requires the development of a process-flow diagram such as that shown in Figure 6-4 for auto repair. In addition to helping visualize the service delivery process, this kind of diagram can be used to identify both points that are particularly critical to the success of an encounter and points at which failure is most often experienced. This allows the development of methods both for fixing problems and recovering in the event of failure. And

Table 6-1 RETURN ON INVESTMENT IN A SAMPLE OF CORPORATE COMPLAINT HANDLING UNITS

Industry	Annual Return on Investment
Retailing	35%–40%
Banking	50–170%
Gas Utilities	20–150%
Automotive service	100% +
Consumer durable goods	100% +
Packaged goods	15–75%
Electronic products	50%

SOURCE: Technical Assistance Research Programs Institute, *Consumer Complaint Handling in America: An Update Study*, Part II, a study performed for the U.S. Office of Consumer Affairs, April 1, 1986, pp. 5–6.

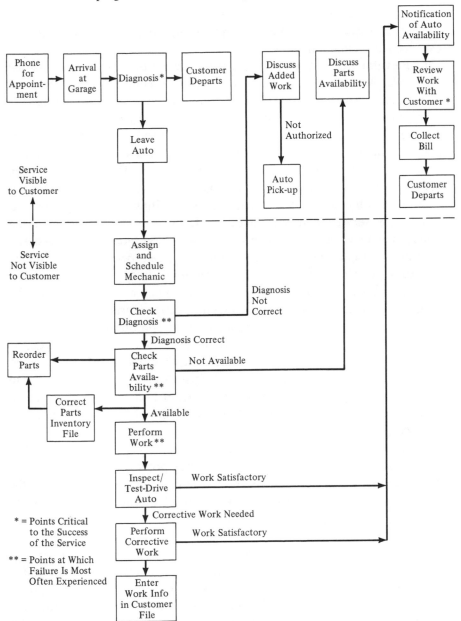

FIGURE 6–4 A Process-Flow Diagram for the Auto Repair Process[a]

[a] Certain concepts shown are adapted from G. Lynn Shostack, "Service Positioning Through Structural Change," *Journal of Marketing*, January 1987, pp. 34–43.

it may suggest the importance of systematically collecting data about failures and recovery performance and measuring such performance against preset recovery standards.

Otis Elevator, for instance, has created a special recovery service, called OTISLINE. A sophisticated database linked to a central 800-number customer service department, OTISLINE helps the company respond quickly and effectively to emergency service (i.e., recovery) calls on its elevators. Moreover, OTISLINE allows the company to produce "excess callback reports," which focus company attention and resources on elevators receiving an unacceptably high number of service calls. The result has been threefold: first, the company responds faster to repair calls; second, faster response gives the company a strategic edge in winning and keeping lucrative elevator service contracts; and, third, by identifying and repairing problem elevators, Otis can reduce service callbacks. Indeed, Otis has determined that if it can reduce service callbacks by one per year per installed elevator, the company will save $5 million annually.[27]

Designing Appropriate Responses. Not only must recovery standards be set and performance measured against them, but appropriate responses must be designed. While Domino's Pizza may find it appropriate to refund customers $3 on a pizza that requires more than 30 minutes to deliver, that is hardly appropriate for passengers on the Concorde who might be inconvenienced by a technical problem. In fact, British Airways refunded $3,200 to each of 62 passengers on a Concorde flight from London when a technical problem forced the plane to land in New York, short of its Washington and Miami destinations.[28]

Assigning People with Appropriate Skills. But perhaps most important of all is the personal manner in which the recovery process is carried out. This requires assigning people with the best listening and human skills to the recovery process, giving them the most careful training, providing them with decision latitude for the use of good judgment, and rewarding them well for their good work.

Breakthrough service companies determine whether frontline personnel have both the capabilities and adequate training to deal with both routine and recovery service encounters. The best seek to staff customer-contact points and train people who can handle all types of encounters, thus reducing communication and speeding up recoveries. However, because recoveries quickly can consume staff resources needed to carry out routine business, personnel may have to be diverted to do one or the other. Envision, for example, the chaos at the airport when a flight is unexpectedly cancelled. Ticket agents, struggling to deal with angry passengers who must make new travel arrangements, begin to neglect other customers who are preparing to board flights from neighboring gates. In short, businesses must plan ahead so that individual problems don't cause the entire service process to hemorrhage.

Once fail points are identified and recovery planning set in place, dry runs or practice drills are valuable in testing and refining a recovery system. The United States Secret Service, for instance, runs its employees through a comprehensive assortment of recovery drills before its agents actually go to work in the field. "We spend hours thinking about what will happen," says Jane Zezeris, a spokesperson for the Secret Service, whose protection agents might be viewed as among the most highly trained recovery specialists. "All of the possible contingencies have been discussed and planned for." Zezeris says that each agent—no matter how senior—receives updated training annually and participates in frequent recovery drills.[29]

The payoff for all this practice and preplanning is the flawless resolution of problems that might otherwise choke the entire service system. Consider the case of an insurance company CEO who had just checked out of the Sheraton Hotel in Boca Raton.[30] While he and his travel companions were loading luggage into a rental car, someone unwittingly locked the keys in the trunk, causing great concern for the departing guests who were en route to the airport and creating a major traffic snarl in front of the hotel.

Seeing a problem in the making, the hotel's bellman took control of the situation and began a preplanned recovery routine. He immediately informed the CEO that a locksmith was nearby and the hotel would have a replacement set of keys made within 15 minutes. Meanwhile, the hotel staff quickly retrieved an auto jack that was bolted on a dolly and stored close at hand. The recovery crew jacked up the car (locked in parking gear) and pushed it out of the way of hotel check-in traffic. Then the bellman telephoned the car's year, make, and serial number to a local locksmith.

The bellman made a special point of keeping the CEO well informed throughout the recovery process, and within 15 minutes, as promised, a hotel employee returned with a replacement key. A potentially costly mishap was turned to triumph. Had the hotel had no such recovery procedure in place the departing guests would have missed their plane, cars would have piled up in front of the hotel, and other guests checking in and checking out would have been inconvenienced. This was an impresario recovery. The recovery system was in place, the players knew their roles, quick action was taken to correct the situation, and the customer was kept well informed of the recovery plan, its moment-by-moment progress, and the problem's resolution.

Breakthrough service companies we have observed often handle recovery encounters in this fashion. To summarize, things we often observe them doing include: (1) recruiting, hiring, training, and promoting for overall service recovery excellence, (2) actively soliciting complaints which are viewed as marketing and process improvement opportunities, (3) measuring both the primary and secondary costs of dissatisfied customers and gearing corrective investments to the level of the costs, (4) empowering frontline employees to take appropriate, pre-planned corrective action on the spot, (5) fostering short lines of communication between customers and managers, (6) rewarding employees for receiving and resolving customer complaints and fixing the sources of such complaints rather than for receiving low numbers of complaints in the first place, (7) including service and recovery excellence as part of a company's business strategy, and (8) most important of all, committing top-level management both to "do it right the first time" and effective service recovery programs.

CONCLUSION

The most important result of service guarantees and associated service recovery initiatives is their ability to change an industry's rules of the game by changing the service delivery process as competitors conceive it. BBBK, L. L. Bean, Domino's Pizza, Manpower, and Marriott, among others, have redefined the meaning of service in their industries, performing at levels that are hard for competitors to match. (According to the owner of a competing pest control company, BBBK "is number one. There is no number two.")

The commitment to deliver total customer satisfaction is one that few service organizations can make publicly with credibility and reasonable levels of financial risk. It can allow for mistakes if service recovery is studied and practiced. Because the causes of service failure and appropriate recovery actions are not always predictable, breakthrough service organizations rely on frontline employees to accomplish effective recovery. Success invariably results from an emphasis on value to the customer rather than cost, empowering employees to deliver value, and trusting them to spend judiciously what is necessary to achieve total customer satisfaction.

Jan Carlzon summed it up nicely when asked recently if there is a danger that empowered employees can spend too much money rectifying a problem. His response:

What's the danger of giving away too much? Are you worried about having an oversatisfied customer? That's not much of a worry. You can forget about an oversatisfied customer, but an unsatisfied customer is one of the most expensive problems you can have . . . the danger is not that employees will give away too much. It's that they won't give away anything—because they don't dare.[31]

This is breakthrough management philosophy. Understanding what outstanding service quality is and some of the most visible, memorable ways for achieving it is important. But as someone has said, quality is a journey, not a destination. It's slugging it out on the road day-after-day with policies and processes that insure sustained effort rather than sporadic, superhuman achievements. Those firms making the journey have found that they have acquired a fellow traveler along the way. It's improved productivity, as we will see next.

7

Managing for Quality and Productivity Gains

The mark of an outstanding service organization is the continued effort it devotes to widening the gap between itself and its major competitors on both service quality and productivity. The effort is both diligent and persistent, almost crusade-like in nature. At firms such as Florida Power & Light, American Express, American Airlines, and The Paul Revere Insurance Company there is almost a single-minded fixation on the challenge. It involves large numbers of people. The process itself as well as the results are made highly visible. The irony is that these are firms that have already established superiority in quality and productivity over all or most of their competitors. They still don't think they're good enough. Whether they are right or not, it's a healthy attitude.

In response to growing concerns about the quality of goods and services produced in the United States, Congress in 1987 enacted the National Quality Awards Law creating the Malcolm Baldrige Awards to be given each year to two companies each in manufacturing, services, and small business. It is hoped that this will be an answer to the Deming Prize program in Japan, a program ironically named after the American whose teachings had fallen on deaf ears in his own country for years after their almost fanatical acceptance in Japan. In 1988 and 1989, the first years Baldrige Awards were given, the board of judges ruled that none of the nine service companies that submitted applications rated high enough on quality to deserve an award.

Ask managers who have made the transition from manufacturing to service operations and invariably they will cite the greater difficulty of controlling quality in services as the biggest difference in managing in the two sectors.[1] Often they go further to attribute their difficulties to the fact that many services are delivered as they are produced, often by the same person; the great sensitivity of service quality to the day-to-day variability in attitudes and behavior of employees; the impossibility of inspecting a service before delivering it; the challenge of supervising a large army of "frontline" servers often found in hundreds of service facilities located close to customers; and the challenge of measuring service quality in the first place.

THE RELATIONSHIP BETWEEN
SERVICE QUALITY AND PRODUCTIVITY

Thoughtful managers responsible for service operations agree on something else. Service quality and productivity vary directly with one another. Quality is not achieved at the cost of lost productivity; productivity gains need not affect quality adversely.

Experiences at a number of leading service companies tend to confirm these beliefs. For example:

Each day that an American Express card applicant has to wait for the card or each day that a cardholder has to wait for the replacement of a lost card was determined several years ago to cost the company the service charge on $2.70 worth of purchases by means of the card. Further, it raised the likelihood that the customer would use a competitive card. With this information in hand, the company formed employee task forces to examine various opportunities for improved performance by breaking down all service operations into their basic elements, measuring each, and then devising ways to improve them. One task force discovered that it took 35 days to process an application for a credit card. A survey suggested that applicants became impatient after 21 days, so that became the new standard of quality. The cause of poor quality was a complex flow of documents and information between different departments. Because managers of the involved departments were included on the task force, one regional director for customer service remarked that "the system forces the walls between departments to come down."[2]

The new standard for quality is now being met, and with fewer people. A restructuring of jobs achieved the same results at a major bank:

At Continental Illinois National Bank & Trust Co. of Chicago, where there are no clerical unions, Christine Szcesniak worked for 17 years on a check-processing line, performing one function over and over.

Now she works at a computer terminal in a "modular" arrangement and performs nearly all the tasks necessary to handle checks sent in by companies that buy goods and services from some 3,000 corporate clients by Continental. "I think it's exciting and different," Szcesniak says. "It's cut down our error ratio, and that's very important for me."

Szcesniak now processes checks that arrive in the mail, deposits them in customers' accounts by computer, telephones customers with up-to-date information on their accounts, and mails the data to them. Under the automated system, each employee processes an average of 50 checks per hour, a 40% increase in productivity over the old approach. "I like it," Szcesniak says, "because you see the package from beginning to end. It's better to be part of the whole thing. Everyone should have change in their life."[3]

In spite of encouraging experiences in individual service-producing companies, productivity in services as it is currently measured is thought to be a drag on overall productivity in many post-industrial societies, especially the United States.

Between 1980 and 1988, manufacturing output per hour of labor rose by more than 3.5% annually, while productivity in nonmanufacturing industries increased at an annual rate of only 1.3%. Poor productivity in the service sector caused the country's overall productivity rate increase to fall to an average of 1.8% annually during the 1980s, a rate far below what it was before 1970 and slower than the rates of other advanced economies.[4] Further, the average yearly growth in the productivity of U.S. service businesses has fallen to a third of what it was in the early 1970s.

If such measures are accurate (a much-debated issue) and productivity and quality levels are thought to be related directly, it would tend to substantiate consumers' perceptions of poor and failing services. And yet, suppliers of breakthrough services have found ways of reversing the vicious cycle resulting from these relationships. How do they do it? It is impossible to understand the complexity and attention to detail associated with such efforts without turning to substantial case examples.

MANAGING FOR IMPROVED QUALITY

The process of managing for improved service quality and productivity begins with an understanding of customers' expectations.

Quality in a service is, as we have said, the difference between the service provided and what a customer expected. It is relative and defined in terms of what each customer expects. The customer, not the server, defines quality. Compare this with the traditional definition of quality for manufactured products, ''conformance to specifications,''[5] suggesting objective measures often defined by the manufacturer, a concept quite inappropriate for most services.

Once customers' expectations have been determined or at least estimated, the analysis necessary to determine causes for deficient service can begin. This naturally leads to the development of service standards. Our concern here is only secondarily with how such standards are arrived at in leading service firms. Rather our concern is primarily with the ways these companies organize themselves to mount the sustained, endless effort required to maintain competitive advantage and dedicated customers.

UNDERSTANDING CUSTOMERS' EXPECTATIONS

Customers' expectations of both results produced by a service and the way it is delivered are, as we have seen, at least as important to perceptions of quality as the absolute level of service quality delivered. The dimensions on which customers think about quality have been researched extensively by Leonard Berry, A. Parasuraman, and Valarie Zeithaml. They have concluded that the most important are reliability (the ability to perform the desired service dependably, accurately, and consistently), responsiveness (the willingness to provide prompt service and help customers), assurance (employees' knowledge, courtesy, and ability to convey trust and confidence), empathy (the provision of caring, individualized attention to customers), and tangibles (the physical facilities, equipment, and appearance of personnel).[6]

Measuring perceptions, however, can be a real challenge requiring creativity. For the most part, if perceptions of quality are measured at all, they are measured through customer surveys, customer complaints, input from employees who interact with customers, quality audits, or on the basis of informal and unsolicited customer comments. Unfortunately, most of these ''methods'' provide an unstructured, uncontrolled, and biased sample because only those customers who've had an exceedingly good or bad experience are motivated to respond. Obtaining an accurate measure of service quality is also a challenge because of the difficulty of directly supervising and controlling the service transaction, because the output of a service often is intangible and the perception of its quality is necessarily a subjective judgment, and because an individual perception often cannot be related to what actually was delivered. In short, the quality of service can't be objectively determined in the way a manufactured product can be inspected to ensure that it meets precise predetermined standards.

In spite of these challenges, managers of leading service firms have devised innovative programs not only for monitoring customers' perceptions but also relating those perceptions to fact. For example, American Airlines regularly monitors a number of customer experiences such as time spent waiting in line to be ticketed, to check and pick up baggage, to deplane after arrival at the gate, to take off and arrive in relation to scheduled times, and others at each of a number of its major terminals.[7] Customers' views that such times are acceptable or too long are then compared to actual time lapses experienced by each respondent. From this, a graph can be constructed showing the point at which customers' perceptions of unacceptability on a particular measure "go critical." For waits for ticketing, for example, this tends to be about five minutes under most circumstances.

But American's program doesn't stop there. At the same terminals, similar measurements are made of the services provided to (and perceived by) customers of its most important competitors. Data showing facts and perceptions about both its own and its major competitors' services provides American's individual station managers with guidelines for staffing, opening up additional capacity at peak periods of demand, and generally adjusting service to competitive levels.

This approach does not insure that every customer's expectations will be met. However, it does provide the basis for deciding what share of customers' expectations American's management can afford to meet.

By way of contrast, until recently the management of British Airways believed travelers measured the level of certain services, such as check-in, by the number of people they saw in front of them in line. Based on its measurement of customer perceptions at its major stations, it staffed its counters to insure that the maximum number of people in line in front of a passenger entering the queue was no more than seven people for economy class, four for business (Club) class, two for first class, and one for Concorde passengers.[8] The simplicity and visibility of these rules of thumb made them easy to manage. (Nevertheless, British Airways has more recently shifted to service standards based on waiting times.)

These differences of approach by the managements of two airlines are less important than the fact that both are diligent in managing for quality. Their excellent performances in recent years, both in terms of quality of effort and profitability, suggest that the method used is less important than management's conviction that quality pays.

ANALYZING AND DESIGNING THE SERVICE DELIVERY SYSTEM

In designing or reviewing the way in which services are delivered, it is useful alternatively to take the viewpoint of the customer, the server, and the firm providing the service. During the process, it is important to keep in mind the cycle of relationships shown in Figure 1–3.

The design process involves the flow-charting of the service delivery process, the identification of quality-sensitive points in the process, the examination of factors influencing performance at quality-sensitive points, and actions intended to anticipate or remedy problems that might arise at such points. In this process, designers of breakthrough services have utilized a number of useful techniques, among them flow-charting, "fishbone" analysis, and Pareto analysis. Their use leads directly to the establishment of service standards. After describing each of them briefly, let's see how they've been put to work in the quality management program developed at Florida Power & Light, one of the most outstanding of its kind in the United States.

Flow-Charting. Charting even the simplest of services provides a graphic view of the steps required in delivering a service. One useful variation on the standard flow chart is the "blueprinting" of a service illustrated in Figure 6–4. Here steps performed in view of or in contact with a customer are charted "above the line" and other steps charted "below the line." This further separation of "front-office" and "back-office" steps in the process helps in the visualization of particularly critical points at which quality is affected in a service delivery process. These may be points at which there is insufficient capacity, intensive human interaction that may be difficult to control, or visible exposure of the service delivery system to the customer. In Figure 6–4 they are designated as failure points.

Once these critical points, which we like to call "pressure points," are identified, they can be prioritized for attention in terms of the amount of leverage (improvement in the difference between value and cost) that can be achieved by each action. This prioritization will require measurements of current quality as well as analyses of causes of quality shortcomings at each pressure point, perhaps using other techniques discussed below.

A second important criterion for prioritization may be established to insure balanced attention to various actions intended to improve quality. For example, in auto repair, the washing of each car delivered back to its owner may cost little and create an immediately positive impression in the mind of the customer. But unless attention is also given to critical steps in the repair process such as accurate diagnoses and effective mechanical work, long-run customer perceptions of high-quality repair service will not be achieved.

Cause-and-Effect or "Fishbone" Analysis. Cause-and-effect or "fishbone" analysis involves the identification of causes of poor performance at a prominent "fail point" or "pressure point." This identification often is carried out by members of work groups experiencing a problem and produces results of the type shown in Figure 7–1 for flight departure delays at Midway Airlines.

The first step in the process is the designation of an important problem symptom, in this case delayed flight departures. Next, the resources required to achieve any kind of flight departure are identified, shown in Figure 7–1 in boxes labeled equipment, personnel, material, procedure, and other. Then problem causes associated with each resource are identified, listed,

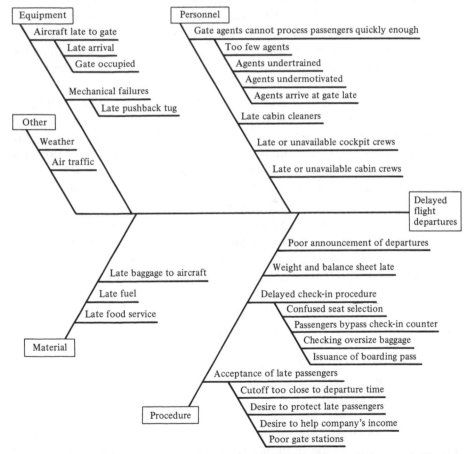

FIGURE 7–1 Fishbone Analysis of Causes of Flight Departure Delays at Midway Airlines

SOURCE: D. Daryl Wyckoff, "New Tools for Achieving Service Quality," *The Cornell Hotel and Restaurant Administration Quarterly*, November 1984, pp. 78–91, at p. 89.

and prioritized, often by means of a voting procedure within the group. For those causes thought to be most critical, such as "acceptance of late passengers" in this case, separate fishbones may be prepared. Based on the identification of and agreement on important causes, corrective actions can be taken. However, before reaching this step, the cause-and-effect analysis may suggest the need for collection of additional data and their organization into, among other things, a Pareto analysis.

Pareto Analysis. Pareto first drew the curve that suggests that 80% of any problem or phenomenon often is due to 20% of the possible causes. Thus, about 80% of most firms' sales are produced by about 20% of its products. About 85% of beer consumed in the United States is consumed by about 15% of the drinkers. Eighty percent of labor grievances or absences from work often can be associated with only about 20% of the labor force. And so it is with service quality. For example, Daryl Wyckoff reports that a Pareto analysis of late departures at three of Midway Airlines' terminals resulted in the finding that more than 80% of all late departures were due to only five causes at each terminal. First on the list at each terminal was "holding the plane for late passengers." Others were "waiting for fueling (all terminals), waiting for pushback (all terminals), late weight and balance sheet (two terminals), and waiting for cabin cleaning and suppliers (one terminal)."[9] As Wyckoff points out:

> Most agents were anxious that Midway not lose the fares of the late-comers, and most agents were also sympathetic to the late passenger (although they forgot the inconvenience to the many passengers who had made the effort to arrive on time). Midway established a policy that it would operate on time and give top service to passengers who were ready to fly on schedule. This discipline was appreciated by the passengers, and the number of late passengers soon declined.[10]

Development of Service Standards. Once analysis has begun to suggest levels of performance that are achievable through improvements in policies, procedures, technology, or incentives, standards can be developed for performance at critical pressure points in the delivery process. These may be stated in the form of both acceptable lower limits and goals. They must be quantifiable, as suggested by the set of standards developed for food service and cocktail service at Rusty Pelican Restaurants several years ago, shown in Table 7-1. Actual performance against such standards can then be tracked either by management or, better yet, by the servers themselves.

The Quality Improvement Program (QIP) at the Florida Power & Light Company employs all of these techniques in the analysis and design of high-quality service delivery systems.[11] FPL's program is particularly note-

Table 7–1 SERVICE STANDARDS FOR RUSTY PELICAN RESTAURANTS

Food-service standards

(1) First contact—cocktail server speaks to customer within two minutes of customer seating

(2) Cocktails delivered—beverage service at table within four minutes of order. If no beverage order, request for food order within four minutes of first greeting.

(3) Request for order—within four minutes after beverage service, customer should be asked whether he or she cares to order.

(4) Appetizers delivered—salad, chowder or wine delivered within five minutes.

(5) Entree delivered—entree served within 16 minutes of order.

(6) Dessert delivered—dessert and coffee or after-dinner drinks served within five minutes after plates are cleared.

(7) Check delivered—check presented within four minutes after dessert course or after plates are cleared if no dessert.

(8) Money picked up—cash or credit cards picked up within two minutes of being placed by customer on table.

Cocktail-service standards

(1) First contact—greeting given and cocktail order taken; seafood bar, happy-hour specials, and wine-by-glass menus presented within two minutes.

(2) Cocktails delivered—cocktails delivered within five minutes after first contact.

(3) Seafood bar delivered—seafood bar and happy-hour specials delivered within seven minutes of first contact; ten minutes for cooked items.

(4) Next contact—check for reorder of cocktail, seafood bar, customer satisfaction, and table maintenance within five minutes from delivery of first cocktail.

SOURCE: D. Daryl Wyckoff, "New Tools for Achieving Service Quality," *The Cornell Hotel and Restaurant Administration Quarterly*, November 1984, pp. 78–91, at p. 87.

worthy for having moved the company from worst case to best in quality, as CEO John Hudiburg puts it, in about six years. In addition to certain of its organizational features, the program emphasizes quantitative analysis, known at FPL as "management by fact," as a cornerstone. A sign outside the office of Kent Sterett, head of the Quality Improvement Department, recently read, "In God we trust; all others must bring data."

FPL's top management implemented its QIP in 1981 at a time when the company, which serves two-thirds of the fifth-largest state in the United States, was in a condition of near-crisis from a second oil shortage, a commitment to the construction of several nuclear power plants, rising costs and rates, irate customers, and possible deregulation of the industry. According to then-chairman Marshall McDonald:

> We had been concerned with keeping rejects down, instead of quality up. We had been busy keeping imperfection under control, rather than trying for perfection. We had sometimes burnt the toast and then scraped it clean, instead of fixing the toaster. Some of us had even learned to like burned toast.[12]

The response was the creation of a Quality Improvement (QI) Department, designed only to support the process, not to provide the leadership for which top and line management were to be held responsible. The effort was begun with ten QI teams, selected and engineered to succeed. Five years later, FPL had 1,400 of such teams organized around functional, cross-functional, and task-oriented problems as well as "lead teams" comprising managers responsible for the success of teams under their direction. Each team followed the same basic steps of what was known as "The Process," involving establishing the reason for improvement, describing the current situation, analysis, the development of countermeasures to problems, the documentation of results, standardization to prevent the problem from recurring, and the statement of plans for work to achieve further improvement. A storyboard format was used to require teams to "fill in the blanks" in an orderly fashion as their work progressed. As a result, storyboards such as the one shown in Figure 7–2 can be seen on the walls of many FPL offices today. The storyboards provide instant, visible reports of progress to supervisors as well as constant reminders of the importance of the effort.

At each step of "The Process," teams were encouraged to adhere to "management by fact," collecting and analyzing data through the use of flow charts, graphs, Pareto diagrams, and fishbone (cause and effect) diagrams.

Several years after the initiation of the program, through a phase called "Policy Deployment," an effort was made to involve both teams and top management in a closer linkage of corporate goals to individual team efforts to encourage teams to concentrate their efforts on projects with the biggest payoffs commensurate with corporate objectives. This process in a sense opened the objective-setting process at all levels of the organization.

Finally, a third phase of FPL's program directed attention to "Quality of Daily Work," the quality of the work environment and service to customers inside the firm. This effort employed the same kind of organization and "management by fact" as previous phases. Throughout all three phases of the program, top management leadership by example and elaborate recog-

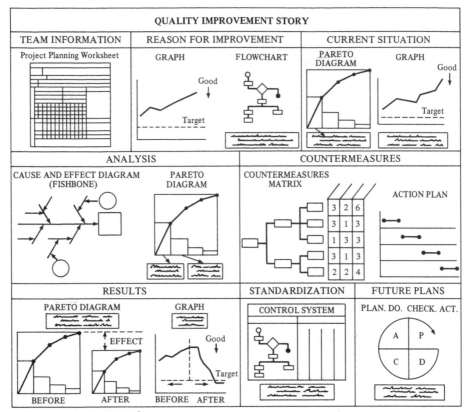

Adapted from the concept of the QC Story, originally named by Mr. Nogawa, president of Komatsu, for the purpose of reporting improvement activities. Professor Ikezawa and others expanded the procedure to include its use as a guide for solving a problem.

FIGURE 7–2 Storyboard Format for Quality Teams at Florida Power & Light
SOURCE: From Christopher W. L. Hart and Joan S. Livingston, "Florida Power and Light's Quality Improvement Program," Case 9-688-043. Boston: Harvard Business School, 1987, page 16. Reprinted by permission.

nition were much more important motivators than relatively modest monetary rewards to teams.

By 1986, "Contribution to QIP" had become an item on every FPL performance-appraisal form and a determinant of pay raises. CEO Hudiburg estimated that he spent 55 days of his time on quality that year. Little wonder that Xerox and Hewlett-Packard, who benchmarked their quality improvement programs against those of other companies, identified FPL's as the best. Or that the President of the foundation created to support the Malcolm Baldrige Award competition, the recently established U.S. Government initiative to encourage quality, was Hudiburg, who did not place his company in competition in order to preserve the credibility of the Awards.

Or that FPL has become the first American firm ever to compete for and win Japan's coveted Deming Award for superior quality.

Once problems in producing quality services have been analyzed, the process of marshaling the resources to produce them begins.

MARSHALING THE RESOURCES

Basic resources in the delivery of high-quality services include facility logistics, technology, information, and people, probably in reverse order of importance.

Facility Logistics. Facilities can be designed to limit options in serving customers, creating a more standardized and high-quality service encounter. Thus, Benetton's typical 600-square-foot store for the retailing of women's ready-to-wear restricts staffing to two or at most three persons and provides little or no "back-room" space. Shelving for merchandize largely is fixed. The facility guarantees high visibility for often-inexperienced salespersons who have no place to hide, encouraging them to occupy their time waiting on customers and straightening merchandise.

In contrast, a Caterair International kitchen is equipped with a great deal of equipment, including work tables and storage racks, on wheels. A rapidly changing set of demands from airlines delaying and cancelling flights from day to day and hour to hour is accommodated by the creation of ad hoc work spaces and processes in a highly flexible setting. This permits a great deal of management and employee latitude and relies on considerable use of judgment by employees, many of whom have been with the company for years.

Both of these facilities are capable of supporting high-quality service delivery under greatly different conditions.

Technology. Contrasting beliefs about the kind of resources that should be marshaled in search of quality in services apply equally well to the use of technology.

McDonald's french-fry machine, with timer and bell, makes it hard for even the most inexperienced employee to produce poor-quality fries, replacing human judgment on the part of a labor force that is, in large part, just entering the labor market and registers a high rate of turnover. In the process, employees are freed to wait on larger numbers of customers while consistently producing high-quality french-fries, something apparently difficult for McDonald's competitors to do, judging from the company's success in taste-test competition. Theodore Levitt has termed this general philosophy "the industrialization of service."[13]

In contrast, diagnostic devices in medicine are improving the process of patient diagnosis by yielding more information sooner about alternative diagnoses that might or might not be correct in a given case. But the doctor still must decide, perhaps with more information sooner about a wider range of alternatives. In this case, the technology may allow consideration and rejection of a larger number of possibilities, leading to creative diagnoses that likely could not have been made with less technology. Instead of being constraining in this case, the technology used in medical diagnosis may have a liberating quality.

Information Systems. Various views of the role of information in a service influence the kind of software design, network communications, and operating unit computing capability that a firm employs.

The information system at Mrs. Fields Cookies was developed by Debbi and Randy Fields to provide central control over the management of several hundred retail shops selling Mrs. Fields products. At the same time, it was intended to insure a high level of both freshness and availability of product, two determinants of quality in the company's service. The system is driven by a database of previous sales results by store for various seasons and days of the week. It generates from this database instructions to each manager about how many cookies of each type and how much labor input will be needed the next day. Based on actual sales patterns as well as weather conditions fed to the system by store managers during the day, the information system issues instructions about when to bake more cookies of each type on unexpectedly high sales days. It also tells when to perform housekeeping and maintenance, when to send out someone with coupons for free cookies, and when to cut back production during periods of slow sales rates. Provided a fledgling manager has reasonably good human skills and high integrity, the information system does much of the rest, including monitoring the manager to see whether its instructions were actually followed.[14]

In contrast, Dean LeBaron and his small coterie of professionals at Batterymarch Capital Management, one of the largest independent money management firms in the United States, use computers both for analysis and to carry out strategies that they have formulated. At Batterymarch, a money manager uses a desktop computer of his or her choice to gain access to a larger central computer to test various securities-picking strategies, such as those involving recession-resistant stocks or stocks with book values far in excess of prices. Once a strategy is determined, responsibility is delegated to the computer to pick the stocks that will satisfy it and to buy and sell them. In addition, the computer has been programmed to ask brokers to bid on fees they will charge for transacting the computer's business. This has resulted in Batterymarch's paying a fraction of the transaction fees paid by other institutional traders.

Employing a computer in this way, LeBaron has leveraged the expertise of his professionals, who are freed from the more tedious work of analyzing and selecting individual stocks. There is no need for a corps of analysts because the computer picks the individual stocks. No traders are necessary. The computer does that too. And results in most years have been so good that there is no need for sales representatives; marketing is by word of mouth. As a result, in recent years Batterymarch has managed several times the capital per professional and realized several times the revenue per professional of its nearest competitor. And it has remained the small group (less than 40 people, all of whom have the title of "trustee") that LeBaron had in mind when he established the business.[15]

People. In most services, people are the largest determinant of quality. And again, views vary widely as to the most effective means of encouraging people to deliver high-quality services. One view holds that the most effective avenue to improved service quality is through increased supervision. Another, in contrast, advocates greater expenditures for training, greater exercise of judgment, and more empowerment for front-line servers. While the latter may be more appealing from the standpoint of quality of work life, again both theories have had their place, often as ingredients of the same high-performance service delivery process.

One of the nation's largest insurance agencies sells insurance to and services claims for members of national associations. Its service department is staffed by more than 50 customer service agents equipped with a highly sophisticated telecommunications system as well as computer terminals providing instant access to central files of customer information. All customer service agents are in one room, facilitating visual supervision. In addition, telephone conversations are monitored for quality and efficiency. Information is computed by the telecommunications system on number of calls handled per service agent, average length of call, and even repeat calls from the same customer (suggesting unsolved customer problems). Little is left to guesswork here.

Contrast this with an organization whose managers supervise largely unskilled labor, The ServiceMaster Company. In preparing people under its supervision to carry out housekeeping chores in hospitals, schools, and industrial firms, ServiceMaster relies heavily on both skill-oriented training and more general educational programs intended to instill a sense of pride and dedication to quality. This is necessary where standards of quality in cleaning services are difficult to set, measure, and administer. Here first-line personnel are deployed in out-of-the-way areas of large buildings and are thus difficult to supervise closely by conventional means.

RECONCILING QUALITY AND COST

If there is one thing that differentiates our conversations with breakthrough service managers and their less successful competitors, it is their attitudes toward the relationship between quality and cost. As we pointed out in Chapter 5, less successful managers assume that quality and cost must be traded off against each other. Breakthrough managers assume, correctly we think, that higher quality and lower cost are totally consistent with one another and that there are ample methods of achieving them in concert. Further, they assume that higher quality leads to higher productivity and vice versa.

MANAGING FOR PRODUCTIVITY GAINS

Doing more with less is generally considered to be both the key to a profitable business and to a better way of life for a society. It's also the basic definition of higher productivity.

PRODUCTIVITY

Productivity is the relationship of outputs to inputs. Outputs may be measured most commonly for manufacturing activities in terms of the quantity of products or other items produced. For services, it is more appropriately (but seldom) measured in terms of results made possible by the service.[16]

Inputs required in the creation of either products or services include labor, capital, and others. Labor is most often the only input measured, with all output credited to it (and called labor productivity). But the mix of labor and capital required to produce various services varies greatly, as suggested by the data from two companies in Table 7–2. Here, we see that the revenue realized per employee in 1988 was $50,300 at United Parcel Service as opposed to $79,900 at one of its freight-transporting competitors, Federal Express. But at least a part of the difference is explained by the employment of much greater quantities of capital in relation to labor, $61,900 per employee at Federal Express as opposed to $31,600 per employee at UPS. Much of this capital is used at Federal Express for equipment and facilities needed for a higher concentration of premium transport services producing

Table 7–2 COMPARATIVE 1988 OPERATING RESULTS, UNITED PARCEL SERVICE AND FEDERAL EXPRESS

Measure	United Parcel Service	Federal Express
Operating revenues (millions)	$11,032	$3,883
Assets (millions)	6,935	3,008
Net income (millions)	759	188
Equity (millions)	3,181	1,331
Employees	219,400	48,600
Revenues/assets	1.59	1.29
Net income/revenues	6.9%	4.8%
Assets/equity	2.18	2.26
Net income/equity	23.9%	14.1%
Revenues/employee	$50,300	$79,900
Assets/employee	$31,600	$61,900

a higher revenue yield than UPS per pound carried one mile, in time yielding more total revenue per employee.

This suggests that several measures of productivity may be most appropriate in a given firm. For example, in an asset-intensive service business, the ratio of sales to assets (or so-called asset turnover) may be the most important measure. In a labor-intensive business, revenue per employee may be more important.

Further, productivity comparisons between firms or even between operating branches of the same service firm with different operating characteristics often have limited validity. Instead, the use of productivity measures by a single operating unit to measure progress against its own previous performance may be much more appropriate.

PRODUCTIVITY IMPROVEMENT

Many different approaches may be used to improve productivity. Two examples illustrate the range of alternatives and the appropriate application of each.

Work Study. This approach to productivity improvement draws upon remnants of the era of scientific management and Taylorism. It identifies critical steps in the service delivery process, breaks them down into their components, and measures the speed (and possibly the accuracy) with which each is performed. Methods of measurement often involve time and motion study carried out by industrial engineers. As a result of such measures, standards are set which must be met within some period of time by service personnel, working most often individually rather than in teams. Bonuses may be paid for exceeding standards. And jobs and equipment often are redesigned as a result of such analyses in order to help people become more productive. The incentive often is monetary and sometimes is substantial.

Tasks lending themselves to this approach to productivity improvement often are repetitive, those for which an objective measure of completion is available, those that are labor intensive, and those over which people have control. For example, United Parcel Service uses time and motion studies extensively to analyze the work of the drivers of its package delivery cars and help dispatchers plan the standard number of deliveries to be expected of each driver on each route. This is critical, because drivers do not work eight-hour days; they work until their assigned packages have been delivered (in the morning) and picked up (in the afternoon and early evening). As a result of such studies, changes ranging from car design to advisories to drivers to knock rather than spend time searching for doorbells at destination residences have been made in package pick-up and delivery at UPS.[17]

Questions have been raised about why UPS drivers, members of the Teamsters union, cooperate in this type of program. But in addition to being measured, drivers receive the benefits of changes and instruction that enable them to work faster and smarter, completing their work days quicker and with less fatigue. Perhaps as a result, they receive above-average wages for the kind of work they do, while their firm has become the world's most profitable transportation company.

Self-Determination. This approach to productivity management stresses the identification of appropriate activities for improvement by teams of service personnel, the establishment of performance standards and goals as well as the tracking of performance by the team itself, and modest, sometimes largely symbolic, rewards for achieving the goals. Typical of this type of approach is the Productivity Indexing program developed at Northern Telecom several years ago.[18]

In this program, teams of personnel are encouraged to follow several carefully prescribed steps in designing a program that reflects the group's mission. This requires first defining what the mission is and then identifying those things critical to its achievement. Critical elements are evaluated in terms of their impact on quality, cost effectiveness, and timeliness. In fact, instead of defining productivity in traditional terms of output divided by input, at Northern Telecom it is defined as value to customer divided by cost to produce, or effectiveness divided by efficiency. This is quite similar to the concept of leverage in the strategic service vision presented in Figure 2–2.

Teams then identify five to seven ouput/input ratios by which their performance is to be measured, place a weight on each, establish a benchmark measure as well as a goal for each, and calibrate and track their own performance from the benchmark (current performance) to the ultimate goal. Weighted progress on each measure contributes to an overall productivity index, one number that reflects the group's progress.

The advantages of this approach are that it is task- or mission-specific; it places responsibility in the hands of those who know the task and how to achieve it best, thus encouraging "buy-in" on the part of team members; it is multidimensional and thus oriented to complex tasks involving quality, cost improvement, and timeliness; and it offers the opportunity for self-appraisal. It is particularly well-suited to services where output is difficult to characterize by one measure.

Matching Approach and Task. These approaches to both quality and productivity management are profiled in Table 7–3. Both have been used successfully, often in the same firm. The key to success is matching approach and task.

Work study often has been employed most successfully for service tasks involving little customization of the service, limited judgment on the part of service personnel, and little or no contact with customers. These are many times entry-level tasks of a repetitive nature requiring limited training. Self-determined multi-attribute initiatives, on the other hand, have been used successfully for tasks in which there is a great deal of customization of the process, the judgment required of service personnel is high, and contact with customers is extensive. It is here that measures of output are varied, often hard to quantify, and somewhat qualitative in nature and the need is greatest for service personnel to believe and participate in the implementation of the program.

IMPLEMENTATION OF QUALITY AND PRODUCTIVITY IMPROVEMENT PROGRAMS

It is difficult to understand the complexity and attention to detail associated with the successful implementation of a quality or productivity improvement program without turning to case examples. Consider the experiences of The Paul Revere Insurance Company in developing its Quality Has Value (QHV) initiative. The effort, initiated by President Aubrey Reid at the urging of executives of Paul Revere's parent, was designed not only to improve performance in quality but also to create a culture of quality at the company.[19]

The first of many actions associated with this effort was the creation of a Quality Steering Committee, chaired by vice presidents of insurance oper-

Service Breakthroughs

Table 7–3 TWO CONTRASTING APPROACHES TO QUALITY AND PRODUCTIVITY MANAGEMENT

	Alternative Approaches	
Dimensions	*Work Study*	*Self-Determination*
Measures determined by:	Management	Employees
Process by which standards are set:	Time and motion study	Measurement of current results
Number of ways results are measured:	Few	Many
Primary emphasis in measurement:	Productivity	Productivity and quality
Tasks for which approach is most appropriate:		
Repetitiveness	High	Low
Labor intensiveness	High	High
Availability of objective measures of task completion	High	Low
Degree of customization of the service	Low	High
Degree of judgment exercised by server	Low	High
Complexity of contact with customers	Low	High
Primary motives for server cooperation	Higher pay, shorter working hours, less demanding workload	More objective methods of compensation

ations and human resources. Because the committee members soon became divided into what one of its leaders termed the "humanists," with implicit faith in employees' recommendations, and the "bean-counters," who sought cost justification for everything, the committee agreed to pursue two avenues centered around Quality Teams and Value Analysis Workshops. At about this time, Patrick Townsend, a former Marine major, was hired to oversee and champion the effort.

Quality Teams averaged about ten people and included every one of The Paul Revere's home office staff of 1,220 people. Members of Quality Teams were encouraged to identify ideas, implement their ideas immediately, and then tell management what they had done. A Quality Team Central was created to develop a Quality Team Tracking Program (QTTP) and certify the value of ideas that had been implemented by Quality Teams. The QTTP was a computerized information system in which the progress of Quality Teams and the implementation of their ideas was made available to everyone. Employees trained as team leader instructors provided direction to Quality Team leaders. As Townsend put it:

A decision to institute a quality team process is, if you will, a decision to allow a revolution. Revolutions come from the bottom up. If there is to be a new American revolution—a service industrial revolution—all the troops must be enlisted.[20]

One of the most important policies associated with the Quality Team process was that no employee would be fired as the result of an idea that led to staff reductions.

Value Analysis Workshops involving managers of each work unit or department were also organized for a one-time look at questions such as "What work do we do?" "How do we do it?" "Why do we do it this way?" and "How can we do it better?" This emphasis complemented that of the Quality Teams. While the Quality Teams asked, "Are we doing things right?," the Value Analysis Workshops asked, "Are we doing the right things?"

Recognition was made a significant part of the process. Its primary reward system was based on the award of bronze pins for teams implementing 10 ideas or projects with $10,000 in annual savings, silver pins and $20 gift certificates to members of teams implementing 25 ideas or $25,000 in annual savings, and gold pins and $50 gift certificates to members of teams implementing 50 ideas or $50,000 in annual savings. By the end of the first full year of the process, 126 teams out of 127 had achieved the bronze pin level, 101 of these silver, 72 of these gold, 10 of these double-gold, and one of these triple-gold. The total cost of these awards was about $80,000.

The awards were made at an annual Quality Celebration at which the Most Valuable Team and Most Valuable People awards were also announced before the distribution of holiday gifts and granting of the remainder of the day off to everyone. But just as important, a Program for Ensuring that Everybody's Thanked (PEET) was implemented, requiring each of 18 senior executives to visit two work areas each month to discuss a Quality Team's quality-improvement ideas with it and hand out at least five "quality coins" to individuals, each good for a free lunch at the company cafeteria. According to one employee, 80% of the recipients elected instead to keep the coins as "a reminder of one of the few times they had actually been thanked for something they had done."

By 1986, the Quality Has Value effort was estimated to be saving Paul

Revere $13 million per year on an annualized basis. Roughly half of this was estimated to have resulted from the 42 Value Analysis Workshops held up to this time. Quality Teams were implementing an average of about 40 ideas per year, in contrast to experiences of Japanese quality circles where teams implemented four or five per year. While Japanese quality circles typically included only about 15% of people in an organization, Paul Revere's QHV initiative included everyone. Even so, pockets of resistance were still encountered, particularly among middle managers, who viewed it as another "program of the month," and field personnel, many of whose ideas required the cooperation of home office personnel for implementation. Nevertheless, by 1987, The Paul Revere Insurance Company was one of nine service companies competing for the U.S. government's Malcolm Baldrige Award for service excellence.

We can draw upon the experiences of managers whose work has been described in the last two chapters to reach general conclusions about efforts needed to achieve quality and productivity improvement.

First, the leadership of Florida Power & Light, United Parcel Service, The Paul Revere Insurance Company, "Bugs" Burger Bug Killers, L. L. Bean, Manpower, Marriott, the Buffalo Bisons, Nordstrom, the Four Seasons, and others all exhibit a great deal of commitment to efforts being implemented in their firms. This commitment goes far beyond general expressions of support or involvement in kick-off ceremonies. It extends to a willingeness to inquire repeatedly about the progress of such efforts, to include such progress in performance evaluations and rewards, to celebrate successes, and to encourage subordinates at each level in the organization to do the same. Ironically, this kind of effort doesn't cost much and its value is priceless.

Second, as we have stated previously, what gets measured is what gets managed. Measurement before, during, and after the implementation of service and productivity improvements is critical to their success. Of course, such measures must reflect the goals of the effort and have an internal consistency of their own to be most effective.

Third, quality improvement is inherently more acceptable to rank-and-file service personnel than productivity improvement. The latter often carries with it a connotation of loss of jobs and has often been opposed by organized labor. As one senior executive of a major hospital put it, "Quality improvement sells. Productivity improvement doesn't." However, quality programs with a hidden agenda of productivity improvement rarely succeed in the long run. It is pretty obvious to everyone, for example, that doing things right the first time will lead to greater productivity. Fortunately, it also leads to increased business volume. As a result, successful efforts have been able to deliver on promises to employees that no jobs will be eliminated as a result of the process.

Fourth, service personnel must be convinced that both improved quality and great productivity can lead to significant increases in business and long-run competitive advantage. This should increase the job and income opportunities at every level of the firm. Firms cited in this chapter have succeeded through extraordinary efforts to both educate prior to the outset of improvement efforts and continue information feedback during and after such efforts.

Fifth, celebration is vital, significant monetary rewards are not. The effort to say "thank you" carries a high value in relation to mere money.

Finally, whether the emphasis is on quality, productivity, or both, those in the ranks must "buy in" to the process. This can be achieved in part by reward, recognition, and participation by top management. But in all successful cases that we have observed, trust between people at all levels in an organization has been the most important determinant of success. Trust is not achieved overnight. It is the result of a mosaic of policies and practices. It is a reflection of basic beliefs about human beings. And it is perhaps the most difficult to emulate and therefore the most potent competitive weapon in an operating strategy. As Patrick Townsend, responsible for implementation of the Quality Has Value effort at The Paul Revere so graphically put it:

I think it's important . . . to realize that the foundation of the whole process is trust. . . . Perhaps it's better put this way. You wake up in the morning. You go out and get in your car to drive to work. On the way to work you use the brakes a hundred times or more. You've never met the person who put those brakes together. You go through all kinds of intersections where other cars stop at red lights or stop signs. You never give a second thought to whether or not they're going to come out and hit you in the side of your car. They're gonna' stop; you trust 'em. You get to your office, you walk into the elevator, and you go to the fifth floor. . . . You don't even look at the name of the guy that inspected the elevator. You trust that it's not going to go plummeting into the basement. You walk into your office and by the time you sit down at your desk at eight o'clock in the morning you have literally trusted your life to hundreds of strangers. And then you hesitate at trusting a 20-year employee with a $50 decision. It's simply not consistent. If you're going to trust somebody, why not trust somebody you know . . . who is committed to the same goals that you are. That's the basis of the quality process.[21]

Leadership, measurement, education, celebration, and trust are all critical in achieving high quality and productivity. Together, they provide an important way of leveraging value over cost to produce profit. In a sense, this is the heart and soul of a breakthrough service. We next turn to products of the "head," including the management of demand and supply, networks, and technology.

8

Managing
Demand and Supply

W isconsin Electric Power Co. charges users of its services more for the
same service delivered during times of peak usage and offers incentives to
customers to buy new energy-efficient appliances that reduce peak energy
demands on the utility. It attempts to alleviate peaks and valleys for a service
that has a somewhat constant level of capacity. It manages the timing of
customer purchases. It manages both physical and human resources to assure that capacity is available to meet customers' expectations of quality.
And it manages customers in ways that make them both more profitable and
more satisfied. How this is accomplished is our concern here.

Managing demand and supply requires a different kind of understanding
about the nature of demand for a service concept as well as efforts to
coordinate the management both of customers and the people who serve
them. In most services, it is the single greatest determinant of profitability.

UNDERSTANDING DEMAND LEVELS,
PATTERNS, AND RELATIONSHIPS

The level of demand keys basic decisions about how much capacity to build
into a service delivery system. The pattern of demand often influences the
kind of capacity developed for service delivery. Relationships between demand for various parts of a multistep service suggest the amount of capacity
to be provided for each step.

The decision about how much and what kind of capacity to build has a
lifelong effect on the success of a service facility and has to be made early

135

in the service design process. Its importance is illustrated in Figure 8–1, showing the way in which demand and capacity characteristics relate to produce two of the most important ways of evaluating potential risk (the percentage of capacity utilization required to break even) and potential return (the profit on investment at maximum sustainable capacity utilization) in a service business.

The need for this kind of information gives efforts to assess demand special significance.

LEVEL OF DEMAND

The developer of a breakthrough service can't observe demand levels of competitors' offerings. By definition, there aren't any. But because service concepts are defined in terms of results produced for customers, developers can observe potential customers trying to achieve the same kind of results through other more conventional means. For example, the developer of a nonexistent home-delivery shopping service can observe and measure the level of demand for other services that achieve similar results, the saving of time from routine chores for busy customers.

Similarly, many smaller brokerage firms process their customers' transactions in-house in order to maintain control over the process even though it may be more costly than using outside services provided by firms specializing in the work. These organizations may be good targets for transaction processing services that empower customers through access to special programs and a comprehensive data base offered along with guarantees concerning the accuracy of the transaction processing.

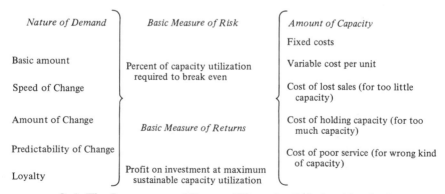

Nature of Demand	Basic Measure of Risk	Amount of Capacity
		Fixed costs
Basic amount	Percent of capacity utilization required to break even	Variable cost per unit
Speed of Change		Cost of lost sales (for too little capacity)
Amount of Change	Basic Measure of Returns	Cost of holding capacity (for too much capacity)
Predictability of Change		Cost of poor service (for wrong kind of capacity)
Loyalty	Profit on investment at maximum sustainable capacity utilization	

FIGURE 8–1 The Importance of Demand/Capacity Relationships in the Service Risk/Return Evaluation

Fortunately, many new service concepts can be tested in action. This is important if prospective demand levels are to be forecasted with even approximate accuracy for a previously unoffered service. Market tests are more feasible for most (non-network-centered) services than for products. Special facilities can be constructed or new services can be offered in existing facilities for such tests, which in reality are business start-ups. But experiences of others have suggested certain caveats in planning and measuring the results of such efforts. These include close attention to the frequency with which a service is purchased, the importance of referrals from other users in the decision to try a service, and the very nature of the innovation adoption rate for particular services.

Responses to some new services, particularly retail consumer services that are purchased frequently such as restaurant services and hair styling, may be rapid. But most require more time, because they are purchased infrequently. These include such things as legal and medical services for individuals and industrial cleaning and advertising services for commercial customers.

Further, the very absence of search qualities for most services means that a referral process for prospective customers is very important. This takes time, although for some services, such as restaurants in New York City, the grapevine works fast if not always efficiently.

In part for these reasons, Valarie Zeithaml has hypothesized that consumers adopt innovations in services more slowly than they adopt innovations in goods and maintain greater loyalty to services they use than to products they use.[1] While these processes may be speeded up through incentives offered to prospective customers, such incentives may take longer to take effect.

Again, these behaviors vary according to other characteristics of particular services, but they suggest extreme care in structuring a market test to allow for the referral process and for repeat usage to take place sufficiently to be able to gauge the potential level of demand for a new service. This may explain why capacity is so often determined on the basis of what one executive has termed "gut fact" rather than scientific measurement. It may explain too why the decision so often is wrong and has to be corrected later, sometimes at great cost.

PATTERN OF DEMAND

A major determinant of success in many services is the degree to which available capacity is utilized. Capacity utilization often varies inversely with the amount, speed, and unpredictability of fluctuations in demand; the degree to which capacity exceeds minimum demand; and the degree to which capacity is fixed. And, as Figure 8–2 suggests, it is a major determinant of service quality.

Unpredictable and rapidly changing demand patterns fall outside the capabilities of market forecasting techniques and are particularly worrisome for service managers. In designing all services related to major stock exchange transactions, for example, daily demand levels and fluctuations cannot be predicted with any reliability. Further, the ability to accommodate peak levels of demand is so critical to the basic mission of the stock exchange that sufficient capacity must be designed to provide it. Even so, a day like October 19, 1987, when the market "crashed," could not be predicted either in terms of its timing or the severity of the demands on market exchange mechanisms. It severely overloaded the system, causing serious deterioration in service levels.

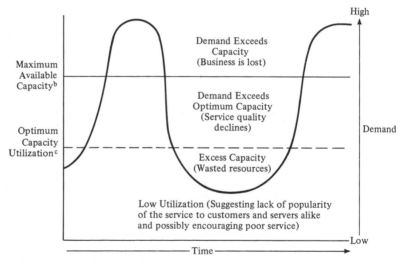

FIGURE 8–2 Implications of Cyclical Variations in Demand Relative to Capacity[a]

[a] Christopher H. Lovelock, *Services Marketing: Text, Cases, & Readings,* © 1984, p. 281. Adapted by permission of Prentice Hall, Inc., Englewood Cliffs, NJ.

[b] For simplicity, this diagram assumes no variations over time in the amount of capacity available.

[c] The optimum capacity is that level of utilization above which the perceived quality begins to deteriorate due to crowding. In some services, such as theaters and sports arenas, optimum and maximum capacity may be the same.

Predictable and less severe fluctuations often allow astute service managers who track such patterns to adjust capacity to accommodate demand in ways we will discuss later. This makes the initial capacity decision less critical, but requires close attention to ways of collecting and analyzing information about demand patterns.

Excess capacity, as suggested in Figure 8–2, often has debilitating effects not only on profits but also on the quality of service experience. A near-empty restaurant both loses money and fails to deliver an important element of dining experience, the social ambience provided by other patrons. Further, to the extent that it discourages servers dependent on business for their income and also influenced by the ambience of a poorly patronized dining room, invariably it leads to a deterioration in service.

While the inability to meet demand may be very serious in many businesses, the condition with the most adverse long-run consequences for others is that of continually operating a facility in which demand exceeds optimum capacity. Optimum capacity utilization for an airline, for example, ranges from 65% to 75%. Below 40%, service deteriorates for reasons mentioned previously. But above 75%, service deteriorates in other ways that can be very annoying to passengers, particularly when it results in rude or abrupt behavior on the part of harried cabin attendants. Failure to do something about this can lead to the alienation over time of valued customers. It has led perceptive restaurant operators, for example, to close tables and refuse to take reservations for tables (or more often individual dining rooms) that can't be properly serviced rather than expose their business to long-term risks of poor service.

For some services optimum and maximum capacity may be the same. Somehow, baseball is better in a full ballpark. A motion picture, particularly a comedy, benefits from reactions from members of the audience, both to the film and to each other. Typically, these kinds of facilities are built well below forecasts of peak demand levels. This explains in part why motion picture auditoriums, on average, have become smaller and smaller, even though the multi-screen facilities of which they are a part have become larger. Smaller facilities for entertainments encourage clients to reserve seats earlier. This can work to the advantage of organizations such as the Boston Red Sox Baseball Club, owners of the smallest major league baseball stadium, Fenway Park. Boston Red Sox fans invariably purchase their seats long before they know the success of the baseball team.

Demand in excess of capacity, of course, exposes a service to a potential permanent loss of business. The seriousness of this condition depends on the intensity of a customer's preference for a service, the primary determinant of a customer's willingness to wait or even experience less-than-perfect service. We'll turn to this in a moment after considering one more element in appraising demand.

DEMAND RELATIONSHIPS

Services made up of multiple features or steps require estimates of demand for each step at which a separate server or facility is required if enlightened decisions about how much capacity to provide at each step are to be made.

For example, a fast-food restaurant estimating peak demand of 160 eat-in customers per hour at lunch and dinner and targeting an 80% utilization rate (to allow for unused portions of booths and tables) will provide a facility with 100 seats if the average length of time to order and consume the meal is 30 minutes. This, in turn, determines the peak demand placed on the pick-up counter. The counter has to be able to deliver 160 meals per hour to eat-in customers (in addition to the number of meals carried out). If carry-out business represents another 80 meals per hour, the service counter has to be able to assemble and collect money for a meal every 15 seconds (sixty minutes divided by 240 meals per hour). If 60 seconds is required to assemble the meal and collect money for it, the fast-food restaurant requires four service counters. This means that the kitchen must be designed to deliver a meal every 15 seconds for eat-in and carry-out customers in addition to meals sold at the drive-in window, which has its own demand patterns and service rates.

We could go on, but the point is that demand level interrelationships require separate forecasts for each stage of a multi-stage service delivery process if facilities are to be designed with step-by-step capacities that are reasonably in balance and do not create bottlenecks that affect overall service levels. This not only requires estimates of demand but also close observation of customer behavior (eating times and willingness to wait in lines at the service counters) as well as serving time and attitudes at various work speeds. Surprisingly few food service managers develop this information. But you can bet that the managers at McDonald's or Benihana of Tokyo (a chain of hibachi-style eating establishments) do.

Airlines have probably spent more time studying the intensity of customer preferences than firms in other service industries. Their work and what they conclude from it is instructive. Even though Delta Air Lines, for example, has devoted a great deal of effort to building customer loyalty among business travelers through quality of service, frequent flyer incentives, and other means, its management knows that if it does not have a flight departing within an hour of the desired time, it will lose targeted business travelers rapidly to competitors who do. All of its efforts have probably only increased this measure of "loyalty" from perhaps 30 to 60 minutes, because the intensity of customer preferences for flying Delta instead of one of the competitors only applies in the abstract, not when it comes right down to available departure times.

On the other hand, preferences for a particular airline's service among pleasure travelers may be more intensive then preferences for specific departure times (although less intensive than for price). In fact, many of these travelers may another day have been the very business travelers described above, perhaps spending frequent flyer mileage they earned earlier in the week on business travel for pleasure travel with their families. These travelers may be more willing to adjust departure times (not dates) to fly their airline of preference.

This helps explain why business travelers drive most airline capacity scheduling decisions. It also suggests why information about the intensity of a customer's preference for competing service in the abstract has to be tested against other factors in a specific purchasing situation. But this information is critical to any assessment of the likely success of various efforts to manage demand, as we will see later.

To the extent that customers are willing to wait for a highly desired service, accurate estimates of demand or capacity-sizing decisions may become less important. But this requires measurements of the intensity of customer desires as well as loyalty.

ANALYZING WAITING LINE BEHAVIOR

We wait in lines, on the phone, and in air traffic control "stacks" over airports. We wait for banking, food, and retailing services. We spend as much time waiting, particularly if commuting waits are included, as in any other activity but sleeping and perhaps eating. New devices, such as "call holding" telephone services, have been designed to make us wait in new, innovative ways. We're told that Russians resign themselves to waiting in lines. The French avoid it. Americans resent it. And one view has it that when the English see a line they join it. Little wonder that an entire body of theory has been developed to study this phenomenon.

The father of waiting line theory was a Danish engineer named A. K. Erlang, who developed it in 1917 to understand the causes of "busy" signals in telephone networks and to be able to size the capacity of switching systems in order to minimize such delays.[2] What's surprising is that it took so long. People had already spent billions of person-years waiting over hundreds of years.

Waiting line theory provides methods for calculating: (1) the average wait in line, (2) the probability that the wait will exceed a given time, (3) the average length of the line, and (4) the probability that the length of the line will exceed a given number, provided we know the time required to serve a person in the line, the rate of arrival of people at the line, and the number of servers. The relatively simple formulas for calculating measures of service in waiting lines do provide general insights into the relationship between demand and supply in waiting lines. For example, as the rate of arrivals approaches service time, the average wait increases exponentially (of course, reaching infinity when the former exceeds the latter). This helps explain why so many services are operated best at around 75% of capacity, delivering good service at a reasonable cost. As the demand exceeds that amount, customer waiting increases rapidly. It also often suggests the importance of seeking ways to add small increments of capacity through improved training or higher compensation of servers rather than through large increments of capacity provided by hiring an additional server and creating an extra queue.

In general, the most practical use is in estimating the trade-off between the costs of service and the expected length of both the line and customers' waiting time when arrivals at the line occur randomly (not in batches). Unfortunately, the cost of waiting time often does not include the costs of customers and business lost because of excessive waiting or perceived waiting line length. The philosophy expressed in the advertisement reproduced in Figure 8–3 that "they also serve who only stand and wait" is the rare exception.

In fact, because it deals in averages, waiting line theory has been of limited use in managing many services. To know that a medical emergency team provides an average of a three-minute response time for patients suffering heart attacks, when patients often have only five minutes to survive severe brain damage or death, is of little comfort. This is particularly true if the emergency service has achieved its record by appearing two out of every three times in one minute and the third time in seven minutes. As a result, more relevant analytic results have been obtained by simulating arrival intervals and service times based on observed occurrences and then assessing variations in the length of the resulting waiting line and waiting times experienced with varying numbers of servers on the line.

"They also serve who only stand and wait."

–Milton

We would like to relieve our customers from having to "serve" and therefore want to shorten our teller lines. If you, or if you know someone who, might like to start a career in banking as a teller, see our receptionist.

Our present President once served his time as a Cambridge Trust Company teller.

Cambridge Trust Company

FIGURE 8–3 A Recent Advertisement by the Cambridge Trust Company (Massachusetts) for New Tellers

Reprinted with permission.

REDUCING WAITING TIMES OR WAITING LINES

When waiting lines or waiting times are judged to be excessive, analysis often leads to decisions to add more servers or reduce service time, thereby increasing the serving capacity of a facility. Service times often are reduced by providing more effective information to servers (such as computerized individual customer account information to bank tellers), somehow simplifying the service process itself (for example, by simplifying the menu in a restaurant), or by reorganizing servers so that they each might specialize in a particular type of service (such as the express lane for people with eight items or less at the supermarket, the check-cashing-only line at the bank, or the special line for people desiring only boarding passes at the airport).

Yet a third tactic might be to spread out customer arrivals in the line by scheduling them or providing incentives for non–peak-hour arrival, increasing the utilization of available capacity. For example, motion picture theaters often charge lower rates for films shown on weekday afternoons, airport authorities are considering the idea of charging higher fees for planes landing at peak time periods, and restaurants reserve tables in order to spread peak demand over longer periods of time and enhance the quality of the service experience for more people taking advantage of off-peak times.

For some services, the length of the waiting line is more important than actual waiting time because it discourages potential customers from entering the line. This can lead directly to a loss of business, particularly where it is easy to switch from one competitor's line to another's. For example, stand near the auto rental counters at an airport when one firm has what is viewed as an excessively long line by business travelers in a hurry to get to their meetings. Even with today's "frequent user" membership programs and advance reservations, potential customers will leave one renter's line and join another's.

Your barber or hairdresser may try to deal with this problem by minimizing estimates of time you may have to wait, delaying your dissatisfaction to the point in time when the wait exceeds the estimate.

The Walt Disney Company is masterful at devising ways to deal with this problem. It should be, because waiting lines are the bane of its best-known service enterprises. At Disneyland and Disney World, signs convey information about waiting time required from each of several points in the line, eliminating questions about the meaning of what appears to be a long line and providing reports of progress to those waiting in a line for a popular amusement. This organization also is masterful at concealing the length of lines by means of partitions and serpentine-shaped queues. As David Maister has pointed out, lines move fast but could look long at the Disney theme parks if they weren't partially concealed.[3] Of course, this only works when the line does in fact move fast and visitors don't feel as if they've been badly misled.

In theory, all of this is nice to know. But in fact, customer satisfaction may be influenced by many things other than the amount of time they actually spend waiting in a line.

Some years ago, Russell Ackoff found that people waiting for elevators in hotels that provided mirrors near the elevators evidenced much less dissatisfaction that those not having mirrors at their disposal.[4] Waiting bank customers provided with information about banking services, perhaps with video units, are less cognizant of the passage of time than others. And cellular phones have greatly reduced perceptions of commuting times. Not only do these examples all involve enhanced waiting environments, but the enhancement in each case has some degree of relevance to the reason for the wait, another feature thought to be important in determining the manner in which the environment is enhanced for those in line. Restaurants that pass out menus to those waiting to be seated realize this intuitively; this practice reduces service time as well.

Timely announcements of reasons for airline delays, clear signs explaining waiting rules, and frequent estimates of progress (as at Disneyland) all have been found to reduce anxiety and enhance waiting experiences.

In addition to reinforcing these ideas, David Maister has added other "principles of waiting" to the list.[5] Included among these are: (1) "pre-process waits feel longer than in-process waits" (suggesting why airline personnel who "work" the back end of waiting lines at ticket counters are so important as they acknowledge the presence of the customer in the line and "officially" end the pre-process wait); (2) "anxiety makes waits seem longer" (as anyone who has waited in a dentist's office can attest to); (3) "the more valuable the service, the longer I will wait" (such as a haircut before an important business meeting); and (4) "solo waiting feels longer than group waiting." And so on.

The importance of this is that many service encounters begin for customers with a waiting line. It is their first impression of the service. An adverse experience in the line may be hard for the server to overcome. And the antidotes to long perceived waits often do not involve great expense, particularly when compared with the cost of adding extra service capacity.

MANAGING CUSTOMERS AND SERVICE CAPACITY

Must a service concept be compromised exactly to meet customer needs? Or customers forced into a mode of behavior in the service of an efficient operating strait jacket? These questions are especially critical in the service sector where few businesses can create the usual inventory buffers between demand and supply differences that are typical in manufacturing firms. Once an airplane leaves the ground with an empty seat, that capacity is lost forever. And yet the best service firms have found their own ways of buffering supply from demand. Winning service organizations have found ways of avoiding these defeating trade-offs by managing both customer buying behavior and service capacity.

MANAGING CUSTOMER BEHAVIOR

Patterns of demand for a service can be managed only if they can be predicted and if customers will respond to incentives to alter the time or place at which they are willing to use services. If these conditions do not hold, as suggested in Figure 8–4, the only alternative may be to manage the supply of service offered to accommodate customer needs.

Methods by which demand can be managed include the usual elements of marketing strategy, service (product) design, advertising, and other forms of communication, distribution, and pricing. As Christopher Lovelock has pointed out, these work best when demand patterns are predictable enough to suggest when such demand-management efforts should be implemented.[6] In organizations able to influence customer behavior but unable to predict demand or easily adjust supplies, efforts may be made instead to inventory demand through reservation systems or what Lovelock has termed "organized queueing."

Predictability of Demand

		Unable to Predict	Able to Predict
	Low	"Chase" demand with capacity or lose business	Plan supplies to meet fluctuating levels of demand or lose business
Ability to Shift Customer Demand	High	"Chase" demand with capacity or inventory demand (through reservations and queues) where capacity is fixed	Manage demand through service design, communication, distribution, pricing, or inventorying methods as well as plan supplies to meet fluctuating levels of demand

FIGURE 8–4 Service Demand-Supply Management Strategies Under Different Conditions

Underlying all of these efforts is, of course, the assumption that customers are willing to alter their demand patterns to accommodate service availability. This is why it is so critical to learn, as discussed earlier in this chapter, how strongly loyal customers are to a service as well as other factors determining their demand patterns. Because no matter how much an individual may want to try a new restaurant or return to a old favorite, few people are willing to eat dinner at five in the afternoon in order to be able to be served, regardless of the incentives given to them to do so.

Managing Through Marketing. Marketing efforts may be used both to increase general levels of utilization of underused available capacity and to reduce general demand to alleviate chronic shortages of capacity through so-called "demarketing."[7] For example, in recent years we have seen imaginative efforts by power utilities to educate customers how to save energy during times of limited power-generating fuel availability. We will see them again as water supplies increasingly become critically limited, prompting advertisements such as the London (England) Water Authority's "Take a Bath with a Friend" billboards of several years ago.

At other times, such efforts may be used to shift existing demand to meet available capacity. They take many forms.

The service package (product) itself may be altered to attract different customers during periods of slack demand. Hotels, with fixed and high-cost room inventories and unable to attract business travelers on weekends, instead may design weekend packages for couples featuring things not offered during the week, such as champagne breakfasts, flowers in the room, theater tickets, and other amenities. Ski resorts increasingly are offering summer entertainment to attract nonskiers to their expensive-to-inventory slopes.

At other times, simple communication through advertising or personal selling may be sufficient to shift demand without requiring changes in the service offering. Curiously, too little information is provided to potential customers by most service managers about the best times or places at which to buy and use services. This information is of mutual benefit, because it not only spreads demand but also enables the server to provide a higher quality of service. Among the more well-known and successful of these efforts are those of postal services in many countries advising customers through advertising to mail early for Christmas; advertising by retailers encouraging customers to buy their winter coats during August, a time of slow store sales, and pay for them later; or sales programs by metropolitan transit authorities to encourage local businesses to adopt staggered working hours to make commuting faster and more comfortable.

In recent years, power utility companies have engaged in some of the most innovative, far-ranging efforts to inform customers about ways to save energy and offer incentives to them to do so. The goal has been to shave peak load demands on power systems that drive needs for expanded power-generating capacity. Uncertainties about construction times and returns on investments in new power plants have convinced power company managers that it is wise to encourage conservation that will enable them to postpone new construction. A leader in these kinds of efforts is the Wisconsin Electric Power Co., whose management has launched an extensive consumer education program. In recent months, the utility has offered its customers $50 to scrap old refrigerators and air conditioners, a free service that will pick them up and take them to the dump, and awards of $40 to $70 for purchases of new energy-efficient models. In all, in 1987 it earmarked $84 million for its incentive program and expected to reap twice that in savings over the succeeding ten-year period.[8]

Distribution strategies can be developed for services that help shift demand to available capacity. Thus, leading hotel chains often cluster their facilities, building two or more in major metropolitan markets. This allows them to encourage customers seeking rooms at a facility that is full to take a room at a nearby sister hotel. At other times, the service can be taken to the customer at times of peak demand at a fixed facility. Thus, the capability of a Burger King restaurant to serve customers is expanded by the introduction of take-out or drive-through service not requiring seats. Routine periodic service to automobiles may be performed by mobile service units frequenting large office parking lots during business hours to alleviate peak weekend demand for such services. And home medical care is offered by medical service organizations to patients that don't need or can't afford long-term hospital care.

Pricing is perhaps the most common of all marketing efforts to influence demand. This requires knowledge of the amount of incentive needed to get customers to alter their behavior. The half-price movie matinee may stimulate demand among senior citizens with few fixed commitments but has little effect on that segment of moviegoers with regular daytime jobs, for whom no amount of price incentive would be enough. Reduced rates for evening use has stimulated the demand for many consumer services, such as telecommunications and computer-driven information services, as well as commercial services such as electrical power.

Pricing strategies employed are influenced most importantly by cost structure. In addition, the degree to which various prices can be confined to certain periods of time or portions of the available service facility may influence their use and the way they are structured in ways illustrated in Figure 8–5. Here, we see that services such as truckload transport (using

Cost Structure with Changes in Business Volume

		Largely Variable	Largely Fixed
Nature of Operating Facility	Indivisible (by Space or Time)	Truckload Transport (Using Hired Truck Owner-Operator) Objective: Price to more than cover variable costs in the short-run and manage capacity and variable costs to short-run demand and revenue for one class of service	Motion Picture Theater (For a Particular Showing) Objective: Price to utilize capacity, with prices quoted on ability to pay (especially for youth, senior citizens) for one class of service
	Divisible (by Space or Time)	Restaurant Objective: Price to more than cover variable costs (food and labor) for lunch with higher value-based pricing for dinner	Airline Objective: Price to utilize capacity, with value-based pricing based on different classes of service, time of week, time of day, and ability to pay

FIGURE 8–5 Relationship Between Pricing, Cost Structure, and the Nature of the Service Operating Facility[a]

[a] Each of these examples basically assumes a simple, one-part service. For a multiple-part service such as a hotel-casino, for example, the establishment might offer low-cost transport to the facility or food at variable costs in order to encourage potential patrons to utilize the high fixed-cost (high-margin) hotel and casino services.

hired contractor/owner-operators paid by the trucking company on a mileage basis) or restaurants (with high variable food and labor costs) are priced at short-term levels which exceed variable costs and, in the long run, exceed full costs if eventual bankruptcy is to be avoided. For services with a high proportion of costs that are fixed, such as motion picture theater entertainment or airline seats (once a schedule is fixed), the objective will be to price to utilize capacity, with prices covering low variable costs, often far below full costs for some customers, through different prices to different customers for essentially the same service. As a result, we have seen half-price seats sold daily for Broadway shows to theatergoers willing to take chances on seat availability by buying tickets on the day of the show in person near the theater district and low-price airline seats made available to travelers willing to ''stand-by'' for flights and take their chances that there might be empty seats available at departure.

Managing Through Inventorying Demand. When excess demand develops periodically for services with relatively fixed capacity, the only alternative may be to attempt to inventory demand through reservation and queueing methods. As customers, we expect to have to reserve ahead for things such as hotel rooms, meals, popular videos, business appointments, and even commercial airline aircraft. Just as we have become used to reservation systems, we have become more expert judges of good and poor ones. Leading service providers understand this and design and deliver their services accordingly. For example, by providing customers with "Wizard" numbers containing information about their auto size and insurance coverage preferences, Avis saves its customers time when they reserve and its servers time in preparing rental contracts. Similarly, leading hotel chains have allayed fears of customers and facilitated their own tracking system by providing clients with numbered reservation guarantees. The objective of many of these systems is to emulate the service of an expert restaurant maître d'hôtel who knows individual customers' preferences for seating and servers.

Queues or waiting lines are often less desirable than reservations as methods for managing demand because they result in greater discomfort and anxiety for customers. But they are often unavoidable and can be managed in expert ways, as we have seen.

MANAGING SERVICE SUPPLY

Up to now, we have assumed that supplies of services are fixed, as suggested in Figure 8–2. This is rarely the case. Creative service providers have found many ways to manage supply whether or not patterns of demand can be predicted in advance. As Earl Sasser has suggested, they fall into two basic patterns, "chase-demand" and "level-capacity" strategies, as shown in Table 8–1.[9] The chase-demand alternative is often elected where demands are highly volatile and unpredictable, the cost structure can be managed on a highly variable basis, and there is a ready supply of relatively low-skilled labor for jobs requiring limited training. This is characteristic of many waterfront materials-handling jobs performed by longshoremen who, for years before they organized themselves into unions, were subjected to the daily "shape up" at which they learned whether they would receive work and compensation for the day or not. It is characteristic as well of many retail sales jobs.

In contrast, level-capacity strategies may be employed where demand is less volatile and more predictable, the consequences of a poorly performed service are serious, and the need for expert providers requiring substantial training (or expensive, complex, specialized equipment) high. This, of course, is the case for many medical services, especially those involving elective surgery and longer-term care.

The undesirable consequences of operating for long periods of time under

Table 8–1 CONDITIONS ENCOURAGING CHASE-DEMAND AND
LEVEL-CAPACITY STRATEGIES AND CHARACTERISTICS OF VARIOUS
OPERATING RESPONSES[a]

Condition Encouraging:	*Chase-Demand*		*Level-Capacity*
Size of fluctuation in demand	Large		Small
Speed of fluctuation in demand	Fast		Slow
Predictability of fluctuation in demand	Unpredictable		Predictable
Cost structure	Highly variable		Highly fixed
Cost of poor service	Low		High
Cost of lost business	High		Low

Operating Responses:	*Chase-Demand*	*"Modified" Chase-Demand*	*Level-Capacity*
Percentage of peak business covered with "base" capacity	Low	Moderate	High
Division of jobs	High	Low	Low
Labor skill level required	Low	Moderate	High
Job discretion	Low	Moderate	High
Compensation rate	Low	Improved	High
Working conditions	Sweat shop	Improved	Pleasant
Training required per employee	Low	(Greater cross-job training)	High
Labor turnover	High	Lower	Low
Hire-fire costs	High	Lower	Low
Error rate	High	Lower	Low
Amount of supervision required	High	Lower	Low
Type of budgeting and forecasting required	Short-run	Long-run	Long-run

[a] Adapted by permission of *Harvard Business Review*. An exhibit from "Match Supply and Demand in Service Industries" by W. Earl Sasser, November/December 1976, pp. 133–140, at p. 135. Copyright © 1976 by the President and Fellows of Harvard College; all rights reserved.

"chase-demand" strategies have led breakthrough service providers confronted with volatile, unpredictable demands to seek ways of modifying such strategies. Those suggested by Sasser include maximizing service delivery efficiency during peak periods, using part-time employees or renting equipment, cross-training employees to perform two or more jobs with different demand patterns, sharing capacity among businesses, and increasing consumer participation in the delivery of service. In addition, through advance facility planning, excess capacity of hard-to-change features may be built into service facilities when they are constructed. Finally, even if none of these possibilities exists, humans are able to deliver what we often call superhuman efforts for short periods of time.

Maximizing Efficiency During Peaks. Effective service organizations concentrate on doing just those things most critical to service quality during periods of peak demand, putting off to the slack times those things that can be postponed. Carefully detailed instructions to managers of Waffle House fast-food restaurants have them performing maintenance, window washing, and cleanup of the grounds as well as kitchen cleanup during mid-morning and mid-afternoon hours in order to be able to devote full attention to customers when they arrive.[10] All recruitment and training of H & R Block tax preparers is carried out in advance of the busy season. To the extent possible, major auditing firms perform pre-audit inspections of records far in advance of the tax and annual report preparation "season" when every company operating on a calendar-year basis calls for its services at the same time.

Using Part-Time Employees and Rental Equipment. Some estimates put the number of part-timers in the U.S. work force at around 30 million, or more than 25% of the nation's work force.[11] Although the figure is growing, it is small compared to the share of the work force that it comprises in Japan. It is estimated that more than half of the new jobs created since 1980 in the United States have gone to part-time workers.[12] A large proportion of these have been assumed by what are known as regular part-timers, those who work less than 40 hours per week on a regular, long-term basis at times during the week when peak demands for their services occur. Leading employers of this resource, such as Nordstrom apparel stores, include part-timers working more than 1,000 hours per year in their benefit and profit-sharing plans, affording them the same kind of training given to full-time employees. At Nordstrom, part-timers record some of the highest sales-per-hour production figures.

Similarly, equipment may be rented or leased to meet peak demands, a practice that has long been used in the airline industry on seasonal vacation routes. In the household moving industry, where most of the year's demand falls shortly after the end of the school year in the spring, a number of the largest moving companies employ owner-operators, either on a per-trip or monthly basis, in effect renting both driver and equipment on a short-term basis.

Cross-Training of Employees. Cross-training not only allows service organizations to staff multiple activities with fewer people, it affords an opportunity for the development of the people themselves through job expansion and higher compensation. There is little reason, for example, why food service personnel in major hospitals might not be able to perform paramedical activities at other times of the day, with both activities requiring interaction with patients. At Shouldice Hospital, for example, everyone is pressed into service as counselors, exhorting their hernia patients to exercise, even though their other duties might range from surgery to housekeeping.[13]

In some cases cross-training has been made more difficult by restrictive clauses concerning job jurisdiction in union contracts. But enlightened managements and their unions have concluded that job flexibility is worth negotiating in return for higher pay, given the increased productivity and employee satisfaction that often result from cross-training programs.

Sharing Capacity. Airlines with heavy demands for summer travel across the Atlantic share aircraft with competitors serving winter vacation routes in the Caribbean. In Europe, more formal pooling arrangements among carriers on the same route restrict the number of aircraft flying in the pool to that which is needed to accommodate comfortably the demand for the route. This is particularly critical in an industry in which it has been shown that the market for a particular route often is divided roughly in proportion to the number of seats flown, empty or full, leading airlines to add unwarranted extra capacity in an effort to capture a larger (and often less profitable after the expansion of capacity) share of market.[14]

Given the large number of people in the U.S. labor force that are holding two or more part-time jobs, it appears that a number of service firms unwittingly are sharing labor capacity. Where this can be done to the worker's benefit as well, in the form of a greater variety of interesting work without the loss of job benefits, everyone is served by the system.

Increasing Customer Participation in Delivery. Self-service concepts employ customers as part of the service delivery system. The most effective insure that customers are trained, through clear instructions, in how to be good "helpers." The range of activities in which customers are willing to engage is rather remarkable. Whether they pump their own gas, as a majority of U.S. consumers do; buss their own dishes; or haul their own furniture purchases, customers enable service providers to reduce demand on the delivery system during peak periods, thereby providing incentives in the form of lower prices to encourage customers to increase their participation further.

Customers are being enlisted to perform increasingly complex roles in service delivery such as medical self-treatment, preventive maintenance on equipment, and various forms of public service. Firms producing high-technology products, such as Stratus Computer, have designed products (in Stratus's case, a fault-tolerant or so-called fail-safe computer) whose problems can be diagnosed by long-distance telecommunications with instructions provided to customers in how to correct malfunctions on their own computers.

Increasingly, customers will be enlisted to perform service delivery, particularly in services experiencing regular, severe peak demands. For example, from time to time consideration has been given to the enlistment of commuting transport buffs to drive their own bus or rail commuter train to work in the interest of shaving peak demands for labor that make most rapid transit systems uneconomical to operate.

Building-In Excess Capacity. Excess capacity of certain hard-to-expand resources can be built into some service delivery systems early in their development. Thus, in construction of commercial office buildings today, it is much more economical to provide electrical and other conduit capacity to accommodate high-technology needs that might be anticipated in the future than it is to rebuild such office structures later. Contractors may run such conduits to the edge of the building where expansion is likely to occur. Extra land may be inventoried to accommodate future expansion, especially where the market value of the land is likely to increase anyway.

Perhaps the most striking example of advance inventorying of capacity is that of the Disney organization in its development of its theme parks. Based on its experience of developing Disneyland in California and seeing developers profit from food, lodging, and recreational facilities built on sites adjacent to its theme park, Disney purchased eight times the amount of land it owned at Disneyland when it developed Walt Disney World in Florida. Even more remarkable is that it quietly acquired 10,000 acres (about 16 square miles) of land outside Paris before announcing its plan to build a EuroDisney theme park there. Nothing of this magnitude had been achieved previously in real estate development in Europe by Europeans, let alone foreign developers.

Calling on Superhuman Effort. Stories are legion about what people can do when they have to. Especially in professional service organizations such as investment banking, consulting, and advertising agencies, where services have to be performed at a client's bidding, excruciatingly intense peaks of activity occur. Rather than staff highly trained, expensive people for any possible peak, such firms have to call on their personnel to perform effectively over long hours at peak times, often with the promise that shorter hours may be worked at other times.

The common thread in all cases where firms rely on superhuman effort is that this is not achieved through supervision or management exhortation. Most often, it is the result of a highly motivated staff with a devotion to a profession as much as to an organization. At peak times, management's role in such organizations is to take part in the work and serve as cheerleaders, making sure that the effort is recognized.

All of this suggests that we rarely know what the capacity of a service delivery system really is. While it may have a "rated" capacity, it is quite likely that its capacity to perform during peak periods of demand is much greater than this, particularly in organizations that recognize this and plan and manage to obtain maximum effort when it is most needed.

MANAGING TO THE RHYTHM OF THE BUSINESS

Businesses have rhythms. Some are induced by customers. They are buying dependable overnight delivery, for example, when they call Federal Express. Or they are buying the delivery of a specially ordered new car in one month if that's what the dealer's sales representative promised.

Some rhythms are created by managers themselves. For some reason, we think that we have to have financial accounting on a monthly basis. This leads to performance measures and sales incentives built around 30-day periods of time, which creates unnatural peaks and valleys in sales patterns and accompanying strains on a company's delivery system. (Who hasn't observed that 40% of the sales of many manufactured products take place in the last three business days of the month when sales commissions and bonuses are paid on a monthly basis?) Accounting conventions and tax laws force nearly every business into one-year time cycles, producing unusual end-of-year activity.

In manufacturing, rhythms imposed by customers can be buffered from those preferred by managers by devices such as product inventory buildups. Few service organizations have this opportunity. Services produced as they are "consumed" march to the beat of the customer, not managers' preferences. Even those that involve a product must practice an extreme form of just-in-time "manufacturing" management; for example, an in-flight airline kitchen must be prepared to respond to last-minute changes in flight plans, load, equipment, and even meal menus.

As a consequence, it's not surprising that at Federal Express phones are answered on the first ring or responses to complaints are forthcoming the same day. In a company with a 24-hour rhythm (jitterbugging as opposed to slow-dancing) there isn't time to let the phone ring twice. The cornerstone philosophy of the company's process for handling complaints is that "the sun never sets on an unanswered complaint." All problems may not be resolved, but all complaints are followed up and responses provided the same day. Complaints carried over to the second day theoretically build up forever.

The surprising thing is that more service company managers don't take note of the rhythm of their businesses and invoke policies, procedures, and standards that reflect them.

Service companies that have tried have found that it is difficult, if not impossible, to jitterbug and slow-dance at the same time. The U.S. Postal Service found this out when it offered different letter postage rates for surface and airmail several years ago. Employees used excess airmail capacity for surface mail to such an extent that the public began assuming that letters sent by surface mail would end up flying anyway. So the use of airmail dropped off, freeing up even more capacity for the use of air transport for surface mail. In recognition of this, the Postal Service finally abandoned two standards of timeliness for letter mail as being confusing to both customers and employees and difficult to manage. Federal Express itself abandoned its Standard (deferred delivery) package service several years ago after having difficulty offering it alongside its Priority One (overnight) service. It's hard to design an operating strategy for a business with a polyrhythmic beat.

A STUDY IN DEMAND-SUPPLY MANAGEMENT: THE AIRLINE INDUSTRY

Of all service industries, the airline industry probably provides us with the best glimpse of what is possible in demand-supply management. Given the difficulty with which competing airlines can differentiate their services, the perishable nature of their inventories, and a cost structure which is largely fixed, capacity utilization, measured in terms of load factor (occupied to total seats flown), and passenger mix are primary determinants of profit. As a result, the hub terminal system has been built to facilitate the batching of passengers for higher load factors, even though hubs often require that passengers fly more miles and spend more time in transit then they would on nonstop alternatives. Incentives for them to do this are the more frequent schedules that a hub system permits and the promise of free transportation through frequent flyer incentive programs that airlines have developed.

In addition, of course, competition has developed among reservation systems which efficiently inform travel agents and, through them, flyers about a myriad of fares. These have become necessary to encourage the largest number of business and leisure passengers with different economic means to fly without encouraging those paying the highest fares to fly at lower fares. Thus, in addition to multiple fare levels for the same basic transport service, lower fares contain restrictions making them less attractive to business travelers, such as advance booking and a required stay at destination over a weekend night.

All airlines practice all of these methods of managing demand. Those that achieve the best performance go one step further. They excel at what has been called "revenue control," with the objects of attracting the largest proportion of full-fare paying passengers possible and the realization of the highest possible revenue per seat-mile over a given competitive route.[15] They do this by managing a somewhat fungible inventory of seats on a flight-by-flight basis, selling some far in advance at low prices and others under fewer restrictions right up to the last minute at much higher fares. And among the airlines, nobody does this better than American Airlines.

Revenue control as the airlines practice it is a little like the game of chicken, seeing who can stand on the railroad track longest before the train comes by. The winner usually has the best sensing device. At American, it is a database that predicts with high accuracy the number of business travelers that will call at the last minute looking for a flight to get to an important business meeting and who will be quite willing to pay full fare. Consider what this involved early in 1987:

> At American Airlines, an average daily schedule has 1,500 departures, and 220 seats available for sale allocated among eight booking classes on a departure. Its controllers thus manage 330,000 seats allocated into 12,000 buckets [departures booking classes] for each schedule day. With flights managed up to 330 days in advance of departure, these controllers are responsible for an inventory of nearly 110 million seats allocated among 3.96 million buckets every day.[16]

This enables American to hold seats in more accurate numbers than other competitors with the confidence that it has a good sensing device. The competitive effect of this capability has been described by Samuel Fuchs:

> Carriers with superior information and decision support systems can introduce deep discount fares with carefully managed allocations. Their

less-sophisticated competitors, matching these fares defensively and without proper control, may accept too many discount bookings and displace some full-fare traffic. Ironically, this displaced traffic may migrate to flights of the sophisticated carriers who initiated the low fares.[17]

As a result, full-fare paying customers make up a larger proportion of American's traffic than that of its major competitors, something that can spell the difference between profitable and losing operations at a time when barely one in six travelers by air pays full fare.

RESULTS

The effective management of customer demand patterns and the supply of services can have a profound effect on profit performance. The above example suggests what is possible today and what will become increasingly possible in other service industries tomorrow. Whether we realize it or not, as customers we will be managed in increasingly diverse ways. Enlightened service providers will insure that such management is for our own good, resulting both in better, more diverse service offerings and more effective utilization of capacity.

9

Managing Networks

Federal Express's record of more than 99% accurate, next-day delivery (when, as the ad says, "it absolutely, positively has to be there") is explained by the company's operating strategy and service delivery system. When Fred Smith conceived the business in a college honors thesis, he elected to employ a network built around a single hub in Memphis, Tennessee. The single hub concept provides service to multiple markets with the least investment in network. Opening up service to a new market requires only the addition of one more route or "spoke" in a hub-and-spoke network. The new market is connected only to the hub, not directly to every other market. And in this case, the hub was located at an airport with a near-perfect record for good flying conditions.

In addition to building a physical network of planes, trucks, and facilities, Smith also funded the design of an innovative information network. He believes that information technology gives Federal Express its competitive edge. As a result, the company's management has put together a system that features computers on board each of Federal Express's radio-controlled vans, computers fed by hand-held "SuperTracker" devices that drivers use to note changes in the status of packages entrusted to them. The on-board computers accumulate data that can be transmitted via cellular phone to local Federal Express offices from where it is transmitted by satellite to a central database. This same database is fed by other computers at the company's hubs, which in turn receive their data from other hand-held SuperTrackers used by sorters who run their optical scanners over bar codes on each of the packages passing their stations at the hub. All of this, combined with the fact that Federal Express has full control over a package from origin to destination, allows customers to obtain updates on the status of their packages every 30 minutes.

Remarkable, you say? Only in the sense that Fred Smith and his colleagues understand so clearly the power of an operating strategy that consistently deploys networks and information technology for strategic advantage. These are matters that link an operating strategy and service delivery system directly to a service concept, as suggested in Figure 9–1. And they are of critical importance in many types of service businesses, primarily because they represent important barriers to entry and sources of competitive advantage. They are the subject of this and the next chapters.

THE IMPORTANCE OF NETWORKS TO SERVICES

Networks are endemic to many service businesses. They take many forms, comprising physical facilities, information, and relationships. They are costly and time-consuming to develop. And they often represent a formidable barrier to entry by competitors. As a result, service firms that have had a sufficient lead on competitors to build networks and utilize much of their capacity have been able to establish nearly insurmountable competitive advantage.

Transporters of both people and freight define their service most basically in terms of origins, destinations, and routes. Utilities distribute power over service areas linked by wire. Images and data are transmitted from origins to destinations by means of sound and light waves and satellite. Credit card issuers are responsible for linking cardholders with retail "service establishments" that have agreed to accept the cards in lieu of cash for purchases.

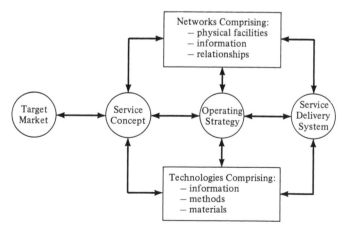

FIGURE 9–1 The Role of Networks and Technologies in a Strategic Service Vision

Issuers, cardholders, and retail establishments are tied together both electronically and by a set of promises associated with a brand name. And brokers of real estate as well as investments increase the value as well as the profitability of their services through networks of relationships encompassing buyers and sellers.

High-encounter services by definition are delivered at the point they are consumed. Until someone figures out how to deliver food and lodging, for example, without having the object of the service at hand, geographically dispersed servers and facilities will be required for their delivery. When these facilities are operated under a common name with the objective of providing a uniformly high standard of service (perhaps involving the reservation of capacity in advance) under a common advertising program, the need for some kind of network arises.

Several times each day we use network-oriented services that are held together by transport routes (whether rail, highway, air, water, or wire), communication channels, relationships, or some combination of these. Because they are costly to build and maintain and often require substantial investment in advance of revenue-producing use, networks exercise a kind of tyranny over service managers. Managers of breakthrough services relying heavily on networks have devoted a great deal of time to their design and management in an effort to overcome the tyranny of networks while enjoying their competitive benefits.

NETWORK DESIGN

The field of network theory has arisen out of the need to do such things as: (1) minimize the miles of expensive pipeline needed to connect several oil terminals, (2) maximize the accessibility of one site to every other site on a network, or (3) simultaneously ''broadcast'' information or product to more than one receiver. As a result, terms such as nodes, links, and connectivity have gained general use among network theorists, as described in more detail in the Appendix.

One assumption is missing from much of the work of network designers. That is the value of time spent by a person or thing in the network. For example, air travelers placing a particularly high value on their time would prefer a network directly connecting many cities with nonstop flights, assuming their departure could be planned to coincide with the departure of necessarily less frequent nonstop flights to their destination. Whether they would be willing to pay more to compensate an airline for the high cost of operating such a network (as opposed to a hub-and-spoke network) would depend on how highly they valued their time and the purpose of their trip. But for high-volume routes, it may pay to create nonstop flights as a marketing strategy as well as one which preserves hub-sorting capacity by diverting some passengers around it. This is what SAS (Scandinavian Airlines System) did when it changed the mix of its fleet to include more smaller DC-9s and began bypassing its Copenhagen hub to provide more nonstop service to business travelers it decided to target in 1983.[1]

The assumptions change with service industry. For freight transportation, the value of transit time for a freight shipment may be critical only when it delays delivery by a day. For overnight package delivery, customers care about pick-up and delivery times, not how much of the 24 hours the package actually spent in transit.

A communications network will have totally different characteristics. Because of the high cost of installing and maintaining wires and the relative insensitivity of the quality of service to the distance a message travels, a telephone company might place a premium on minimizing the ratio between miles of network line and people served. A communications network relying on satellite or radio wave transmission would be more concerned with the concentration of senders and receivers (nodes) in a given geographic area within range of a satellite or transmitter.

A credit card processing network relies on existing telephone networks for the transmission of credit inquiries from retail stores accepting customers' credit cards. But the critical determinants of service in this kind of network are the capacity to accept incoming calls and the processing time at the "sorting" hub, the credit authorization center. We as consumers do not like to experience waits of more than a few seconds for the credit approval of our purchases, waits made to seem longer than they are, as we know from our earlier discussion concerning the psychology of waiting lines, by the anxiety over whether our credit is going to be judged by the system to be good.

Brokerage networks employed in services ranging from investment banking to real estate succeed or fail because of relationships. Good communication networks (and even transport networks where face-to-face relationships are important) are necessary but not sufficient. The strategy of PHH Corporation, which offers a range of services to business including vehicle fleet management, employee relocation and real estate management, and office facilities and design management, illustrates this.

PHH Corporation identifies the four key underlying principles behind its successful performance as "anticipation, simplification, relationships, and vision."[2] Of these, the effective management of relationships with suppliers has been particularly important.

In the case of PHH's vehicle management companies, quality relationships with automobile manufacturers are critical. PHH orders over 100,000 cars and trucks each year for its corporate clients, through direct computer link-ups to the manufacturers. The vehicles are then built according to individualized specifications and shipped to delivering dealers around the United States, Canada, and Europe, as close as possible to each client's individual drivers. Other vehicle-related services include on-the-road maintenance and repair assistance, fuel purchase programs, and national discount programs for automotive supplies, all of which mean that PHH is also in the business of managing relationships with an enormous array of automotive service and parts suppliers, gas stations, towing and car rental companies, and dealer service locations.

PHH relocation and real estate management companies rely on solid relationships with another powerful and interwoven network of suppliers. PHH Homeequity handles the physical moves of clients' employees from one location to another. The process involves the appraisal and purchase of the transferee's original home, the management and resale of that home, the mortgage of the new home, the movement of household goods, and many ancillary services as well. In order to offer this range of services, PHH manages a network that includes its clients and their transferring employees, real estate brokerage firms through which PHH buys and sells real estate, appraisers, moving companies, and titling attorneys, as well as the capital markets that supply the company with sources of low-cost capital.

The key ingredient in PHH's ability to provide quality delivery of this complex mix of services is effective relationship management. (The network may even, in some cases, involve PHH competitors from another side of the business. However, according to PHH management, when a relationship with a competitor is required for the successful delivery of the service to the client, "it is accepted, and managed successfully.")[3]

As part of its philosophy of relationship management, PHH Corporation management has constructed a "success template" that sets forth the elements of a "win-win" relationship, shown in Figure 9–2. It suggests the extent to which this company has gone in setting itself apart from its competitors by working hard at relationship management. And it may help explain how the PHH Corporation has been able to put together earnings increases in 119 out of 120 quarters while building revenues to more than $1.7 billion.

Relationships may be quite fluid, even though they can be costly and time-consuming to establish. Information is the coin of the brokerage realm, and it is easy to compress, transport, and multiply (through sharing). For these reasons, Harlan Cleveland has suggested that it is very difficult to conceal and confine.[4] As a result, networks that lend themselves to control

Elements of a Win-Win Relationship

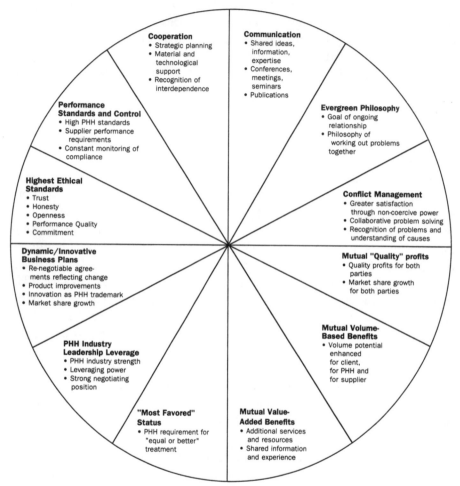

FIGURE 9–2 PHH Corporation Supplier Management Success Template
SOURCE: Marketing Department, PHH Corporation, 1989.

over the flow of information may be favored by brokers. For these purposes, the hub-and-spoke network is ideal, assuming that the broker sits at the hub and buyers and sellers at the ends of spokes.

NETWORK BUILDING AND MANAGEMENT

The value of a network to a customer often is directly proportional to its size. The number of destinations served by a freight carrier may influence a potential shipper's choice of service. The more subscribers there are to a cellular telephone network, the greater the value to the cellular telephone owner. And the larger the number of past graduates of high quality from a business school, the greater the value of its MBA degree to potential students. Existing routes and relationships make new ones more valuable to potential customers. New routes and relationships feed more traffic onto existing ones, increasing the extent to which available capacity on existing ones is utilized.

This explains the advantage of being the first in a service industry to build a network, particularly one to which competitors do not have access. But networks are costly. And in their haste to gain competitive advantage, network builders have built too fast, becoming mere memories in the process. Let's concentrate our attention instead on those who have built carefully and well.

Consider the experience of CompuServe, Inc.[5] This company operates separate businesses offering both information and network services. It operates a large company-owned central computing capability and a national communications network which is partially leased and partially owned. Its information services include both an executive information service, largely utilized during business hours, and a consumer information service, for which demand is greatest during nonbusiness hours. Both offer subscribers access to literally hundreds of databases as well as a communications link to other users of the services. Both utilize CompuServe's computing resources and communications network.

In addition, CompuServe helps client companies organize and operate internal communication networks as well as networks that link them to their customers and suppliers. Both of these services utilize CompuServe's network and message-switching capacity, largely during business hours. Yet a fifth major activity, computing services, provides traditional data processing capability to other business clients who elect to have their data processed in batches at off-peak times or on a real-time basis during business hours on CompuServe's huge bank of computers. This service uses both network (communication) and computing capacity during both day and evening hours.

The way in which CompuServe's various service businesses utilize its network and computing capacity is summarized in Figure 9–3. As hard to sort out as a can of worms? So much so that CompuServe's management cannot rely on profit measures for each business but rather strives for pricing which maximizes the use of network and computing capacity both day and night by balancing and matching demand and supply by resource and by hour of the day. It's this high and balanced use of available capacity both

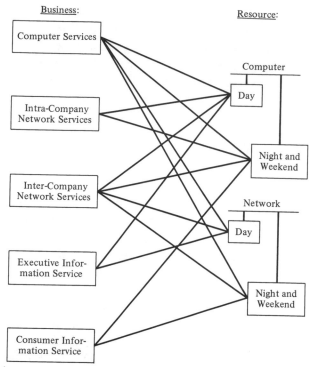

FIGURE 9–3 Joint Utilization of Resource Capacity at
CompuServe, Inc.

day and night that enables CompuServe to price each of its services competitively and still operate its overall business profitably. Several years ago,
consultants attempted to allocate all of CompuServe's costs to the five
businesses in a manner that had worked with the consultants' manufacturing
clients. As a result, they pronounced most of CompuServe's businesses
unprofitable in a year in which the company overall achieved record profits
and operated what was acknowledged to be the only truly successful consumer information service in competition with much larger and better-
financed competitors.

CompuServe's consultants missed the point. In services, success is more
often determined by effective capacity utilization than by the profitability of
all services sharing common facilities and other resources. Internally, the
most relevant piece of information is the share of available capacity needed
to achieve break-even operations or a particular profit goal. (Fortunately,
CompuServe's management ignored the consultants' analysis.) Information
systems which allow management to adjust either demand for, or supply of,

capacity are of much greater tactical and strategic value than those which attempt to measure the profitability of individual services.

On the other hand, internally oriented information systems that track profit performance by geographic location, particularly for retail or industrial services delivered through multi-unit chains, are highly relevant for many services. This is especially true where the proportion of total costs attributable to and controllable by the management of a given retail branch is high. Again, however, the need for a multi-unit chain to maintain a presence in all major markets or in close proximity to important customers' facilities may mean that some sites are operated at a loss as part of a consciously determined marketing strategy.

BUILDING COMPETITIVE ADVANTAGE WITH NETWORKS

Clustering of network nodes can be particularly beneficial where service quality is associated with service availability and control. In the retailing of convenience goods, where store name advertising and recognition are important, market share often is built most effectively by offering merchandise at more than one site in close proximity to where potential customers live or work or both. Repair services, in particular, may provide more effective sales support when they are clustered near the point of use for various durable goods.

Some years ago, Sears, Roebuck set out to increase its share of the Los Angeles market by securing attractive sites located near clusters of potential customers. In addition, these sites were spaced roughly 20 miles apart across Orange County in recognition of information gained from marketing research that customers in Southern California were willing to drive up to 10 miles to shop at a Sears store. This clustering of stores allowed Sears to obtain increased efficiencies in advertising and physical distribution costs.

The Xerox Corporation built its competitive advantage in its years of greatest growth in office equipment sales through offering good products and superior service. The latter was delivered through a service "army" so large, 12,000 strong, that it could physically get to any Xerox copier in the United States within 30 minutes of a call for help. The density of the location of Xerox equipment enabled the company to operate its service army profitably. And the availability of the service army was the primary reason many new customers chose Xerox. No competitor could afford to offer the level of service that Xerox did.

Desired density for a motel chain catering to long-distance travelers by highway and emphasizing its reservation service may be a facility every 500 miles, roughly a reasonable day's drive. A similar organization targeting business travelers, on the other hand, may need several facilities clustered around each of several major business centers.

SECOND-MOVER COUNTER STRATEGIES

How do you counter a Sears or a Xerox, particularly if it has a five-year head start in building its network? For this lesson, we can turn to a Montgomery Ward or a Ricoh.

Recognizing Sears, Roebuck's strategy to space its stores systematically across Orange County, California, the management of Montgomery Ward, wishing to improve its share of market several years later, had to decide whether to attempt to locate its stores next to those of its major competitor. Instead, the decision was made to build a similar network but in such a way that Ward's stores were located approximately equidistant between Sears stores. Because of the fact that population by this time had spread itself somewhat evenly across this vast county, Ward's strategy guaranteed that it would be closer than Sears to roughly half of all potential shoppers. It enabled the chain to secure a position as a substantial runner-up to Sears in Los Angeles market share for mass merchandisers.

Similarly, Ricoh, a Japanese manufacturer of copying equipment, could not possibly afford to match Xerox's service army in the early days of competition for the market. But it could instruct its dealers to sell only within a certain radius of selected major business centers where it could concentrate its small but hardy band of service personnel in a way that could emulate Xerox's vaunted service in selected areas.

Both Montgomery Ward and Ricoh used clustering and density to counter formidable competitors that already had established significant service advantage.

MANAGING FOR MAXIMUM UTILIZATION

Networks are costly and often must be put in place in advance of their use. This perhaps explains why Federal Express to this day represents one of the largest venture capital start-ups from scratch in the history of American business. Even by leasing when it could, the company's management had to obtain $52 million in financing by 1973 to establish a sorting hub in Memphis, offices and terminal facilities in 55 cities, a fleet of 26 Falcon jet aircraft, and a fleet of pick-up and delivery vehicles.[6] To make matters worse, much of the money had to be spent before one package was picked up and delivered by the company. This tends to focus a manager's mind on building the utilization of network capacity.

The key to capacity utilization in networks is balanced usage. As we saw at CompuServe, the company balances the use of its communication network linking computer users by pricing its services for different times of the day to attract the volume of business users it desires during working hours and the amount of demand it can accommodate from individual "consumers" during nonbusiness hours. The former pay more because the value of their time slot is more significant to them. And they are not personally responsible for paying the bill. The incremental cost of an added unit of business in a network with available capacity often is small, affording a great deal of latitude in pricing this business. Why else are airlines able to sell seats at deep discount prices to those willing to endure a number of restrictions, including the possibility of not flying at all?

Efforts are made as well to balance usage through marketing effort calibrated to the availability of excess capacity. This may require a high degree of flexibility in allocating sales or advertising effort.

The overall objective, of course, is to obtain economies of flow or density. The success of leading firms in deregulated U.S. service industries to do this has led some to conclude that the power of these firms to control both markets and prices "derives largely from the major companies' extensive networks of transportation and communication facilities."[7]

OVERCOMING THE CREEPING BREAKEVEN

One way to increase the utilization of existing network capacity is to add new routes or relationships. But the new routes or relationships, until demand for them can be developed, pull down the average utilization and profitability of the entire network. This produces a phenomenon known as "creeping breakeven," illustrated in Figure 9–4.

Fred Smith will not likely forget his encounter with creeping breakeven as CEO of Federal Express. After beginning operations at possibly the worst time imaginable, in a period of recession and rapidly rising fuel prices in 1973, the company flirted with bankruptcy as it expended a total of about $90 million (raised through a series of financings) over the succeeding three years in pursuit of the elusive break-even point. Having projected profitable operations within a year after the beginning of operations, it became more and more frustrating to approach breakeven with existing equipment and routes only to realize that additional investment in equipment and routes were required if the company's service was to be brought to the point of

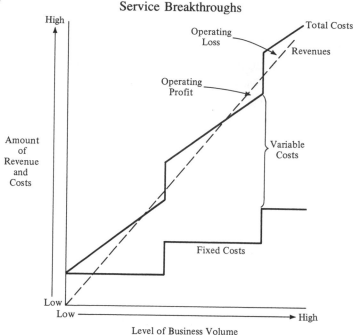

FIGURE 9–4 The Creeping Break-Even Phenomenon

being requested by customers.[8] It wasn't until early 1976 that cash flow and finally profits turned positive as the high utilization of the company's older routes more than balanced out the low utilization of new routes that were feeding older ones to produce an average utilization of planes, trucks, sorting hubs, and personnel in excess of breakeven.

If this process is prolonged overly long, a number of organizations have been forced to halt expansion, regardless of competitive service implications, to get both cash flow and profits under control. Once having achieved breakeven, managers under these circumstances often are psychologically driven to make whatever decisions are necessary not to allow operations to fall below it once again.

Through a highly creative decision, the management of the Williams Cos., a large owner and operator of oil pipelines, was able to put the threat of the creeping breakeven behind it quickly. In 1986, it purged 1,000 unused miles of its pipeline network of petroleum, strung fiber-optic cable in it, and in a short time became the fourth-largest long-distance telephone company in the United States.[9] Though a newcomer to the industry, its Williams Telecommunications Group, Inc., subsidiary became profitable much faster than its larger competitors, thanks to the new use of a largely depreciated, low-cost network for which expensive right-of-way was already established.

This has enabled it to expand through a combination of its own low-cost facilities and more costly conventional methods while operating profitably.

MANAGING QUALITY IN NETWORKS

The importance of quality excellence is a direct function of the degree to which multi-site operations are linked by name, by the need for timely response, or by trust.

LINKAGE BY NAME

Two restaurants operating under common ownership but different names and in different markets have little need for a common standard of quality imposed by a network relationship. But both company-owned and franchised McDonald's outlets are linked so strongly by name that ownership doesn't matter with customers. A poor experience at one location reflects on all McDonald's stores.

LINKAGE BY THE NEED FOR TIMELY RESPONSE

To be effective, communications networks require timely response. With improved technology, our standards for timely response are becoming more and more demanding.

Reservation systems inherently are associated with a substantial degree of customer anticipation and anxiety that requires high standards of response. Witness an airline passenger attempting to make alternative travel plans after having had a flight cancelled due to weather. This often occurs at precisely the time that other passengers are scrambling to use the same capacity. It explains why airline personnel must have special numbers they can dial for high-priority response from personnel of other airlines in order to be of maximum assistance to travelers at times of greatest need (and probably peak demand).

Either capacity has to be built into systems to handle peaks (a "level" supply strategy) or temporary help has to be commandeered under a "chase" supply strategy to provide timely response. The former is much more feasible when technology plays a major role in service delivery. Where people comprise much of the delivery effort, a "chase" strategy utilizing part-timers or people with other responsibilities who are cross-trained to help out at peak times often is most feasible.[10]

LINKAGE BY TRUST

The world's financial system, made up of many networks of relationships, operates to a great degree on trust. Capital is traded on the basis of verbal agreements that are only later confirmed and honored. That's why the violation of trust that occurred with the illegal use of insider information by several Wall Street traders in 1986 and 1987 was so devastating to the "networks" embodied in the financial community.

This is true of many brokerage services in which the quality of relationship is paramount. Those who can't be trusted are boycotted by other brokers, whether the item being brokered is real estate or credit.

The management of quality of this type of linkage is perhaps most difficult of all. Violations of trust may be discovered long after a transaction, if ever. But because of its importance, network participants often pursue vigilante methods involving word-of-mouth advice and references intended to isolate violators.

In general, shared interest in the success of a network often argues for mutual assent and adherence to controls over the quality of linkages of all kinds. It is a case where the value resulting from quality control is mutually recognized to be greater than the cost of conformance to mutually shared standards. In particular, successful franchisers have recognized and used this as a lever in controlling matters of quality with franchisees. We'll have more to say about this later when we focus our attention on franchising.

10

Managing
Information Technologies

While technological innovation in manufacturing most often emanates from materials or methods, in services the primary wellspring is information. And since the benefits of new information technologies are often more difficult to estimate, their application may require either greater amounts of "faith" or larger estimates of eventual financial return.

John B. McCoy, like his father before him, has set aside annually a portion of the gross profit of the organization he leads, Banc One Corporation, for research and development into both information and methods technologies. The decision was made originally when the bank was insignificant in its industry. The amount currently is 4% of gross profits, much higher than at most other banks. Much of this money has been spent to support the work of John Fisher, a former radio advertising executive and a technological visionary whom few banks would have considered hiring several years ago. In banking circles today, Fisher's name is mentioned whenever the subject of technology and innovation come up. This prolonged, constant commitment of human and financial resources has produced a stream of technology-based successes and failures.

Banc One was, for example, the first bank to install automated teller machines and the first bank to issue BankAmericard, the forerunner of Visa, outside of California. It developed state-of-the-art technology for processing credit card information both for itself and for other organizations such as credit unions and savings and loan associations. At one recent count, it processed information for nearly seven million cardholders. At the same time, experiments in home banking services and point-of-sale purchasing using debit cards to automatically deduct purchases from bank accounts have not been successful. But Banc One has become known as the most innovative and one of the most profitable in the U.S. banking business in the process. McCoy's goal has been to be "successful by being different. The market appreciates that we are not dependent 100% on the old-fashioned banking business."[1]

Similarly, at Federal Express, for example, it has taken 11 years to develop COSMOS, its package-tracking information system. The project has required several leaps of faith on the part of CEO Fred Smith, who continues to maintain (even in the face of the failure of another technology-based venture at Federal Express, ZAPMAIL) that technology is at the core of the company's competitive strategy. But one of Smith's great fascinations in life has been with technology. That may explain why he had the motivation to back up his vision of an increasingly high-tech society in need of appropriate supporting services with actions reflecting the values of that same society. As Smith proclaimed in an early communication to potential customers:

> This company is nothing short of being the logistics arm of a whole new society that is building up in our economy—a society that isn't built around automobile and steel production, but that is built up instead around service industries and high technology endeavors in electronics and optics and medical science. It is the movement of these support items that Federal Express is all about.[2]

What better way to distribute high tech than with high tech?

MANAGING INFORMATION

Data is the most valuable raw material that many service firms possess, yet it never appears on a balance sheet. This accounting practice is probably excusable to the extent that most data is never processed into information on which management decisions can be based. But information isn't given any specific value by accountants. Perhaps that explains in part why more of this asset than any other is wasted in business. And it may explain, but not excuse, why databases with special power to describe customer behavior patterns are so hard to find even today.

Decision quality is a function both of the quality of available information and managers' abilities to use it. Information systems often contain elements of all types of information shown in Figure 10–1. Here we find internally oriented information about the costs of various resources used in producing goods or services as well as capacity utilization and the profitability of the business or component parts such as products, individual facilities, or entire

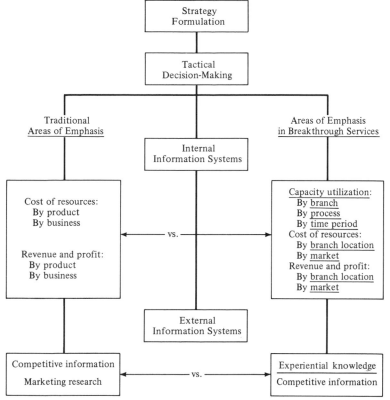

Underlined items = special areas of emphasis in information systems
for breakthrough service management.

FIGURE 10–1 Contrasts Between Areas of Emphasis in Traditional
and Breakthrough Service Information Management

subsidiary entities. This is often combined with externally-oriented information about competitors and the needs and behavior of customers, in a few cases even extending to efforts to estimate the profitability of selling to various customers or groups. This information may be obtained from more or less formal marketing research as well as the accumulation of knowledge from selling to and serving customers. It is this latter that we call experiential information.

INTERNALLY ORIENTED INFORMATION SYSTEMS

Traditionally, internally oriented information systems have allowed manufacturing organizations to track the costs of resources such as labor, materials, real estate, capital, and management. Often it has been possible to combine this with information about sales volume and prices to track and manage profitability by business entity or even by product. This approach has proven to be largely irrelevant for most services.

Many services are delivered by processes in which delivery facilities are shared and the resources devoted to a particular service are only a small fraction of the costs which must be recovered in the pricing of that service. Putting it another way, costs that can be identified with a particular service "product" are such a small proportion of the total that it is often futile and misleading to attempt to track the profitability of one in a line of services.[3]

EXTERNALLY ORIENTED INFORMATION SYSTEMS

For the most part, externally oriented information systems have emphasized the collection of data about competitors and customers, either through more formal marketing reserach or less formal sales experiences and patterns. Breakthrough services more often are built around the development of what we have called experiential information that profiles the behavior of customers or products to be serviced and is collected and analyzed over time, adding to a server's knowledge in ways that make it increasingly valuable. This is often of much greater value than the more traditional forms of external data.

Manufacturing firms have for years constructed experience curves which reflect the way in which production times and costs decline with each unit produced, tangible evidence of the value of experience. But learning about customers is a field in which service firms have pioneered. It has provided the same kind of competitive advantage and barrier to entry for service competitors that the experience curve represents for manufacturers. It is at the core of breakthrough service management.

Experiential information is not free. It requires the development of data collection and processing routines that refine data into usable information. Its value often is not realized until years after efforts are first made to develop it. Like the king who, when apprised by his gardener that there was no rush in planting a tree that would take 50 years to achieve maturity, commanded the gardener to "plant the tree immediately if that is the case," breakthrough service firms "plant their experiential information trees" immediately. The resulting long-term harvest often is bountiful.

CREATIVE USES OF EXPERIENTIAL INFORMATION

Those firms that recognize the value of data (particularly data about customers and competitors), marshal it carefully, and organize it into information, have built formidable competitive weapons in their industries. These weapons continue to serve them for years, taking on increasing value with the passage of time. The role is not long. It includes, among others, American Express and Dun & Bradstreet in financial services, Schlumberger in oil field services, Federal Express and American Airlines in air transportation, the Progressive Corporation in insurance; The ServiceMaster Company in facility management services, and L. L. Bean and Mrs. Fields Cookies in retailing. These are the firms that have gone beyond the development of internally focused cost information and management control systems and the construction of customer-centered information based largely on marketing research studies. They have developed what we will call experiential information based on the effective capture of data drawn from their experiences in serving customers.

The list could be longer, particularly considering the immense potential for information-based competitive strategies in firms that already possess vast amounts of data in their files. For example, in 1989 AT&T files contained the addresses, calling patterns, and credit worthiness of more than 93 million customer accounts. Roughly 66 million people held Sears, Roebuck credit cards, not counting the 27 million holders of Sears's Discovery cards. Banks, through the VISA and MasterCard organizations which they sponsor, theoretically had access at that time to buying patterns of nearly 200 million U.S. cardholders; American Express had similar information for its 22 million U.S. card owners and another 8 million in other countries.[4]

Major issuers of "plastic," whether in the form of credit, frequent flyer, or other membership cards, are just beginning to explore the potential for linking two or more "cards" to obtain increased patronage for each party to the linkage. Thus, frequent flyers earn miles (for free transport) by using special bank credit cards for their purchases. Other card users are entitled to discounts or purchases at cooperating establishments. These linkages provide a good example of the way in which information technology and network concepts are being married to provide more complete customer services and powerful operating leverage. To the extent that they involve the exchange of information concerning customer behavior patterns among service membership programs, they will enhance the experiential information base available to each. They will require critical strategic decisions as the "sides are chosen" for the information-driven service competition to come.

The list of organizations making heavy use of experiential information is not confined to the giants of the service sector. The Shouldice Hospital in Toronto does one thing, repair one type of hernia. But it is the world's most complete repository of data about tens of thousands of people who have had inguinal hernias repaired there, one reason why the hospital has a success rate about 12 times better than the average of other North American medical hospitals.

Similarly, the Hartford Steam Boiler Inspection and Insurance Co. knows more about the behavior and use of steam boilers than the companies that manufacture them. Its engineers have inspected and insured such equipment for more than 120 years. And the tiny Rural/Metro Fire Department has built its ability to provide quality fire protection privately at significantly lower costs than its municipal competitors not only by developing innovative fire-fighting techniques but also by collecting and using extensive information about the premises it protects. It even prepares microfiche diagrams of building plans that can be scanned by crews on a microfiche reader en route to a fire. Why shouldn't Rural/Metro be able to provide a more effective fire-fighting service? Even more important, the inspections required to develop such information yield important recommendations for actions that prevent possible fires.

Even in public service, more than one political candidate has used experiential learning about candidates to target messages to potential voters at lower cost. For example, Father Robert Drinan, the first Catholic priest to be elected to the U.S. Congress, achieved a major political upset in this manner in a primary campaign against an incumbent who had been in office 26 years. Drinan's campaign manager, John Marttila, with little money but several thousand volunteers, deployed the volunteers on a house-to-house survey to find the issues of importance to each voter in Drinan's Massachusetts district. The resulting data, when processed by computer, was used to direct the mailing of Drinan's position statements only to those voters interested in each issue addressed. The startling campaign success was achieved well below the initial budget estimates.

Schlumberger over the years has built an extensive profile of experiences encountered in the drilling of 70% of the world's oil wells. This data, in the form of profiles of geological formations, electronic "soundings" obtained from applying the company's "wire-line" technologies to clients' drilling efforts, drilling experiences at different depths with different technologies, and information about ultimate results, is the finest, most complete database of its kind in the world. Schlumberger has invested large sums of money in both hardware and software to insure that the data is processed into relevant information that can be made available in actionable form to its more than

2,000 engineers working in the field at out-of-the-way drilling sites. In spite of a badly depressed market for oil field services, Schlumberger has remained the most profitable firm in the industry in large part because its database and related information system carry the highest value, offering the greatest opportunity for leveraging value (price) over cost.

Dun & Bradstreet has built a diversified service firm on experiential data. For 149 years it has collected and sold information that allowed users of its D&B credit service to determine the credit worthiness of companies with which they did business. At first slowly, and then more rapidly, D&B began processing this data in ways that might signal potential credit problems in companies in which it collected information. D&B credit ratings became the standard of the industry. More recently, the company has expanded its experientially based information services by acquiring Moody's, Inc., a leading rating service for the quality of bonds issued by public and private organizations based on Moody's file of data reflecting their credit worthiness. Subsequent acquisitions of other data-based companies such as A. C. Nielsen, which regularly audits such things as retail purchasing and television viewing behavior of consumers, have made it possible for D&B to begin developing new information service products that utilize two or more of its experiential databases, adding to the value of its traditional services. The information that D&B has would take a potential competitor decades of time and billions of dollars to collect. That's the competitive power of experiential data and information.

American Airlines has tracked its customers' flying patterns more closely than its competitors. As we saw earlier, the result is the most sophisticated load planning (or revenue control) program in the business.[5] It is based on information about the numbers of passengers, by class and fare category, on each flight in American's system. More important, it identifies when each reservation was made prior to flight time, allowing American to know how long to hold available capacity at a higher fare level before releasing it to travelers seeking low fares. It has allowed American to price its flights more selectively than its competitors.

Major airline efforts to track customer behavior by route and flight and to reserve and price seats accordingly is credited by one former competitor with driving his company out of business. According to Donald Burr, who founded and led People Express to its early success with its low-cost, low-price strategy and innovative human resource policies, the airline failed because of the power of its competitors' computer technology. "They were able to harness that technology to set their prices at or lower than People Express on a point-specific basis. . . . They were able to compete with low-cost producers in a very specific way without trashing their yields."[6]

We tend to think that Burr still does not know what hit him and his airline. While it may have been superior technology in part, it most certainly was the combination of that technology with superior information management, suggesting again that breakthrough service providers combine technologies for competitive advantage. How do they manage technology to achieve this?

MANAGEMENT OF TECHNOLOGY

If by technology we mean hardware, then technology is vastly overrated as a source of competitive advantage in services. For example, the world's commercial aircraft are produced by only three manufacturers. Their products are available to all airlines. Automated teller machine (ATM) networks now connect the smallest banks with the largest, providing all customers with convenient access to their accounts on a national basis. And computers with superchips will make machines with the power of today's mainframe computers available to any firm that can afford an increasingly modest price tag.

In an industry such as lodging, there have been few technological breakthroughs to equal the electronic wake-up call and the in-room mini-bar, which are hardly proprietary. McDonald's has been said to employ technology effectively, but a close examination suggests that its most effective devices are simple timers on cooking. They include utensils such as the french fry machine and a 4×4 system of cooking hamburger patties (16 at a time) that results in the right amount of cooking time and allows condiments to be applied through a four-headed (2×2) applicator that reduces application time by 75%.

But when we speak of technology, we'll also include software, the logic that controls the hardware. This is the link between hardware and data that, for example, makes American Airlines such a formidable competitor with its yield planning and seat "blocking" and pricing programs. Technology in a broader sense that includes software as well as hardware and extends to methods and materials has been a potent force in the competitive strategies of breakthrough services. But its application generally to services is thought by many to have produced sometimes disappointing results, and currently is the source of some amount of soul-searching. For possible reasons, let's review first the nature of technology and the way it has been used in services. Then we can take a more detailed look at the recurring reasons why some service companies have been able to make technology a core element of their offerings and why many others have not been able to realize the promise of information technology for improved quality and productivity.

THE HOLY TRINITY OF TECHNOLOGY

Technologies concern themselves with materials, methods, and information. Materials technology is basic to the other two. Thus, the development of strong, lightweight aluminum made possible the construction of more efficient aircraft that changed the technology of methods used in the air transport business. Current research in materials that are superconductors will change the way information is transmitted and processed.

Methods technology relates to the development of new machines, processes, and ways of working. It includes the design of the workplace and the scheduling of activities taking place there. In services, it can be as simple as the introduction of box beds to eliminate a difficult cleaning problem for hotels or as complex as the redesign of a bank to reflect the restructuring of tellers' and officers' tasks to provide improved levels of service to preferred clients.

Information technology encompasses computing and communication, the handling of data, and methods for converting data into actionable information.

These technologies are both interrelated and interactive. Thus, while new materials may make new forms of computing possible, new forms of computing provide information used in the development of new materials. These relationships are suggested by the intersecting rings in Figure 10–2.

COMBINING TECHNOLOGIES

Firms that have experienced the greatest success in changing the technological face of an industry often have combined basic technologies, working at the intersections of the diagram shown in Figure 10–2. In the early 1960s, for example, modern ships and terminal facilities were designed to handle containers that could be transported equally easily by rail, highway, or ship with great economies in the transfer of containers (rather than the individual items of freight they contained) from one transportation mode to another. Within several years, most of the merchandise freight moving on some of the world's most heavily used international trade routes was moving in containers as opposed to older methods. However, profits did not accrue immediately to containership operators flush with rapidly increasing volumes. They found instead that their assumptions concerning the number of containers required in the service delivery system per container actually being carried on board a ship were much lower than had been programmed into their business plans and prices. The reason? Shippers were using con-

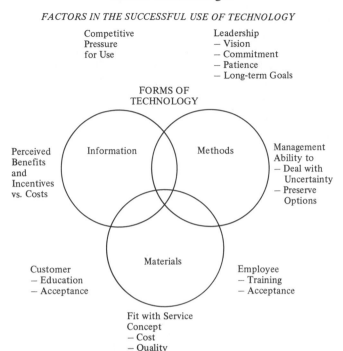

FIGURE 10–2 Relationships Between Forms of
Technology and Factors in Their Successful Use

tainers for storage rather than returning them to "active duty" as assumed.
Worse yet, the container service operators were losing track of containers in
the system. It wasn't until improved information technologies, in the form
of better tracking and inventorying systems, were combined with the significant change in methods technology (containerization itself) that the real
breakthrough in improved service, lower cost, and profits occurred.

Similarly, in 1978, Merrill Lynch first introduced its Cash Management
Account (CMA) which offered customers checking, savings, credit card,
and securities brokerages services. More important, through its newly developed information processing systems, Merrill Lynch could combine information about all these services on a single statement supplied monthly to
account holders. (Incidentally, it wasn't by accident that Merrill Lynch
turned to Banc One Corp. for help in processing its credit card information,
a service that earned Bank One criticism from other banking institutions for
allowing a "nonbank" to enter banking.) But Merrill Lynch then combined
methods with information technology by promising to "sweep" idle funds
in accounts into interest-bearing money market funds on a daily basis. The

combination of comprehensive transaction-based information services and the allure of a method for putting all of a client's funds to work at all times attracted more than $100 billion into CMA accounts and assured Merrill Lynch the dominant share of the market for years.

ServiceMaster's customers that we have interviewed, hospital administrators and school superintendents, repeatedly tell us that one of the major influences in their decisions to contract with the company for housekeeping and other services was the positive impression they received in visiting ServiceMaster's laboratory and education facilities in Downers Grove, Illinois. Through the years, this company has built competitive advantage not only by assembling information about cleaning tasks and developing information systems for staffing and work allocation on individual jobs, but also by developing superior methods and materials in its laboratories. For washing windows, the company replaces ladders with specially designed, lightweight, long-handled squeegies using easy-to-remove velcro-backed, washable cleaning cloths soaked between uses in fluids developed in ServiceMaster's laboratories. This perhaps explains why ServiceMaster's chairman, Kenneth Wessner, is so enthusiastic about giving a short lecture on the ServiceMaster method for washing a window or mopping a floor. The enthusiasm suggests the source of continuing support for the laboratory's budget.

ENLISTING CUSTOMER AND EMPLOYEE SUPPORT

Introducing new technology into any organization is a bit like transplanting a human organ from one body to another. The organ may function perfectly, but the body may nevertheless reject it. This is a particularly complex process for many services where customers and services must interact both to provide information important to the service and to produce the service itself. Both must believe that there are personal benefits to be achieved by using a new technology. The benefits are not always apparent without education and incentives to use it.

Automated teller machines (ATMs) nearly failed where banks did not take precautions to educate potential users adequately, particularly concerning the safeguards against the misuse of someone's account by another customer. Direct dialing had to be sold by AT&T with the appeal that it would save customers time and cost less. And at Federal Express, couriers objected to the early tests of hand-held shipment tracking devices because they were being asked to input information that hadn't been required of them previously, thus slowing down the pick-up and delivery process. The software used in the device had to be improved to reduce the 12 questions asked for each delivery "exception" (such as package delivered next door because the receiver was not at home) to only three or four required for a specific type of exception. With this change, the positive aspects of the technology (such as making couriers look "high tech") began to outweigh negative ones for the couriers.

American Hospital Supply Corporation (AHSC), which distributes medical supplies from its own as well as other manufacturers' factories to more than 10,000 hospitals and medical laboratories, launched a massive education program when it established computer links to its customers in the 1970s under a program called ASAP (Analytic Systems Automatic Purchasing).[7] Managers had to be convinced that the use of the system would result in better service to hospitals (who entered orders through terminals supplied by AHSC), lower inventories for both hospitals and AHSC, lower sales costs, and larger volumes of sales for suppliers. By the mid-1980s, successive "generations" of ASAP allowed AHSC's customers to place orders using personal computers and a hospital's own internal stock numbers rather than AHSC's; build files for standing and repetitive orders; inquire on-line into pending back orders, prices, and delivery dates; and place orders through a bar code scanning device for reviewing hospital shelf stocks. As a result, AHSC's market share soared as the use of its system by customers increasingly locked competitors out of their hospitals. By 1985, AHSC had also implemented VIP, a "reverse ASAP" that linked the company to its suppliers on a computer-to-computer basis. As more and more customers and suppliers joined the system, the value to all participants increased as order trends could be identified and communicated to everyone more quickly.

EMPOWERING PEOPLE THROUGH TECHNOLOGY

Managers of information-intensive services increasingly face decisions concerning the degree to which they should automate or informate their services or, as Earl Sasser and William Fulmer have suggested, the degree to which they should empower the customer or the service provider.[8]

Empowering the Customer: Automating. New technologies are making possible automation that empowers customers. These technologies range from automated teller machines for banking to computer-assisted home shopping and information-oriented services. Consider, for example, the implications of one of the simplest of technologies in medicine, the device allowing patients to administer their own medication for controlling pain.

Traditionally, painkillers have been administered by nurses or their assistants, usually at the request of the patient. Often, patients do not call nurses until they experience relatively high levels of pain, many times out of deference to a busy nurse. Upon being unable to summon nurses immediately during busy periods at a hospital, patients suffering pain in addition begin to experience rising levels of trauma. When they appear, nurses typically administer dosages of painkiller sufficiently large not only to deal with the high level of current pain, but also to reduce the frequency of future calls. Increasingly, the administration of painkillers through service providers has become a "no-win" process for patients and nurses alike.

Recently, a device has been developed that allows a patient to push a button on a wristband, activating a small dose of painkiller in a container placed near the point of need. The size of dosage can be regulated by a doctor. As a result, nurses have been saved a number of routine calls. And research to date shows that patients not only are able to regulate levels of pain within much tighter upper and lower limits, but use less painkiller to do so.

In a completely different service arena, Accu-Weather, Inc., has developed an $89.95 software-and-service product that's designed to let customers plot their own customized, local weather forecasts whenever they desire. The Accu-Weather Forecaster enables users to tap into the company's database, which compiles comprehensive weather information from the National Weather Bureau and other sources. The software allows transportation and insurance companies, pilots, farmers, fire departments, and other customers to manipulate the data on a personal computer to help tailor their forecasts for local target areas.[9]

Where the accuracy of information input is essential to good service, the decision to empower customers has, at times, shifted responsibility for poor service caused by inaccurate information to customers. Firms employing this approach have found it essential to provide troubleshooters to assist customers in installing procedures to correct problems leading to poor quality before customers begin blaming the service rather than themselves.

For the consumer, these types of technology-enhanced service systems are liberating. Technology has *automated* the service process, empowering customers and providing them with personalized convenient service superior to that which they could obtain through encounters with other humans.

Empowering the Service Provider: Informating. Other information technologies empower people in different but equally exciting ways. They empower service providers, enabling them to deliver superior service to sometimes astounded and often very satisfied customers. Shoshana Zuboff has called this form of empowerment informating.[10] It is the process through which service providers are supplied both with superior information and ways of retrieving it, combining it, and otherwise using it intuitively to solve customers' problems in ways that are both effective and personal. It can lead to significant learning and development on the part of service providers as well as the development and possession of information at the lowest operating levels of the organization that may not exist at middle or even upper levels of management. As a result, managers have to come to terms with not having all the answers first in an informating organization.

Informating is most successful when service providers are empowered to act on their new-found knowledge, to make judgments concerning corrective action, and to act first and report on actions later. Where such latitude is not provided or where employees are not prepared sufficiently to exercise it well, Zuboff's research suggests that unusually high levels of frustration and unsatisfactory performance among employees can result.[11]

The full potential for learning in other systems may not be realized until service providers not only are given the authority but actually encouraged to "override" instructions provided by the system. The much-heralded management information system of Mrs. Fields Cookies is a case in point.

The creation of Debbi and Randy Fields, Mrs. Fields Cookies basically is focused around an effort to maintain control of a rapidly growing, totally company-owned chain of retain cookie baking shops through a computer system that both controls and supervises store managers. Over 500 Mrs. Fields store managers start each day by calling up the system's Day Planner program on their individual workstations. Each of the managers tells the computer what day of the week it is, and whether it's a normal day, sale day, school day, or holiday. Then:

> the computer goes back to . . . (each) store's hour-by-hour, product-by-product performance on the last three school-day Tuesdays. Based on what you did then, the Day Planner tells each manager . . . here's what you'll have to do today, hour by hour, product by product, to meet your sales projection. It tells him how many customers he'll need each hour and how much he'll have to sell them. It tells him how many batches of cookie dough he'll have to mix and when to mix them to meet the demand and to minimize leftovers. He could make these estimates himself if he wanted to take the time. The computer makes them for him.[12]

Based on information concerning hourly sales directly fed from the cash register, the computer might direct the manager to have more or less cookies baked than originally planned or to send employees out into the street to distribute flyers that stimulate demand. In addition, a manager can use the computer system to help in scheduling crew, interviewing crew applicants, preparing personnel evaluations, and looking up information concerning the maintenance of store equipment.

This strategy worked as long as Mrs. Fields confined herself to the domestic cookie business. But more recently, expansion into foreign markets and the extension of store product lines into other bakery products has made it more difficult to control operations centrally by means of information technology.[13]

Empowering Both Customer and Service Provider. In a U.S. commercial banking industry that is spending heavily for information technology, Wells Fargo & Company stands out. It is distinguished too by the way it has empowered both customers and employees in both its consumer and commercial banking services.

Like many other banks, Wells Fargo has supplied its tellers with terminals that speed customer transactions by providing fast access to account information. However, this bank's terminals allow tellers to handle up to a hundred different transactions for consumers. At the same time, the bank has empowered customers not wishing personal service by providing one of the highest concentrations of automated teller machines in the country. And recently, 71% of the bank's checking account customers were using them, the highest percentage for any bank at the time. In tandem, these developments have enabled the bank to reduce employment at some of its branches by 60% and centralize many functions at headquarters.[14]

But it's in its commercial banking business where Wells Fargo stands out. Again, it has empowered both its own officers and its customers. Wells Fargo's Integrated Office Support System helps officers explore new financing alternatives for business customers in a fraction of the time previously required. According to Michael James, head of one of Wells Fargo's commercial banking offices:

> What used to take a day—studying things in a deal like cash flow and the sensitivity of the figures to changes in interest rates—can be done in 15 minutes. . . . We can use that information as a marketing tool, particularly when approaching small companies that have never been able to do that kind of thing.[15]

Commercial customers are now able to manage their own cash accounts by tapping directly into Wells Fargo's computer system through electronic data interchange. For example, the Hilton Hotel Corporation's computers query Wells Fargo's computers during the night to prepare reports on Hilton's cash accounts. Similarly, the Catholic Archdiocese of Santa Rosa, California, uses its direct access to pool funds from its various religious and educational facilities by means of Msgr. Thomas Keys's portable computer. The impact that this has had on the relative roles played by the bank and church is described by Msgr. Keys:

> It allows me to use a program I wrote that tracks the deposits, withdrawals and average daily balances of the different entities and generates a monthly interest check for them. . . . We pay Wells a fee of $3,500 to $5,000 a month, and the diocese gets the float. They are a conduit and we have become the bank.[16]

All of this in combination with other Wells Fargo efforts to empower employees through improved computer-assisted just-in-time purchasing systems, electronic mail, and other devices may sound as if the bank is pioneering. But the bank's chairman and chief executive, Carl Reichardt, says, "I am much more interested in reliability than being on the leading edge. . . . There's nothing worse than selling technology-driven services that do not work."[17]

INVESTING IN TECHNOLOGY AND PEOPLE

Good service organizations look for ways to substitute technology for people. But in what sometimes becomes a single-minded quest for substitution, many fail to realize their expectations by spending too much on technology and too little on the training of employees to use it effectively. This is confirmed by a recent study by Martin Starr of Japanese and European firms operating in the United States. The Japanese firms were found to be outperforming other foreign-affiliated firms. Starr's data suggested this was due in part to larger relative investments not only in technology but also in training and research and development.[18]

Superior service performers invest both in technology and people, sorting out the functions to be performed by each and spending enough on personal development to insure not only the more effective use of technology but greater employee and customer satisfaction.

Sorting Out the Roles of Technology and People. Many service jobs are being performed better with technology in both its hard (equipment and materials) and soft (information) forms. Clues to the potential for this can be gained from the communications and railroad transportation industries which have had the greatest success in providing steadily improving service with rapidly increasing productivity. In both, we have services performed through what we might call "fixed option" service delivery systems consisting of massive networks restricting the opportunity for the effective use of human judgment in the operation (as opposed to the maintenance) of the system. Further, the demands of communication and rail networks for rapid switching and continuous monitoring are beyond those that humans can perform, either efficiently or, in some cases, at any cost.

At times, "high touch" may detract from the perceived quality of service. In addition to providing 24-hour transaction capability, automated teller machines may provide service improvements over "high-touch" methods by making it possible for customers to transact business while avoiding unwanted human interaction.

Other "fixed option" technologies make it possible for inexperienced operators to produce excellent french fries at McDonald's, control space availability and direct traffic flow in airport parking lots, and make accurate change at retail counters.

Just as these "hard" technologies have changed the face of several service industries, "soft" technologies have been employed by other breakthrough service firms to achieve similar results. For example, the collection, analysis, and dissemination of information concerning the merchandising of women's ready-to-wear has led to rapidly increasing labor productivity in retail outlets specializing in this type of merchandise.[19] Firms like The Limited in the United States and Benetton in Europe have taken responsibility for the retail merchandising of their goods, not only in terms of designing and installing store fixtures, but also instructing store managers (whose management is largely confined to relatively inexperienced people) in the proper ordering and display of merchandise and the staffing of their stores. This, combined with centralized attention to consumer fashion trends, sourcing, and the most effective store layout and merchandise display patterns, has revolutionized ready-to-wear retailing, making available better design quality at lower cost in a format that facilitates consumer shopping and increases the effectiveness of sales people.

Achieving Higher Employee Satisfaction through Technology. Most service firms underestimate the cost of employee turnover, confining their analysis to a comparison of the cost of hiring and retaining more capable people to that of enduring high turnover and training costs. The very best service providers place a value on quality of service over time and the retention of employees as a means of retaining customers.

The cost benefits of investing in people as well as technology are realized all too rarely. For example, in the long-haul, irregular route, truckload highway transport business, drivers traditionally have been regarded as so interchangeable that most have been hired as independent owner-operator contractors on a "per-trip" basis. Johnnie Bryan Hunt, majority owner of J.B. Hunt Transport Services, Inc., concluded that if he was going to maintain control in a highly cost-sensitive business, he needed to operate with his own equipment and drivers.[20] Further, with a rapidly developing shortage of new drivers drawn from the 20- to 24-year-old age range in the trucking industry, steps needed to be taken to increase productivity, and reduce both labor (by far the highest component of trucking cost) and turnover costs.

Hunt developed an information system to facilitate the more effective scheduling of equipment and drivers. As a result, he has been able to run his trucks 126,000 miles per year as opposed to an industry average of about 115,000 miles per year in recent years. More important, Hunt's trucks run loaded 92% of their miles compared to an average of 88% for his competitors, while the base pay of Hunt's drivers is roughly comparable to that in other firms (about 23 cents per mile in 1987). The company's management calculated that a reduction of five percentage points in its annual driver turnover rate of about 100% would be worth $1 million in reduced training costs alone.

As a result, J.B. Hunt has guaranted its drivers a minimum of 2,100 miles of driving per week, has increased the number of its "terminals" (used in the truckload transport business largely for equipment maintenance and dispatching) to provide increased opportunity for drivers to switch loads to improve their work schedules, and has allowed drivers to trade for loads headed in their homeward direction. In addition, the company began testing a satellite communications device in each truck cab that allows drivers to communicate directly with dispatchers, eliminating calls from truck stops that require roughly two hours per trip per driver, increasing driver productivity and potential income.

Partially because of these efforts, J.B. Hunt, by 1987, had become the second-largest irregular route truckload hauler in the United States, with about $390 million in revenues. Operating more than 3,000 tractors and more than 7,000 trailers, the firm's ratio of operating costs to sales in late 1988 were 82.8% in comparison to an industry average of 97%.[21] This has all made it worthwhile for Hunt, contrary to his habit, to wear a tie just as his drivers are required to do.

IMPLEMENTING TECHNOLOGY

A number of other issues confront organizations placing heavy emphasis on technology in a competitive strategy, but they are not unique to services. Among them are decisions about: (1) being a leader or an adaptor in the development of technology, the equivalent of the classic make-or-buy dilemma, (2) adapting a technology to a service concept or vice versa (as in the development of one-hour photo processing capability which basically changed the service concept for this business), (3) incrementally developing elements of a system with or without an overall long-term plan for the service delivery system as a whole, (4) attempting to utilize portions of a technology during development as opposed to waiting for the completion of the full development process, (5) making a full commitment to one alternative or electing less satisfying alternatives that preserve flexibility, (6) testing results on a localized basis or "rolling out" the entire system, and (7) following a strategy of proprietary development in the firm as opposed to participating in a consortium or an industrywide cooperative effort.

How a firm decides these issues depends on such things as the ability of its leadership to suspend disbelief, the presence of both a "champion" and a "sponsor" (à la John Fisher and John McCoy, respectively, at Banc One), the size of the investment in time and money required, the importance of the technology to the service concept and the establishment of competitive advantage, the resources of the firm, and the general state of the technology itself. Some highlights from Federal Express's development of its COSMOS package tracking system give us an insight into one breakthrough effort in technology development.[22]

We've already documented Fred Smith's ability to suspend disbelief concerning matters of technology at Federal Express. Early on in the conception of COSMOS, he identified his champion, Harry Dalton, who had spent his early days with the company as a station manager in Philadelphia. Far from flamboyant, Dalton nevertheless had a strong interest in, aptitude for, and pragmatic attitude toward technology that Smith was looking for. Perhaps even more important, he had a bulldog-like tenacity once he became involved in a problem. As Dalton often says, "The only thing we know for sure is that we won't get it quite right the first time, but we'll come back and fix it."[23]

COSMOS was vitally important to a company whose CEO realized it served customers who bought the service as much for its one-courier shipment control as for its speed. There was little doubt that the technology would have to be developed to complement the service concept. And an exhaustive survey of available technology confirmed that Federal Express either would have to assume leadership in developing some components of a package tracking system or would have to resign itself to waiting for others outside the industry to do so. Had Smith and his colleagues realized how much time and effort this would require, they might have quit then and there. But they didn't.

Instead, Harry Dalton was sent off to Colorado Springs to help develop a technology center and the technology required for COSMOS. This required (1) the establishment of close working relationships with potential suppliers of what later became known as a SuperTracker hand-held scanner that could enable couriers to read bar-coded labels on packages at the point of pick-up and delivery; (2) the DADS mobile terminal that could be mounted in the courier's van to receive information from the SuperTracker and transmit it to a local Federal Express office; and (3) a "Smart Base" computer that could receive information from a DADS unit as well as customer requests for pick-ups and provide courier routing recommendations, message services, and other information processing capability as well. It required coordination with other groups developing software to support both computers and the network management process, and the satellite communications systems needed to link the network. Different suppliers were expert at each of these technologies, requiring several development projects to be managed and coordinated in parallel. Dalton did not wait for the development of the "ultimate solution," instead implementing pieces of the system as his group progressed. Compromise ruled over pride and perfection. Alternative competing designs were developed in parallel to preserve flexibility and speed the work. The order of the day was not to allow "best" to get in the way of "better."

All of this required sizable commitments to potential suppliers and a constant attention to communication and training. Project task force meetings were held weekly. Monthly project reviews had to be held in auditorium-size conference rooms to handle the number of people attending. After local testing of new equipment and systems, and the ongoing usage of various generations of equipment as they were developed over an eight-year period, Federal Express, in 1987, committed to the purchase of 30,000 "nth generation" SuperTrackers, enough to equip all of its couriers with a capability of reporting the status (five minutes after each event in the "life" of a shipment) of many more than the 750,000 packages it was handling on a daily basis at the time. This required educating 20,000 people how to operate the technology, necessitating the development of professional trainers who could train information coordinators from each terminal who could in turn train all terminal personnel.

It's impossible to convey the sweat and tears required to develop and implement the technology for this service strategy breakthrough. But it's a good bet that having made the investment and effort, Federal Express is not likely to make its system available to others even if it could. For there is some basis for concluding from its experience that there is as much magic in the chemistry that made implementation of the technology possible as there was in the original vision and ongoing belief that supported the work.

Those managers that have been able to (1) involve all levels of management in the development and adoption of information technology; (2) focus investments in technology on specific groups of people or tasks; and (3) appraise and follow such investments on a rate-of-return basis have achieved significant results. It is happening in both the public and private sector, as suggested by results achieved by the U.S. Forest Service:

The U.S. Forest Service, one of the few organizations that has done before-and-after studies of its automation efforts, signed a $125 million contract with Data General Corp. in 1983 to automate and electronically link its 900 offices. Environmental-impact statements now take 39% less time, while timber sales contracts take 27% less time to draw up. The service has sliced 30% off the hours needed to do its work and cut staff by 25%, to 37,000. "In 1985 alone we had savings of $125 million," says Charles R. Hargraves, associate deputy chief for administration. He "conservatively" expects a 250% return on investment between 1983 and 1990.[24]

Along with Banc One, J.B. Hunt Transport, Federal Express, Wells Fargo, and other leading service firms, the experience of the U.S. Forest Service suggests that good people are vital to the implementation and effective use of technology. At the same time, information technology in these organizations has mobilized their people in one of several ways we will explore next.

11

Mobilizing People

At a recent meeting we held with CEOs of major service firms, it quickly became apparent that issues concerning people and organizations dominated the list of challenges they felt were most critical. This is hardly surprising, given the people-intensive nature of many services and the fact that multisite services may require literally hundreds of general managers, setting them apart from comparably-sized manufacturing companies. Near the top of the list were: (1) becoming the employer of choice for people with "the right stuff" in their industry or the communities in which they had operating facilities; (2) developing and retaining such people with what one CEO has termed "ministering"; (3) promoting good managers toward rather than away from customers; (4) "dieting" the organization, especially at middle levels; and (5) empowering frontline managers while maintaining adequate control. They provide us with an agenda for this chapter and the next.

The CEOs concluded as well that a firm successfully meeting one of these challenges would probably deal with several. Experiences of breakthrough service managers bear this out. Because the accomplishments of these leading firms cry out for attention, we've donated two chapters to them. Our division is arbitrary. There is nearly complete overlap between the mobilization of people and the organization of work. That's why the same firms keep coming up again and again in examples we will use to illustrate these important levers for achieving service excellence.

BECOMING THE PREFERRED EMPLOYER

Things that attract people to service jobs vary with the type of job and qualifications required. What holds for the fast-food service job may not be applicable for the professional service firm. Further, people often do not articulate accurately why they join a company and why they continue to work for it.

Being frequent travelers, we stay in many hotels. And being students of service management, we continually ask people what they like about a company or a job, particularly when we stay at the same hotel periodically where we encounter the same staff members on the job month in and month out. This is true of a Courtyard Hotel by Marriott that one of us frequents. An informal survey of the restaurant staff at this hotel recently surprised us. Employees were saying that the thing they liked most about their job was the benefits, particularly the health insurance coverage. And yet they genuinely seemed to be enjoying what they were doing, and perhaps more important, who they were doing it with. They were a team. And team players don't quit the team. What we were told didn't reflect what was going on. But the result was the same: low turnover, a matter of critical importance in service businesses involving face-to-face relationships and frequent repurchase from the same person or facility by customers.

Perhaps inspired by the Courtyard example, Marriott selected a small group of managers led by a "maverick" not likely to be influenced by traditional hotel practices to come up with a breakthrough concept for the budget hotel business in which Marriott's competitors had gotten a head-start. The first thing this group of managers did was to isolate itself from "the establishment," other members of Marriott's vast hotels group. Next, it came up with the concept called Fairfield Inn, one with all the makings of a breakthrough service.[1]

Based on marketing research, the Fairfield Inn team determined that there were a large number of potential inn customers that wanted only hospitable treatment and clean rooms at a reasonable price. This resulted in a series of decisions to: (1) adopt the goal of impressing (not just satisfying) guests; (2) commit to a creed emphasizing good value, expressed in hospitality and clean rooms for a price not to exceed $39 maximum per room per night; and (3) develop a program centered around the selection and retention of excellent employees, rewards for performance, and the design of efficient physical facilities.

Rather than hire and then sort out poor employees, with attendant high costs of recruiting, training, and business disruption, the Fairfield Inn management team concentrated on hiring and keeping people with "the right stuff," defined primarily in terms of mental attitude and talent, not demographics. This required the development of a specially designed recruiting questionnaire that, along with an interview, provided separate measures of prospective employees' guest orientation (human skills), reliability, productivity, and loyalties as well as possible enthusiasm for an incentive program, which at Fairfield Inn is called Scorecard.

Training of new recruits under this program includes technical skill building. But the primary emphasis is on the enhancement of human skills to reflect the company's goal of excellence in hospitality.

In addition to receiving market-level wages, the thirty or so receptionists and housekeepers (the only two job categories) at each Fairfield Inn can earn up to an additional 10% through guest evaluations of their work. A simple PC-driven check-out game called Scorecard, requiring about 15 seconds to play, encourages guests to provide feedback on the cleanliness of their rooms, the level of hospitality at check-in and check-out, and the overall value of their experience. In contrast to the more traditional ''Will You Let Me (Bill Marriott) Know?'' Marriott hotel room questionnaire which provides under a 5% response, Fairfield Inn's customer feedback rate is around 50%. This is essential because responses keyed to specific check-in and check-out times and room assignments provide daily customer feedback by employee. This data is accumulated at each inn weekly, posted monthly, and used as part of a quarterly performance review for every employee. Bonuses, too, are paid quarterly. Half of each quarterly bonus is based on individual performance and half on the performance of the entire staff, thus ensuring some amount of peer pressure for good individual performance. Michael Ruffer, Fairfield Inn's general manager, cites a familiar philosophy regarding management compensation. ''If you don't reward by ego, they'll leave.''[2] But he's talking about entry-level employees, not senior managers.

To counter ''no show'' employees, the bane of every employer of entry-level people, a system of paid leave was developed. In addition to one week paid vacation per year, Fairfield Inn employees earn up to two weeks of additional paid leave for perfect monthly attendance on the job. They can maintain their attendance record either by appearing themselves or arranging in advance for a colleague to appear. Those achieving perfect attendance for an entire quarter are given added paid leave bonus. When inn managers do find themselves short of staff, they can pay cash for added work by housekeepers on a daily basis, thus recognizing the fact that most people agree to such extra work because of an immediate need, not the prospect of a fatter pay check at a later date.

Inn managers can earn up to 40% of their compensation in bonus. Half of the bonus is determined on Scorecard ratings and 25% each on occupancy rates and other individually determined objectives for the quarter.

We'll leave it up to you to decide whether this is a breakthrough concept or not, but it is unlike any other we've seen in the innkeeping business. And it appears to be eliciting strongly positive responses from the "right" customers, the "right" managers, and the "right" inn personnel.

Preferred employers don't always offer the most glamorous jobs. That is why experiences of two great service competitors, UPS and Federal Express, are instructive. Both seek ways of encouraging people to self-select for jobs that might not appeal to everyone and then reinforce the "rightness" of an employee's self-selection decision by rewarding behavior emphasized in the selection process.

Both firms hire large numbers of employees for work in their package-sorting hub facilities. At UPS, a large proportion of these jobs are full-time. Success at the hub often leads to an opportunity to drive a delivery car. Success in driving a delivery car results in a supervisory position and ownership of stock in a highly successful company. Success in a career of supervision provides wealth sufficient to make an employee economically independent at retirement. The work is hard. The routine, particularly at the hub, is sometimes boring. The hours in the delivery car may be long; the day is over only when all packages have been delivered. But expectations are made very clear and communicated in the Policy Book, a copy of which is issued to every new employee. The UPS "factory" is not for everyone. But those who sign on expecting to work hard for good pay are not disappointed. And they are constantly reminded through job design, the design of equipment from the sorting conveyor to the specially designed and manufactured delivery car, uniform dress, and company communications that they are the best at what they do, a source of job satisfaction that is just as strong and important at UPS as in the U.S. Marine Corps.

The high levels of productivity that are sought at UPS sometimes lead to complaints by Teamsters union managers representing large numbers of UPS employees. But when quizzed, Ron Carey, president of Teamsters Local 804 in Long Island (New York), said several years ago: "If UPS announced it had 1,000 openings for drivers tomorrow, there would be 100,000 applicants."[3]

The Federal Express "factory" crew also thinks it's the best at what it does. But the culture is one that appeals to a different type of person than at UPS. Because of its emphasis on overnight delivery for all of its business, the main Federal Express hub at Memphis (supplemented by several smaller hubs elsewhere) must be designed and staffed to sort over a million pieces of freight and express mail in the period of only four hours to enable these items to reach their destination cities in time to be loaded onto delivery vans for next-morning delivery. This requires a greater emphasis on part-timers with both high energy and intelligence levels. As a result, Federal Express is one of the great benefactors of Memphis State University students. For this group, the attraction may be in large part the very high hourly wages. But what seems to keep them on the job is their participation in an intense four-hour nightly fire drill carried out with good humor, a circus-like atmosphere, and an intense effort. The thrill of a good job done once-and-for-all occurs nightly. And the company celebrates the good job done, both with promotions for people who are interested in a career with Federal Express and, more commonly, by paying the college tuition for all part-timers (as well as full-time) employees, offering them the right to fly free in the "jump seat" of Federal Express freighters, and including them in a number of other company programs. Not everyone is attracted to this kind of working environment. But among those who elect to work there, it is rated as tops, a truly preferred employer. This explains why it has been recognized as one of 100 outstanding employers in the United States[4] as well as one of the best workplaces for women.[5]

Other large employers of entry-level personnel, such as retailers, are making a concerted effort to become employers of preference in their communities. For example, Younkers, a 35-store regional department store chain in the Midwest, has implemented a Satisfaction Plus program in which sales associates are paid on the basis of their sales productivity, measured in terms of dollars per hour. This was instituted in response to the knowledge that the company's sales productivity was below the industry average in a business with extremely high asset costs for inventory and expensive buildings, placing a premium on capacity utilization.

Satisfaction Plus is the culmination of a sequence of efforts over three years to measure, recognize, and reward quality and productivity in its sales force. It involved raising the minimum wage paid every associate significantly above what it had been, developing dollar-per-hour sales productivity standards for each sales department, evaluating salespeople against these standards monthly, and adjusting their hourly wage rates every six months based on their sales productivity performance on a rolling 12-month basis. Sales associates exceeding so-called standard performance in many cases earn more than double what they did previously. Those failing to meet standards are given 30 to 90 days to improve, along with training to help them. The program is accompanied by a continuing "mystery shopper" effort in which sales associates are judged by criteria including their facility in greeting incoming customers, courtesy, and sales skills.

The early results of Satisfaction Plus were striking. By the end of its first year, the average hourly wage of salespeople at Younkers was increased by 21%. Top performers, in most instances, had more than doubled their salaries. At the same time, because of a 20% increase in dollar sales per selling labor hour, Younkers' selling costs as a percentage of sales fell by 0.4 of a percentage point, worth roughly $1.2 million in operating profit. The quality of sales effort, according to mystery shopper reports, increased significantly. The turnover of sales personnel rose by 35% in this first year, largely comprising those people unable to meet standards after a 90-day probation period. And perhaps most significantly, salespeople were becoming less tolerant of poor performers in the organization, having concluded that a good department attracts more customers and more selling opportunities.[6]

The Younkers program is based on assumptions similar to those under-lying compensation at Nordstrom, among them the belief that low productivity in retailing results largely from the way people are hired, developed, and compensated. Although Nordstrom has for years employed an incentive system centered around commissions averaging between 6% and 7% of sales for its salespeople, the results are much the same at Younkers.[7] Those who survive the first four months of employment become loyal advocates of the Nordstrom philosophy, at least based on our informal store conversations with them. They earn upwards of $30,000 to $40,000 each. But, even though Nordstrom has its pick of potential retail salespeople in every market in which it operates, the turnover rate among new recruits is high. The standards are high and the system is demanding, sorting out all but the very best.

Organizations such as Fairfield Inn, UPS, Federal Express, Younkers, and Nordstrom are not for everyone. But for those wishing to associate with high-performance, high-reward organizations, they represent rewarding op-portunities and are giving these companies an edge over other employers in finding and keeping the best people in the highly competitive, difficult entry-level labor pool.

MINISTERING TO PEOPLE

Growth is a common objective, often unfulfilled, in most companies. It is considered one of several alternative strategies. But there is no alternative to fast-paced growth at The ServiceMaster Company Limited Partnership, employing roughly 18,500 people, 4,000 of whom manage employees of ServiceMaster's hospital, school, and industrial clients who are engaged in support services such as housekeeping, maintenance, and food service, or franchises that provide such services to individual homes. The company's objectives, published in its annual reports and displayed prominently in its offices, allow no possibility for lack of growth. They are: (1) to honor God in all we do; (2) to help people develop; (3) to pursue excellence; and

(4) to grow profitably. Even more important, CEO C. William Pollard points out that the first two objectives are *ends* objectives and the third and fourth *means* objectives toward achieving the ends:

> The first is meant to provide a common starting point for all of us, not to convey a religious point of view. In combination with the second, it guides us by suggesting ways in which we treat people. The last two objectives not only provide the means for achieving the first two, they keep us in balance and provide a kind of creative tension for the management.[8]

Bill Pollard puts it this way: "Because this company is dedicated both to the development of the individual and our ministry to an increasing number of people, growth is an imperative."[9] As a result, The ServiceMaster Company seeks to double its size and the people under its management every five years. Starting with about 120,000 clients' employees in 1985, the number should reach seven figures by the turn of the century.

When Pollard uses the word ministry, he does not use it in a strictly religious sense. When executives of The ServiceMaster Company use the word God, they do not impose their personal views of God on others. But they do require a commitment to be masters of service (hence the company's name) through the development of people. And at ServiceMaster, people development is carried out with a vengeance. The vice president for people is not an empty title. The person holding this job presides over a department that designs and runs internal training programs ranging from orientation for entry-level managers up to a three-year MBA-equivalent and turns out reams of training material annually. Managers' offices prominently display shelves of books, both on management and inspirational topics, that are widely circulated, read, and discussed. Compare the following recent description of the planning process at ServiceMaster by one division vice president with others with which you may be familiar:

> In setting our financial goals, we take into account such things as market potential and trends in operating costs for our region, including training and development costs. We are also asked to state our personal goals, including the sponsorship of the development of other individuals in the organization as well as the amount of time I might want to spend, for example, with my division manager for sales contacting CEOs of existing and potential customers; classes I might want to take; and community service activities in which I'll be involved. These are reviewed by the person I report to and then sent . . . to the people who report to me. For example, I get Bill Pollard's personal

goal statement. . . This year, I've programmed eight days of training for each of my direct reports (functional division managers), eight days for area managers who report to them, ten days for each regional manager, and fifteen days for each facility manager who works "next to the customer."[10]

Clients' employees (housekeepers, cooks, repair people) managed by ServiceMaster similarly receive on-the-job training, group training sessions in job skills, periodic educational meetings led (for the first time in many cases) by professionals in the organization, feedback meetings with managers, and even basic educational opportunities to learn reading and writing skills. As Kenneth Wessner, ServiceMaster's chairman, puts it: "We want to help people be something before we ask them to *do* something."[11] Little wonder that ServiceMaster is an effective competitor even in Japan, where it employs more managers in one of its fastest-growing markets than any other foreign firm.

While other leading service performers may call it something different, they minister to people in their own way.

For example, the Red Lobster chain operated by General Mills, the largest table service restaurant chain in the United States, utilizes human development as a critical means of attracting and retaining the best talent of its kind available in each market in which it operates. At the same time, this enables the chain to deliver a high level of service through a network of more than 400 restaurants.

Red Lobster recruits are put through an intensive four-day training program prior to the opening of a new restaurant. This includes classes, memorization exercises, simulated situations, quizzes, and contests. Some of the exercises emphasize the honing of personal skills in a system which requires a minimum of uniform codes and avoids, to the extent possible, rote routines for servers. According to one account:

. . . while stock descriptive phrases are taught in the seminars, the servers are encouraged to improvise their sales pitch.

"We try to remove the spiel and inject the personality," explained Jeff O'Hara, president of Red Lobster USA. "We're trying to bring it down to an intensely personal experience."

The company is also well known among waiters and waitresses, in most areas where it is found, as a good employer that offers solid benefits, a chance for advancement, and flexible hours. Most of all, it is known as a restaurant where the tipping is good. . . many students spoke of their hope to make more than $100 in tips on good nights.[12]

At Red Lobster, the initial training is only the beginning. All staff members are required to attend monthly classes to polish their service skills. The objective is personal as well as corporate growth. It represents another kind of ministering.

Not surprisingly, one of the most rigorous human development programs in the service industries doesn't even involve employees. It's the program operated by McDonald's for prospective franchises. Once selected, they are expected to work for 20 hours per week for two years at a local McDonald's restaurant. And they work for no pay. According to one account:

> They do it all—working the counter, flipping hamburgers, cleaning toilets, fixing milkshake machines, and handling the book work—and most continue holding down their regular jobs . . .
>
> On top of that, trainees rotate through classes at regional company locations, working their way through a thick four-volume training guide and cramming for periodic exams. The program culminates with a two-week advanced course at Hamburger University, the residential training center at McDonald's headquarters in Oakbrook, where students have to pay as much as $700 a week for room and board.[13]

The objective? A coveted McDonald's franchise, generally thought to be the most profitable in the fast-food industry. And a partner that is known for providing ongoing support to franchisees. Even McDonald's franchisees who have not succeeded praise the support provided them by the company in difficult times.

HYPER GROWTH THROUGH MOBILIZATION

People are the major constraint on growth in most service businesses. Leading people-intensive service companies have alleviated this problem. Some have elected to do it through what one executive has called the "enfranchisement of people," not the franchising of the business. Others have elected to do it by franchising, but in a manner designed to encourage franchises to develop loyalty equivalent to that of an employee of the company. Both approaches have unleashed powerful forces for hyper growth.

ENFRANCHISING PEOPLE

Au Bon Pain (ABP), a company operating a chain of upscale stores offering meals featuring French-style bakery products, recently was encountering

what its management termed the "cycle of failure" in store management.[14]
The "cycle" confronts most operators of food and lodging chains and is
characterized by: (1) poor pay, (2) jobs with little responsibility, (3) a
continuing crew labor shortage, (4) chronic turnover, (5) an inadequately
motivated management staff, and (6) continued poor pay. Its management
decided to test the concept of empowerment by implementing a Partner/
Manager Program (PMP) in two of its stores. The objectives of the PMP
were to achieve rapid growth in revenues and profits as well as provide a
human resource mechanism which freed ABP to grow at an accelerated rate
without great pain. Under the PMP, the manager and associate manager of
each store split with the company on a 50-50 basis all controllable profits
over an amount negotiated annually on the basis of past performance.

Concurrent with the PMP, Au Bon Pain's management continued efforts
to maintain control over quality. These included a mystery shopper program, surprise white glove (eight-hour) inspections by senior management,
and an organized customer feedback project. The mystery shopper program,
for example, was organized around twelve so-called "moments of truth"
such as: (1) no customer waiting in line more than three minutes; (2) customer recognized within 30 seconds after approaching the counter; and (3)
no table left soiled more than two minutes after customer departure. Mystery
shoppers' reports of all moments of truth being satisfied were celebrated by
senior management with appropriate recognition at the store level.

Expected benefits from the program were reduced management turnover
with attendant savings in recruiting and training costs as well as dramatic
increases in sales. Anticipated problems were that managers might experience burnout from overwork resulting from reducing costs while increasing
revenues. In addition, there were concerns that as managers strained the
physical capacities of their stores or encountered bottlenecks, they might be
frustrated at not being able to capitalize fully on the program.

Nevertheless, the experiment was implemented in two stores, with the
architect of the program, Leonard Schlesinger, executive vice president and
treasurer, taking personal responsibility in serving as district manager to the
two stores whose managers were given an opportunity to participate in the
experiment. Management expected dramatic results. But it was not prepared
for what happened.

Managers reduced staff, brought in low-cost support people, developed
wholesale customers whose product could be baked during off-peak or store
closing hours, let out repair work on a bid basis, and worked longer hours
themselves. During the first six months of the experiment, sales increased
over the previous year in one store by 60% and in the other by 200%. The
compensation of managers nearly doubled in one store and more than dou-

bled in the other. Controllable profits for the company after salaries and bonuses nearly tripled over the previous year. As Schlesinger puts it, "What we did was provide each store manager with a franchise without requiring payment for it."[15]

The PMP is Au Bon Pain's response to the need for growth in sales and profits through an ability to attract good managers and associates. At Younkers department stores, it's Satisfaction Plus. And at Nordstrom, the retail chain, in addition to rewarding its salespeople by commission, it empowers them to meet competitors' prices and encourages them to develop their own minibusinesses by creating files of customer preferences for certain types of merchandise and even having merchandise routinely delivered to offices where shoppers work. Similarly, managers are given wide latitude in developing policies for their individual stores as long as the focus is on serving the customer. This has insured the availability of a ready supply of people needed to fuel Nordstrom's fast growth.[16]

The Nordstrom case highlights both the benefits and drawbacks (if not administered carefully) of a pay-for-performance system with extensive manager and sales associate empowerment to serve customers. It has produced a backlash from current and former employees with lagging sales results (and commissions) who claim that they have been placed under undue stress and forced by zealous managers to perform duties such as preparing customer "thank you" notes for no added pay outside of normal working hours. This is being used as a rallying cry in union efforts to bring pressure to bear on Nordstrom's startled management, pressure far out of proportion to the relatively small minority of the company's associates that the union represents. As Jim Nordstrom, Co-Chairman, recently put it, "We were naive to think that the product would speak for itself."[17] This is a strong testimonial for the importance of careful attention to both customers and service providers in mobilizing people.

Other competitors have elected to achieve rapid growth through franchising. The best have avoided the ill will that this alternative can provoke.

"HIRING" THE FRANCHISEE

Franchising has been an important concept for organizations that produce and deliver fast food, auto repair, cleaning, real estate brokerage, and other services at many market-oriented locations.[18] Typically, it has been thought to be a means of rapid growth for a franchisor through reliance on the capital of franchisees, in other words, largely a financing concept. But a close look at the most successful franchising efforts leads to the conclusion that they are managed as extensions of a human resource strategy to attract scarce, motivated management talent to an "extended organization."[19]

FRANCHISE MANAGEMENT

Urban Ozanne and Shelby Hunt have pointed out that franchise contracts have several somewhat standard clauses.[20] They require that, in return for the use of the franchisor's name, service concept, operating strategy, advertising, and managerial assistance such as site selection, training programs, operating manuals, and ongoing advice, a franchisee agrees to pay an initial fee or otherwise invest up-front in facilities and inventory. In addition, the franchisee agrees to pay royalties, often a percentage of sales, to the franchisor. A franchisee may also agree to restrictions on suppliers to be utilized, prices changed, sales of competitors' products, accounting practices, and the general condition in which operating premises are to be kept. Finally, such agreements have termination clauses specifying the franchisor's right to repurchase the franchise or otherwise control the use of its name.

THE FRANCHISING LIFE CYCLE

Franchise relationships are like marriages, including the fact that they too often end in divorce. We all know the stages: courtship, marriage, mid-life crisis, and possible divorce. The courtship often sows the seeds of a poor marriage and a poor franchise relationship. It is here that the benefits of the franchise are oversold in an effort to line up franchisees.

Marriage is the easiest. Accompanied by assistance with location, the design of a facility, sources of store fixtures, training, and ultimately free balloons for the opening, it is the stage in which the franchisee too often gets the most in exchange for the franchise fee or subsequent royalties. Too often it is the high point of the relationship.

Mid-life crisis occurs from months to several years after the marriage. It usually results from the general perception that the services being provided by the franchisor are not worth the continuing charges to the franchisee. It often is triggered by a specific action regarded as unfair by one or more franchisees. The most common of these results from perceived shortcomings in quality or service provided by suppliers from whom franchisees may be required to buy or overstoring which results in competing franchisees being located too closely to one another. In other cases, the crisis results from the failure of the franchisor to provide continuing assistance, adequate or high-quality advertising, an adequate stream of new products or ideas, or efforts to freshen up an outmoded theme or "format" for the franchise. In nearly every case, however, the crisis results from the failure of a franchisee to achieve expected profits.

SUCCESSFUL FRANCHISING PRACTICES

Franchising was first developed on a large scale by U.S. auto manufacturers who elected early in their development not to sell and service their products, concentrating their limited funds on the capital-intensive manufacturing process. But the fast-food industry has had the greatest amount of experience with the concept in terms of numbers of contracts and operating franchises. Comparative information about two of the better-known fast-food franchisors, McDonald's and Burger King, is shown in Table 11–1. Based on the operating characteristics of each, you can probably guess which has had the greater number of crises in dealing with its franchisees, even though both organizations have been relatively successful compared to others in their industry and to franchisors of other concepts. How do they and many other successful franchisors do it?

STRUCTURING THE DEAL

The starting point for successful franchisors is an appraisal of the value of a service concept, operating strategy, name, and support package to a prospective franchisee. This can be translated into an income stream with a calculated present value.

It is at this point that the investment required and the targeted return on investment (ROI) for the franchisee can be estimated. The excess of the value of the expected income stream over the targeted franchisee ROI is the amount of value brought to the agreement by the franchisor. This value is reflected in some combination of the franchise fee, most often paid at the outset by the franchisee, and a continuing royalty, often stated in terms of a percentage of sales, as in the McDonald's and Burger King agreements. Any additional profits made by a franchisor through the sale of fixtures or supplies to a franchisee is taken into account in determining fees and royalties.

Finally, mutual obligations designed to ensure the quality of the service delivered as well as the profitable operation of both franchisor and franchisee are devised, along with penalties for failure to meet them.

But note that the process begins with an inventory of benefits to the franchisee. Those who start instead at the end and work their way back to the beginning of the items noted here more often end up in divorce court.

Table 11-1 COMPARATIVE PROFILE OF TWO COMPETING FRANCHISORS

Burger King	Per Restaurant[a]	McDonald's
$1 million	Annual Revenues	$1.5 million
$140,000	Annual Profit	$234,000
$40,000	One-Time Franchise Fee	$22,000 and $15,000 security deposit
3.5% of monthly revenues	Royalties (paid to parent for use of name and for marketing and training support)	3.5% of monthly revenues
$1 million (assumes franchisee buys land and constructs building)	Cost of Starting Up	$435,000 (assumes franchisee rents land and building)
50–60	Number of Employees per Restaurant	60
1,125	Number of Hamburger Patties Sold per Day	1,382
	For the Chain	
3.5	Average Number of Restaurants Held by Franchisee	2.8
$0.63	Average Cost, to Consumer, of Hamburger (U.S. only)	$0.63
Independent food companies supply Burger King's in-house procurement and distribution arm. Independent distributors also used by 40% of franchisees.	Supply System	Independent food companies supply independent national distributors.
Burgers are flame-broiled and warmed in microwave.	Cooking Methods	Burgers are grilled. Microwave ovens are not used.
Total: 5,578 Franchisee-operated: 4,760 Company-operated: 818	Total Number of Chain's Restaurants, Worldwide	Total: 10,190 Franchisee-operated: 6,936 Company-operated: 2,494 Joint ventures by McDonald's and a franchisee: 760
$215 million for local and national advertising, fiscal 1988 (ended May 31, 1988). Franchisees give 4% of revenues to a national ad fund; half goes to regional ads, half to national ads. Groups of franchisees may contribute extra money for additional local ads.	Advertising	$918 million for local and national advertising, 1987. Franchisees contribute varying percentages of revenue, averaging 6.4%, to a national fund for national ads. They also contribute to a local fund for local ads.

[a] Average franchisee-run outlet.

SOURCE: Company reports and estimates provided by analysts, as reported in Eric N. Berg, "How Two Burger Flippers Stack Up," *The New York Times*, November 20, 1988, p. F-4. Copyright © 1988 by The New York Times Company. Reprinted by permission.

Of course, all of these calculations depend in part on the market potential for the area surrounding the prospective franchise location. So the decision must be made early on concerning those locations to be owned and operated by the franchisor and those to be sold to franchisees. The former often are those in urban markets with the highest sales potential but also requiring the highest investment in land, facilities, and management talent. But in more successful franchising strategies, these are held to a minimum to enhance opportunities for franchisees. Unfortunately, these often are the locations that are used as demonstration outlets, building expectations in the minds of visiting prospective franchisees that can't be fulfilled in markets they'll be serving.

SELECTION OF FRANCHISEES

One model for selecting franchisees is the "Mom and Pop" strategy that seeks out individuals capable of owning and operating one or at most several units. While their franchisees might not agree with the characterization, this is basically the model that has been followed by McDonald's. This provides the franchisor with greater power in the relationship and the opportunity to reserve stores in larger markets for franchisor ownership and operation.

Another model involves the search for a small number of prospective franchisees with strong management potential and the capital necessary to develop entire territories. This essentially is what Wendy's, a competing fast-food franchisor, has done. It characterizes, too, the approach of another well-known retailer, Benetton, whose system is based on the designation of areawide agents who in turn select individual licensees for stores. This approach simplifies the selection process, but may lead to less power for the franchisor and less control over the franchisee. In addition, it may lead to uneven geographic development of a chain, depending on the management and financial capacities of franchisees.

There are few franchisee selection processes more rigorous than McDonald's. It knows exactly what it wants, and this does not include absentee owners, those who are not going to be active in the business, professional people, or "other experts used to having people come to them."[21] A prospective franchisee must be willing to operate one unit rather than receiving territorial rights, work up to 18-hour days, and be on the job seven days a week. According to one account:

> People most likely to get interviews are those with "ketchup in their veins"—a McDonald's expression for outgoing high-energy types who'll devote their lives to the Golden Arches.[22]

In addition, a prospective applicant in 1989 had to be willing to invest initial equity ranging from $66,000 to more than $200,000, depending on whether facilities were to be leased or purchased. The lure, of course, is the prospect of high returns on a franchisee's investment of time and money.

Expectations created in the minds of prospective franchisees during the selection process are most critical to the success of the relationship. What a prospect hears may be conditioned by what he or she wants to hear, again not unlike many courtships. Successful franchisors resist the temptation to overrepresent the potential benefits of the franchise.

ON-GOING MANAGEMENT

The challenge of the successful management of franchisee relationships results from the nearly irreconcilable aspirations of the two parties to the agreement. On the one hand, there is a franchisor who may see the franchise as a vehicle for funding expansion while maintaining extensive control over the franchisee. On the other hand, the franchisee sees the franchise as a stage on which he can play out his entrepreneurial dream. In reality, neither is accurate.

Successful management begins with a training program keyed to the needs of the business and the caliber of the franchisee sought. This often is part of a package of services that may include the selection of a location, the design of the facility and its equipment, the codification of methods, and, in the case of McDonald's, a lease on both the building and the land on which it sits.

Regardless of the package of supporting services provided by the franchisor, they should roughly correspond to the magnitude and timing of the fees and royalties paid by the franchisee. The more visible they are, the better. For example, advertising designed and placed by the franchisor using a fund provided by franchisees, often collected as a percentage of gross sales, is both visible and timed roughly by its very nature to correspond to franchisee contributions.

The preservation of franchise value through the control of the quality of franchisees' operations is particularly important where the name alone provides important information to prospective customers, usually in situations in which they patronize more than one unit in the chain. Paul Rubin has suggested that this should influence the way in which initial fees and royalties are structured:

> In those businesses where there is much managerial discretion (or greater problems of control), we would expect a higher percentage of the revenue of the franchisor to come from the initial fee and a relatively lower percentage to come from royalties; where there are relatively few managerial decisions to be made, we would expect more of

the income of the franchisor to come from royalties . . . where the trademark is more valuable, we would expect relatively more of the franchisor's revenue to come from royalties, for this would create an incentive for him to be efficient in policing and maintaining value.[23]

This may explain why McDonald's has maintained a firm quality control program among its franchisees, a program supported by the franchisees themselves who realize that they rise or fall together.

END-GAME ACTIONS

Franchise agreements contain so-called termination clauses specifying the conditions under which a franchisee's operation may be passed on to heirs, sold, bought by the franchisor, or simply closed. Often they are heavily weighted in favor of the franchisor, with some justification to the extent that the franchisor also represents the interests of other franchisees in a chain. In fact, termination clauses are so difficult to invoke that leading franchisors conclude that the most practical way to terminate an unsatisfactory relationship is to help the franchisee turn it around, move it, or sell it, often back to the franchisor. The difficulties of the legal alternative are illustrated by McDonald's experience in France when it decided in 1978 to file suit against its franchisee for the Paris area, Ramond Dayan:

> His 12 restaurants ran into serious trouble in 1977 when a team of McDonald's inspectors said he failed to meet company standards for quickness, service, and cleanliness. The next year McDonald's sent another team of inspectors with French court-appointed officials, who snapped photographs of dog droppings in the stores and found Mr. Dayan's stores charged for catsup and hid straws behind the counter.
>
> Mr. Dayan . . . said in the litigation that McDonald's inspectors were a pretext for abrogating the franchise agreement, maintaining that it felt it was not obtaining sufficient royalties from him.
>
> Nevertheless, Judge Richard L. Curry of Illinois Circuit Court ruled in 1982 that McDonald's had the right to take away his franchise, stating that the company was acting to "rid itself of a cancer within its system before it grows and further infects" other stores. The judge added: "Its price for disassociation from Dayan will be to turn its clock back 10 years and be forced to start anew in Paris."[24]

Indeed, McDonald's did disappear from Paris for more than a year.

Just as common are franchisee complaints against their franchisors. Quite often these are settled out of court by franchisors who realize the difficulties of arguing a legal case against a smaller opponent. And several operators of major chains, such as Benetton, use a license agreement that apparently does not, at least under U.S. law, qualify as franchising because it requires no fee for the use of the company's name, relying instead on exclusive purchases of Benetton merchandise by its licensees. (In Benetton's case, litigation is further complicated by the fact that the company uses no written agreements with its licensees.)[25]

Recently, efforts have been made by innovative franchisors to shift some responsibility for quality control efforts to advisory boards comprised of franchisees themselves, a kind of approach used by condominium owners. Such advisory boards often have been more strict in their recommendations for corrective action to maintain quality than the franchisor could be.

Leading franchisors often retain the right of first refusal on the transfer of stores to new ownership by franchisees. And frequently they exercise buy-back clauses, taking back ownership at a more mature stage in the development of a chain when the franchisor can marshal greater human and financial resources.

When the success of the franchisee is insured by the franchisor, end-game actions aren't needed. Success often depends on the degree to which development and other support programs are supplied to franchisees. This is not unlike the relationship any employer has with its employees. As Paul Rubin has pointed out:

> Legally, the franchisee is a firm dealing with another firm, the franchisor. This legal classification is apparently a result of the fact that the franchisee must pay for the franchise. But . . . the economics of the situation are such that the franchisee is in fact closer to being an employee of the franchisor than to being an independent entrepreneur.[26]

Perhaps there is a lesson here. We have seen earlier that firms that have been most successful in attracting, retaining, and developing the best employees have found ways of empowering and enfranchising them, as in the case of Au Bon Pain, Fairfield Inn, Younkers, and Nordstrom. Conversely, the most successful franchisors such as McDonald's have found ways of making their franchisees feel as if they are members of an extended organization, with all of the enthusiasm and loyalty to the corporation typically exhibited by valued employees. Both types of organizations place a great deal of emphasis on the design and conscious development of an internal strategic service vision. Both have unleashed powerful forces for hypergrowth.

Outstanding people constitute the core of any breakthrough service strategy. But the way they are organized to achieve an objective plays a large role in their effectiveness. It's our next concern.

12

Organizing Work

Gary Aronson is living proof that a college degree is not required for breakthrough service leadership. Aronson was one of two managers of Au Bon Pain French bakery restaurants who agreed to participate originally in the company's Partner/Manager Program, described in Chapter 11, in which managers split profits above an agreed threshhold amount 50-50 with the company.

Perhaps as a reflection of his human nature, Aronson decided to "beat the system" by working harder, taking immediate responsibility for everything from construction projects to employment policies in his store. Almost immediately, his work week ballooned to 80 or 90 hours. In order to see more of him, his wife went to work for him (eventually obtaining a store of her own to manage).

Just as Au Bon Pain's management encouraged Gary Aronson to break the "cycle of failure" of: (1) low pay, (2) jobs with little responsibility, (3) chronic turnover, (4) a shortage of talent, (5) inadequate motivation among its store managers, and (6) continued low pay, he decided to do the same thing among the entry-level people staffing his store. He reasoned that it was absolutely essential for a business dependent on customer loyalty from the "regulars" who frequented his store day after day expecting to see and greet the same faces on a daily basis. How he went about doing it illustrated several aspects of how breakthrough service companies are going about the very reorganization of work.

Aronson's first action was to begin cutting the "head count" of employees in his store nearly in half, from 40 to 22. This allowed him to pay higher hourly wages and guarantee a minimum of a 50-hour work week (with at least 10 hours of overtime at time-and-a-half pay). It also allowed him to offer those prospective associates who were willing to sustain the pace an opportunity to double what they could make at any competing non–table-service restaurant such as McDonald's. Even in a very tight labor market, he had little trouble attracting the best available candidates.

Aronson's reasoning was simple. He raised pay, created larger jobs, reduced turnover, reduced barriers to hiring the best people, and motivated his work crew, creating a "cycle of success." Further, because associates were on the job at least 50 hours per week, it became difficult for loyal customers not to find their favorite servers on the job, just as it was hard for associates not to find Aronson there. Associates began thinking twice even about calling in sick, because it invariably meant losing a full day of over-time pay. And they began thinking twice about returning to the "cycle of failure" at competing restaurants. The first year of his new policies, the annual turnover rate among Aronson's associates dropped from 200% to less than 10%.

Because his service concept and operating strategy significantly increased the volume of business done in his store, Aronson's labor costs as a pro-portion of sales dropped dramatically even as associates' salaries began to multiply. He accomplished this by selecting people (or helping them select themselves) who fit a profile, his "vision" of the business. Without both-ering to conceptualize what he had done, Aronson implemented a human resource "mix" in a masterful way. Both he and Au Bon Pain's senior management found ways of replacing supervision with positive incentives for accepting increased responsibility, thereby opening the door for a sim-plified organization structure. They relieved the pressure to create opportu-nities for promoting the best people away from customers by enlarging the jobs carried out in contact with customers. In the process, they altered significantly the role of management. In a sense, Gary Aronson has helped us define our agenda for this chapter. His experience suggests first of all the importance of matching the service concept and elements of human resource strategy to achieve maximum service impact and operating leverage.

THE HUMAN RESOURCE MANAGEMENT "MIX" UNDER DIFFERENT OPERATING STRATEGIES

We tend to generalize about elements of the human resource management "mix" of decisions concerning staffing tactics, recruiting, selecting, train-ing, assigning, rewarding, and generally building organizations. But few would argue that we approach these tasks similarly for management consultants as we do for dishwashers. Similarly, within the same firm, policies on these matters might differ greatly for positions requiring different skills, such as management consultants and secretaries.

How do we think about these differences? David Maister and Christopher Lovelock have provided us with one useful way of doing so based upon the degree of service customization and customer contact associated with a job, as shown in Figure 12–1.[1] Here we see a range including the "factory service" (characterized generally by the electric utility generating plant) at one end and the "professional service" (bringing to mind legal, medical, and management consulting services) at the other. The range includes mass services such as fast-food restaurants and technological services such as computer-driven information services.

Degree of Service Customization

	Low		High
	The Mass Service		**The Professional Service**
	Recruiting and Selection:	Broad-based effort, with criteria primarily based on human skills and attitude.	Recruiting and Selection:	Highly selective, based on technical and human skills.
	Training:	On-the-job, with little or no follow-on.	Training:	Professional schooling and on-the-job, with periodic updates.
High	Assigning:	To specific unattended tasks.	Assigning:	Given great care to facilitate personal development.
	Rewarding:	Modest, based on time on the job.	Rewarding:	High, on basis of value of output to clients.
	Goals:	Minimize job complexity and training time required for frequent replacements.	Goals:	Build expertise through minimum turnover.

Degree of Customer Contact

	The Factory Service		**The Technological Service**
	Recruiting and Selection:	On basis of criteria such as basic knowledge, health, attitude.	Recruiting and Selection:	Selective, with criteria primarily based on technological skills.
	Training:	On-the-job, with limited follow-on.	Training:	Prior to selection, with technologically oriented update seminars.
Low	Assigning:	To cover unattended production tasks.	Assigning:	To specific unattended tasks.
	Rewarding:	Varied, often based on time on the job.	Rewarding:	Varied, based on technological skills.
	Goals:	Minimum training costs and minimum turnover only of key people.	Goals:	Minimize turnover to provide technological expertise and continuity.

FIGURE 12–1 Human Resource Management "Mix" Under Different Operating Strategies[a]

[a] Based on a framework presented in David H. Maister and Christopher H. Lovelock, "Managing Facilitator Services," *Sloan Management Review*, Summer 1982, p. 22. © 1982; used with permission.

THE PROFESSIONAL SERVICE FIRM

High levels of service customization and customer contact characterize these tasks, requiring that people ranging from lawyers to engineering consultants be selected on the basis of both technical and human skills. Because this may be a hard combination to find, great care and considerable expense typically is invested in both recruitment and selection. Training often is obtained before employment, but added on-the-job training typically involves assignments in which the recruit can become familiar both with customs and colleagues in the firm. This places a premium on the care with which assignments are made to balance the need to serve customers (who desire continuity in their relationship with an individual) with the need to develop the professional (suggesting more of a variety of assignments and clients).

Because the value of a service to the customer is often embodied in the skills of the individual professional, the goal here typically is to minimize turnover and the high cost of replacement and the loss of customers. Compensation levels are high. They may include high proportions of incentive payments in firms emphasizing individual performance, as in merger and acquisition "brokering," or lower proportions in firms stressing the collaborations of teams of people in temporary work groups organized around projects such as in management consulting.

THE FACTORY SERVICE

Here there is neither much customization nor much personal contact with customers. Whatever skills are required can be taught quickly, thus often leading to a personnel policy under which little time is spent in recruitment, training costs are minimized, selection takes place after hiring, and assignments are routinely made to standardize jobs. Compensation in wages, which often are keyed to seniority rather than to performance and turnover, is managed to insure that the mix of personnel at various levels of seniority and thus compensation levels are maintained. Even so, turnover in the service factory often is very uneven, with supervisory or near-supervisory personnel turning less slowly and some of the labor force turning over several times per year. This allows many service factories to practice "chase" strategies in which staffing levels are adjusted upward or downward to reflect customer demand.

The extremes of the professional service and the service factory are clear, explaining (without necessarily commenting on) the differences in the human resource mix for each. It is when we turn to the technological service or the mass service that management practice becomes less clear-cut.

THE TECHNOLOGICAL SERVICE

Services centered around technology, in which the service is delivered electronically with little contact between customer and server (as opposed to the service) are among the most rapidly proliferating today. For much of their staffing they require people with stronger technical skills than human skills, people who like to engage in mechanical or electronic tinkering. Recruitment and selection are critical, with on-the-job training intended to supplement more extensive formal training received before employment. Compensation is often substantial but rarely involves high bonuses or other incentives for short-term performance, often because incentives are thought to be hard to administer in jobs emphasizing innovation and the design of such things as software, mechanical devices, or electronic networks.

Sandy Trevor, executive vice president in charge of operations at CompuServe, has put together such a technology-driven service.[2] It is responsible in part for the company's ability to deliver a wide range of effective, low-cost network and information services. Trevor's people are tinkerers par excellence. They early on took over responsibilities for maintaining CompuServe's huge bank of Digital Equipment computers from DEC's service people. And they have reprogrammed them so they run at three and four times the capacity claimed by DEC in its own sales literature. They have redesigned and manufacture network switches that can be repaired remotely, thus reducing the need for field engineering. They have contributed greatly to the company's operating success, explaining in large part why CompuServe's is the only consistently profitable consumer information service. But don't ask them to interact with customers on a face-to-face basis; that's not why they came to work at CompuServe.

THE MASS SERVICE

Fast-food chains, with little customization of product but high levels of customer contact, are stereotypical mass services. Theoretically, this should place a premium on the recruitment and selection of people on the basis of human (versus technical) skills. Training similarly should reflect this emphasis, as should rewards. Too few organizations understand this. Those that do prosper handsomely, as do their employees. Often this involves a breakthrough vision of what the business is and how company personnel fit into the vision. What goes on at The Walt Disney Company reflects such a vision.[3]

The cast members (please, not staff) at one of Disney's major attractions or adventures (please, not amusement park), Walt Disney World, number 21,400, of which 2,400 are managers, 14,800 permanent hourly personnel, and the remainder casual personnel working weekends and holidays performing about 900 different roles (not jobs). They are recruited locally, with one out of every three interviewed actually hired, and paid minimum wages with no incentives. They don costumes (please, not uniforms) to work both on-stage (in public areas) or backstage on Walt Disney World's 28,000-acre stage, rain or shine, every day of the year. They serve an audience (not a crowd) of 23,000,000 guests (not customers) per year that arrive expecting a fresh performance, courteous performers, and a clean stage. Guests apparently are not disappointed. Because in spite of hard-to-control elements such as weather and occasional problems such as "technical difficulties" with equipment, 62% of Disney's guests are repeat visitors and 49% return on average every two-and-a-half years. These sound like breakthrough service numbers, particularly when the economics of repeat business that we explored at Club Med earlier are applied to Disney.

Perhaps most remarkable is that the turnover rate among full-time employees at Walt Disney World is only 21%, a fraction of what it is in most mass services. While some part of this can be explained by the positive working environment (to which cast members themselves contribute by sharing work, picking up waste paper, and involving themselves in other customs), some credit has to be given as well to Traditions I. Regardless of the role for which they are hired, all newly hired Disney cast members (including those assigned to retail units of the newly opened Disney store chain) take the one-day Traditions I course. It not only introduces them to company customs and values, but also gives them practice in human skills through projective exercises asking them to interpret pictures such as one showing elderly guests with a small child with tears in his eyes standing in the rain at Disney World. Cast members are then given an opportunity to suggest what might be done to help their guests feel better. Practice in helping make things easier for guests, accepting guests as they are, and even smiling is a part of Tradition I. And while it may sound corny in the telling, it apparently makes a big impression on cast members.

Traditions I is followed by training in the park. Typical of this phase is the emphasis on human skills. Sanitation hosts (not custodial people), for example, spend little time practicing the use of broom and trash pan. But they do rehearse answers to many questions that guests might ask of the nearest Disney cast member they see, often a sanitation host. And they practice sweeping while maintaining eye contact with guests, eye contact designed to invite questions. They also build the patience required to answer the same question ten times a day with continuing enthusiasm.

The scheme shown in Figure 12–1 can be used to understand important industry trends in the organization of human resources. For example, the Ledgeway Group, a consulting organization specializing in information services, concluded recently that an important trend in this service industry will be the refocusing of tasks, as illustrated in Figure 12–2. Today's "field engineers" and "product and service sales representatives" will be de-emphasized in favor of increased use of both "account engineers" and "board swappers." According to this view of information and after-sales computer services:

> Tomorrow's service management team will require a new combination of technical and account-management skills. The team leader will be an "account engineer" who will exhibit the strong account manage-ment skills of the traditional sales representative, combined with the technical skills of the traditional field engineer. The account engineer will have a systems orientation to service problems and will be able to coordinate multi-vendor solutions in complex environments. For simple hardware remedies, the future "board swapper" will require relatively low technical or account management skills.[4]

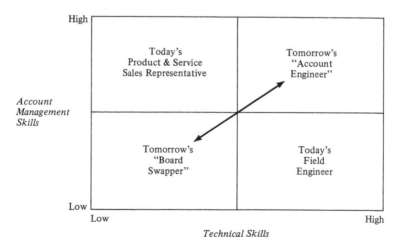

FIGURE 12–2 The Changing Job Requirements of Successful Service Marketing and Delivery in Information Services
SOURCE: *ServiceTrends Trends and Forecast, Customer Service Industry,* 1988 Annual Edition (Lexington, Mass.: The Ledgeway Group, 1988), p. 49.

LEVERAGING HUMAN RESOURCES
THROUGH DIFFERENTIATION AND INTEGRATION

Organization effectiveness can be improved by defining jobs that enable people to specialize their efforts. However, it is important that holders of these so-called differentiated jobs somehow coordinate their activities through what has been called integration.[5] Charles Moritz, CEO of the Dun & Bradstreet Corporation, describes the need for people in such jobs to understand the importance of their work with the following anecdote:

> A few years ago, a young employee who worked in the computer room at one of our divisions asked me a question that profoundly affected my thinking about the organizational implications of customer focus. His question was eloquent in its simplicity: "Mr. Moritz," he asked, "where does my work go and is it important to anyone?"[6]

Outstanding service executives have to manage the tension between differentiation and integration. They have found a variety of ways of doing it. These include focusing efforts around the service "front office" and "back office" while seeking ways of coordinating marketing and operations through vehicles such as internal service contracting.

FOCUSING THE "FRONT OFFICE" AND "BACK OFFICE"

Richard Chase has argued that an important way to improve the economics (and often the quality) of services delivered is to clearly identify "front office" (in the Disney parlance "on stage") and "back office" functions, regardless of the type of service business under scrutiny, and organize, staff, train, and reward differently for each.[7] This is the way in which the output and time of highly paid "front-line" personnel is leveraged through the delegation of tasks requiring less judgment and customer contact to the "back office."

This concept is an outgrowth of an earlier concept set forth by Wickham Skinner called focusing the factory.[8] It argues that customized one-of-a-kind services require one type of factory (akin to the job shop in manufacturing) and that repetitive services involving little judgment or different kinds of judgment should be carried out in something more resembling an assembly line. Of course, the degree and nature of customer contact involved in either type of service complicates the analogy to manufacturing and suggests another dimension around which focus (and leverage) can be achieved. Complications arise, however, when service organizations following this philosophy seek to promote from within.

For example, at United Parcel Service, a great deal of effort has been made through the years to focus the organization around basic tasks of package delivery, package sorting at hubs, and engineering. The one thing that all associates hold in common, however, is that they all have driven a UPS-brown delivery car, getting a good infusion of "brown blood," in company parlance, in the process. Further, the company follows religiously the practice of promoting from within. But when the need arose recently for people who could upgrade UPS's computing and communications technology, questions arose as to whether they could be found in the UPS organization, and if not, whether newly hired computing and communications professionals should similarly be required to get an infusion of brown blood.[9] The problem was made more acute by the fact that attention in recruitment, selection, and training had been given in the past to skills and attitudes reflecting the basic operating needs of the organization, not the changing technologies that the company might employ in the future.

Investment banking is an activity that requires both finely honed human and technical skills of senior personnel. But it also requires a great deal of back-up research and financial analysis. Entry-level professionals are hired for their technical skills and given jobs as analysts. For only a few do these jobs lead to the more senior positions involving close client relations and business development. This "finders-minders-grinders" hierarchy provides a way of leveraging the scarcest, most highly valued skills in most professional service firms. If it is combined with a policy of promoting from within, however, it requires hiring entry-level people with both human and technical skills suggesting the potential capability to assume a senior position. It also requires an extensive program of employee development and appraisal administered alongside an "up or out" promotion and retention policy. The unwillingness or inability to implement such policies may help explain why the attrition rates in many professional service firms, including public accounting, management consulting, and investment banking, are so high.

COORDINATION BETWEEN MARKETING AND OPERATIONS

Having differentiated front-line, marketing-oriented tasks from back-office operations, many service organizations find that some means have to be preserved for building a cross-functional understanding and cooperation between the two groups. Most banking organizations traditionally have so well differentiated front-office, interest-earning lending activities from banking operations departments that it has been difficult to create mechanisms for bringing them back together for purposes of designing and delivering other increasingly important fee-earning customer services such as payment processing and cash management that require functional cooperation and integration. It was this very problem that prompted Chemical Bank several years ago to adopt a product management organization in its operations department to foster coordination between operations and customer relations personnel.[10]

Interactions with "customers" inside the organization are every bit as important as those with customers outside the firm. One group's back office may be another group's customer. This has led several large service organizations that have become excessively functionalized in the eyes of their senior managers to encourage the negotiation of internal service contracts.

INTERNAL SERVICE CONTRACTING

The management of a large industrial casualty insurance company recently experienced so much friction between its underwriting (pricing), marketing (sales), claims (customer service), and administrative (premium collections, etc.) groups that it decided to turn to a process familiar to it, contracting. After all, insurance underwriting is a contracting process.

The procedure involved getting representatives of various groups together to talk about the most important needs existing in their own group that were either being met or not and the needs they thought they were fulfilling for other groups. Through this process, gaps between what one group thought it was delivering and what it was actually delivering in terms of service to another group were discovered. Perhaps more important were the gaps between what one group thought was important and another thought was important that were also identified.

For example, the marketing group complained that it was getting to be more and more time-consuming to get price quotations out of underwriting. The delays had increased up to two weeks, far in excess of what marketing felt reasonable or, more important, competitive. On the other hand, members of the underwriting group expressed concern about work overload, caused in part by frivolous requests on the part of marketing. Because each industrial casualty contract is unique, underwriting was quoting rates (prices) on every contract being processed. When the two groups collected and analyzed information about the contracts, however, they found that 90% of the risk exposure was represented by only 20% of the contracts. With top management's blessing, it was agreed that marketing representatives would be allowed to price small insurance policies, freeing up underwriting to provide three-day response time and more careful review of larger policies. Marketing became more responsive to customer needs and the load on the overworked underwriting group was relieved. An important source of friction between the two groups was removed by rewriting the implicit contract between them, making more explicit the needs and expectations of each as well as the way in which they would be met. And because the underwriting group had more time to examine and determine prices for the most complex proposals, risk to the company actually was reduced.

In successful service organizations, the "factory" markets itself to its internal customers, those involved in managing client relationships. This suggests the need for training "factory" personnel to be better marketers and those responsible for client relationships to be better "customers" of the factory.

KEEPING THE BEST TALENT NEAR CUSTOMERS

The story is all too familiar. We observe an outstanding operating manager in a hotel, restaurant, or transportation company, and what do we do? We move that person to a larger facility in the name of greater opportunity or to a higher-level job in the belief that he or she can develop other good managers. Whether the premise for the promotion is valid or not, we often have succeeded in promoting our best operating and marketing resources away from the people who matter most, their customers. Increasingly, breakthrough service managers are seeking ways to avoid doing this by expanding job opportunities "in place" and broadening the meaning of the term promotion to include increased job opportunities.

At The ServiceMaster Company, for example, the most frequent complaint of hospitals served by the company's support services management force was that managers were rotated too often and not left in their jobs long enough. The complaint was that good ones were promoted too fast and poor ones had to be moved to another facility they were more capable of managing. The result was a lack of continuity in relationships.

In response to this concern, ServiceMaster reorganized, creating a kind of hierarchy "in place" by identifying a group of good managers deserving promotions but not wishing to relocate. Rather than moving them, the company offered to expand their jobs and compensation by giving them responsibility for one or two additional adjacent hospitals. The fact that their "home base" hospital administrators might see less of them under this arrangement was preferable to their being moved out of the community entirely. As a result, the average time in a geographic assignment for a

ServiceMaster manager increased measurably and the company's management costs declined in relation to revenues through job enlargement.

At ServiceMaster, Au Bon Pain, and other leading service organizations, job enlargement has played a major role in keeping good first-line managers near customers. Mitchell Fromstein, the CEO of Manpower, Inc., feels so strongly about problems of promoting good people away from customers that he and about thirty of his top managers each maintain personal responsibility for one of the company's offices in order to stay close to the customer. In Fromstein's words, they "adopt a market." In addition, each recently spent a week, including training, occupying one of the company's four front-line positions. They took calls from clients and interviewed, tested, and placed applicants for temporary employment positions. According to Fromstein:

> Senior managers come back with all kinds of ideas including making first-line jobs easier rather than more difficult to perform. If you're going to be a general you have to remember what it was like to be a private.[11]

What is left unsaid here is that by doing this, Fromstein and his senior managers stay close to first-line managers.

TURNING THE ORGANIZATION UPSIDE DOWN

At SAS, Jan Carlzon went to great lengths to convey the importance of customers and those from SAS serving them directly. He stood the airline's organization on its head, as suggested in the 1981 chart of the organization shown in Figure 12–3. It is an arrangement that has changed since then only in degree, not in basic philosophy. Sandra Vandermerwe described what happened:

> Front line workers with the most customer contact had formerly been at the bottom of the chart. Carlzon put them on top. It became everyone else's responsibility, including his, to "serve" those who directly served the customer. . . . The company was divided into various profit centers varying in size from the airline division down to a particular route where a route manager was regarded as an entrepreneur who was free to decide the time and number of flights between the two cities, contingent on the approval of the government involved, and who could lease . . . airplanes and flight crews from other divisions.[12]

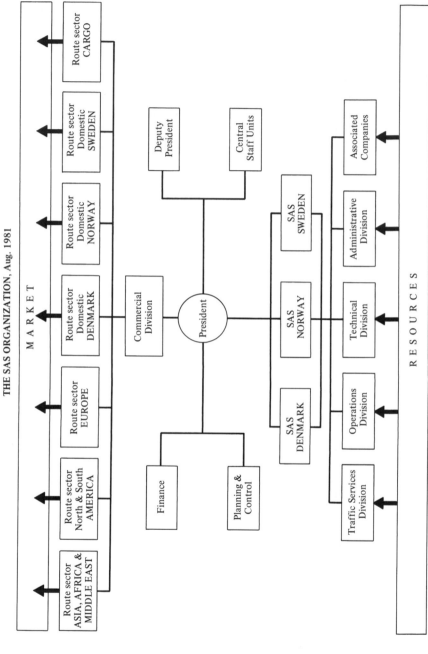

THE SAS ORGANIZATION, Aug. 1981

MARKET

Route sector ASIA, AFRICA & MIDDLE EAST

Route sector North & South AMERICA

Route sector EUROPE

Route sector Domestic DENMARK

Route sector Domestic NORWAY

Route sector Domestic SWEDEN

Route sector CARGO

Commercial Division

Finance

Planning & Control

President

Deputy President

Central Staff Units

SAS DENMARK

SAS NORWAY

SAS SWEDEN

Associated Companies

Administrative Division

Technical Division

Operations Division

Traffic Services Division

RESOURCES

FIGURE 12–3 SAS Organization Chart

SOURCE: "Scandinavian Airlines System SAS (A)," (Geneva: International Institute for Management Development [IMD], 1985), p. 23.

Anyone can turn an organization upside down on paper, but if it is to be more than a symbolic act, it has to be accompanied by other changes in the way employees are organized and motivated. At SAS, this involved a reorganization of the operating arm into profit centers identified by geographic route sectors, oriented around domestic and international (outside Scandinavia) travelers. Along with profit centers go increased responsibility and authority for front-line operating managers. It requires too that performances of others in the organization be altered to reflect the way they serve front-line operating entities. Effective response to front-line needs often requires shorter lines of communication and fewer intervening levels of management. Even with all of these changes at SAS, it still required time for the members of the organization to absorb the profound changes that accompanied the act of redrawing the organization chart as shown in Figure 12–3.

DIETING THE ORGANIZATION

Service organizations, especially those with many operating sites, are particularly vulnerable to pyramid-building in the organization. After all, if a firm operates at 3,000 sites and the maximum number of operating managers that any one manager can supervise is thought to be seven, by definition the operating organization alone must have five levels of management. The resulting pyramid not only makes jobs manageable, but also provides a ready avenue for promotion for successful operating managers. The other side of the coin, of course, is that it makes communication and coordination more difficult, slowing an organization's competitive responsiveness and stifling initiative at the lowest ranks.

In recent years, leading service organizations have done an about-face on this matter, expanding jobs, increasing compensation, and cutting out layers of management, often starting with headquarters staff. This is organizational weight-watching.

For example, at the same time that it expanded the responsibility of its hospital facility managers, The ServiceMaster Company also eliminated one of its four levels of operating management, areas comprising several hospitals each, by promoting some of its area managers to regions and reassigning others to large facilities. In the words of one manager: "Those who were able to handle the area management job well were ready for a promotion and those not doing well were relieved to be able to return to the management of individual facilities."

At Au Bon Pain, Executive Vice President Leonard Schlesinger took personal responsibility for the Partner/Manager Program experiment, even though he was fully occupied with other matters at the time. The decision was intentional. As Schlesinger put it:

> One of the basic ideas behind the Partner/Manager Program was that it would reduce the need for supervision of store managers. I wanted to see if we could eliminate the need for district managers. Because I didn't have any time to supervise the managers in our experiment, I assumed that would be the best way to test the idea.[13]

The Au Bon Pain initiative empowered store managers. But we can't forget that it did so under a stringent system of controls on those elements of quality that the company could not afford to compromise.

EMPOWERING AND CONTROLLING

Some uses of information and technology, in combination with incentives, control and restrict the latitude of personal behavior. Other uses empower and teach people. Shoshana Zuboff has written eloquently about these alternatives.[14] Each use may have its advantages under certain conditions. But each must be supplemented in ways designed to enhance the working environment and satisfaction for humans, particularly in companies whose managers lose sight of the fact that the satisfaction of servers is inseparable from that of their customers.

CONTROLLING AND RESTRICTING BEHAVIOR

Recently one of us was taken on a tour of an impressively large open office by a senior executive of one of the nation's largest insurance brokers. The office contained open cubicles for at least 100 customer service representatives, all busy answering incoming telephoned questions concerning correct addresses, premium payments, claims, and related matters. Each representative was equipped with not one, but two electronic display devices with keyboards. Like a rock music keyboard setup, one was for the right hand and one for the left. Because this left no hands for answering the telephone, representatives were equipped with telephone harnesses with both earpieces and mouthpieces. Finally, each cubicle contained a mirror facing each representative on which was stenciled, "Smile, you sound just like you look."

A page out of *1984, Brave New World*, or the worst of Taylorism you say? Maybe. And if so, it could lead to the same kinds of labor dissatisfaction and militancy leading to adversarial relationships between labor and management that have plagued the industrial sector for so many years. But before reaching a judgment, it was necessary to know the range of questions a representative was permitted to address and resolve, the kind and quality of information available in real time with which to do it, and the incentives and measures of performance associated with the job. Unfortunately, in this case the measure of performance used (number of calls handled per hour) and the executive's obvious pride that some of the better customer service representatives were able to handle up to 150 calls per day did not suggest much opportunity for job enrichment here. And the presence of the mirrors did little to quiet a growing feeling that information, technology, and incentives were designed to control and restrict behavior in this case.

Of course, control and restriction may be what is absolutely necessary in a particular service. Few of us would like to see free spirits and entrepreneurial behavior in an air traffic control tower, for example. But where this is absolutely necessary, other means must be sought to provide job satisfaction, whether on or off the job. Failure to achieve this probably accounts for the fact that air traffic controllers experience a high incidence of job-related ailments such as mental stress.

EMPOWERING PEOPLE

Technology and information systems that place large amounts of information in the hands of service personnel, when combined with the latitude to act and performance measures and rewards that encourage creative problem resolutions, can be empowering and the source of considerable satisfaction to servers. Much of the satisfaction apparently arises from customer amazement at the range and speed of responses that their requests elicit. Where this is combined with a control system that measures results in terms of customer satisfaction or problems resolved rather than number of calls handled, it creates a powerfully positive working environment in offices like the insurance brokerage agency described above. In this case, the physical environment becomes secondary to the latitude of decisions entrusted to the server, the tools provided in support of the job, and the learning that is encouraged as part of the job.

Jan Carlzon of SAS has eloquently described the difference between the use of instruction for control and the use of information to empower people:

> Instructions only succeed in providing employees with knowledge of their own limitation. Information, on the other hand, provides them

with a knowledge of their opportunities and possibilities. . . . To free someone from rigorous control by instructions, policies, and orders, and to give that person freedom to take responsibility for his ideas, decisions, and actions, is to release hidden resources which would otherwise remain inaccessible to both the individual and the company. . . . A person who has information cannot avoid taking responsibility.[15]

Empowering, teaching, and supporting service personnel are particularly important in situations where there is little time to refer decisions to a higher authority, where direct supervision is difficult, and where the first-line service personnel are the company in the eyes of customers. This is certainly true in the Wire-Line Division at Schlumberger, providing advice on the probability of success to those drilling for oil around the world based on electronic ''mapping'' of drilling sites on a continuing basis during the drilling process.

Schlumberger's wire-line engineers must go where their customers think the oil is. But they go armed with a million dollars' worth of equipment (including a truck and computer), the world's best database of profiles of geological conditions in which both dry holes and producing wells were found elsewhere, and substantial training in how to use the data to save customers large amounts of money. Because they are Schlumberger to those drillers, they go also with a deep understanding of and loyalty to the company's principles and business values. And they are rewarded well for helping their customers both avoid and solve drilling problems.

INVOLVING MIDDLE MANAGEMENT

Making change in organizing work is much easier in the telling than in the doing. Invariably it involves opposition, either open or tacit, from middle managers. Just as the effects of most successful dieting plans are seen around the waistline, middle management often is most affected by such moves. This is what occurred, for example, at SAS.

The process by which the plan to turn the organization upside down at SAS was devised was one in which a small group of senior managers was sent off to plan the change while their colleagues continued to manage the airline. When the ''shadow'' management was then charged with implementing its proposals, it naturally encountered resentment from some of the managers who had been left ''minding the store.'' In one of the few statements of things he wished might have been done differently, Carlzon later commented that:

> . . . what I know is that . . . if a company has to change, it needs both the creativity and the structure—it's a balance. I gave them the vision without the systems and structure, the tools to execute the vision and know if they were successful or not.[16]

Similarly, a number of firms have concluded that more involvement of leaders among middle management in designing and managing dieting programs can facilitate such transitions.

Efforts to alleviate adverse effects on middle managers have included salary increases, transfers to other parts of an organization, or even early retirement. But the most successful efforts have been carried out with advance consultation, the inclusion of middle management, and a reasonable allowance of time for the transition. Even so, opposition and a certain amount of disillusionment may occur until improved operations alleviate the hunger pains.

IMPLEMENTING A COHESIVE INTERNAL STRATEGIC SERVICE VISION

Outstanding service firms have a clear internal strategic service vision. The vision sets forth basic values on which the firm is built. It reflects basic beliefs in people. And it targets certain kinds of people and structures a working environment, embodied in a service concept, operating strategy, and service delivery system designed to appeal to them. Questions posed in the design of an internal strategic service vision, set forth in Figure 12–4, mirror those asked in structuring its external counterpart shown earlier in Figure 2–1.

In breakthrough firms, the elements of the vision convey a consistent message designed to appeal to the people that are targeted. This consistent message and the people it attracts are the cornerstone of what has come to be known as an organization's culture. A clear, consistent message and people that understand and support it results invariably in a strong culture. If the culture is appropriate for the service and the clientele toward which it is directed, it can be a potent competitive force.

Our students have little trouble identifying firms with a strong internal service vision. Their opinions have been fashioned by work experience in those organizations. Among the firms on their list, selected from among only a few service industries, are Delta Air Lines, American Airlines, Arthur

Target Employee Group	Positioning	Service Concept	Value-Cost Leveraging	Operating Strategy	Strategy-Systems Integration	Service Delivery System
What are common characteristics of important employee groups? What dimensions can be used to describe these employee groups? Demographic? Psychographic? How important are each of these groups to the delivery of the service? What needs does each group have? How well are these needs being served? In what manner? By whom?	How does the service concept propose to meet employee needs? How do competitors meet such needs? How are relationships with employees differentiated from those between competitors and their employees? How important are these differences? What is "good service" to employees? Does the proposed service concept provide it? What efforts are required to bring employee expectations and service capabilities into alignment?	What are important elements of the service to be provided, stated in terms of results produced for employees and the company? How are these elements supposed to be perceived by the targeted employee group? How are these elements perceived? What further efforts does this suggest in terms of the manner in which the service is: Designed? Delivered?	To what extent are differences between returns to employees and the level of effort they put forth maximized by: The design of the service concept? The design of the elements of the operating strategy? Job design? The leveraging of scarce skills with a support system? The management of supply and demand? Control of quality through— Rewards? Appeal to pride? Visibility? Supervision? Peer group control? Involving the customer in the delivery of the service? Effective use of data?	How important is direct human contact in the provision of the service? To what extent have employees been involved in the design of the service concept and operating strategy? How desirable is it to: Increase employee satisfaction? Increase employee productivity? What incentives are provided for: Quality? Productivity? Cost? How does the strategy address employee needs for: Selection? Assignment? Development? Evaluation? Compensation? Association?	To what extent are the strategy and the delivery system for serving important employee groups internally consistent? To what extent does the integration of operating strategy and service delivery system ensure: High quality? High productivity? Low cost? High morale and "bonding" of the target employee group?	What are important features of the service delivery system, including: The role of people? Technology? Equipment? Layout? Procedures? What does it require of target employee groups? Normally? At peak periods of activity? To what extent does it help employees: Meet quality standards? Differentiate their service from competitors? Achieve expectations about the quality of their work life?

◻ = Basic element   ⌐ ⌐ = Integrative element

FIGURE 12–4 Elements of the Internal Strategic Service Vision

Reprinted by permission of *Harvard Business Review*. An exhibit from "Lessons in the Service Sector" by James L. Heskett, March/April 1987, p. 121. Copyright © 1987 by the President and Fellows of Harvard College; all rights reserved.

Andersen, Bain & Company, Goldman Sachs, Chase Manhattan, McKinsey, Citibank, Salomon Bros., Coopers & Lybrand, Schlumberger, Peat Marwick & Main, Federal Express, United Parcel Service, and Booz, Allen & Hamilton. In addition to sharing a strong culture, we hear repeatedly that members of these organizations have high regard for their companies and regard themselves in some respect as being "No. 1." But they pursue very different paths toward that result.

DECIDING WHETHER TO FARM OR HUNT

In describing their experiences in these firms, our students paint pictures from different palettes. On the one hand, some of these organizations are described as placing strong emphasis on teamwork, group development, and loyalty to the organization first and to a field of expertise second. When they go into competition, they march as an army and serve customers through teams of experts. David Maister coined the term "farmers" in describing the internal behavior of members of these organizations; he has called this type of organization the "one-firm firm."[17] Figuratively speaking, they band together, repairing each others' barn roofs and harvesting each others' crops, in fighting against a hostile external environment. However colorful the language used to describe it, these firms have an internally cooperative vision.

Other organizations are described as comprising outstanding individuals who collectively serve customers in very effective ways. Inside the organization, however, they are encouraged to develop their individual skills, perhaps by observing other outstanding colleagues. Compensation and other programs encourage them to perform in ways that benefit both themselves and the company, sometimes at a cost to other members of the organization. They have been characterized by Maister as "hunters," foraging for themselves and shooting everything that moves, sometimes including their own associates.[18] Variations on this theme have been "a pack of wolves," who forage individually but, upon finding a kill or encountering danger, cooperate to achieve the desired result. In less graphic terms, we'll describe these firms as having an internally competitive vision.

This kind of imagery can be carried too far. It can conjure up unintended positive or negative impressions. It is too simplistic. But it is useful in describing two "poles" of a range of internal strategic service visions near which successful service firms are often found. Some of the elements of these poles are presented in Table 12–1. We can cite some examples in comparing them.

Table 12–1 TWO CONTRASTING INTERNAL STRATEGIC SERVICE VISIONS[a]

	Internally Competitive Vision	*Internally Cooperative Vision*
Target Market:	Smart, hard-working, ambitious, self-reliant, competitive, "inner-oriented" people	Smart, hard-working, ambitious, nice, "other-oriented," team players
Service Concept:	Service with satisfaction through financial success; Individuals above institution, with the firm creating a stimulating environment in which outstanding people can compete with one another; Emphasis on having the best individuals	Service, financial success, and fulfilling work lives; Institution above individuals, with the firm more than the sum of its parts; Emphasis on having the best firm
Operating Strategy:	Candidates screened for skills plus competitive drive	Candidates screened for skills plus "right" personality, character, and values
	Emphasis on training for skills improvement	Significant investment in firmwide training, often evidenced by a company "university," in part as a means of socializing people
	Significant hiring of top performers from outside plus an "up or out" system of promotion	Promotion and growth from within with emphasis on continuity
	Substantial migration of top performers among competitor firms	Little "voluntary turnover"
	Growth by merger and from within, as opportunities present themselves	Emphasis on controlled growth from within

INTERNALLY COOPERATING AND COMPETITIVE VISIONS

There are as many similarities as there are differences between internally cooperative and competitive strategic service visions. Remember, we're

Table 12–1 (Continued)

	Internally Competitive Vision	*Internally Cooperative Vision*
Operating Strategy (continued)	Compensation based primarily on individual performance, assessed objectively	Compensation based primarily on total contribution to the firm, assessed subjectively
	Limited communication, with sharing achieved through financial incentives, with meetings regarded as intrusive to main task	Open communications and sharing of ideas and business "leads" through frequent meetings
	Interdepartmental respect only for good people based on their capabilities and demonstrated performance	Mutual respect across organizational departments based on both capabilities and regard for the group's mission
	Leadership by example, based on past or current performance	Leadership through a consensus-building style
	Change achieved through the encouragement of the internal competition of people and ideas	Change achieved through the sharing and support of group-developed ideas
Competitive Advantages:	Ability to move fast, with individuals leading the way	Ability to bring many resources to bear on competition as a second- or third-mover
	Highly entrepreneurial	Capable of capitalizing on competitors' good ideas
	Continual improvement through self-criticism, new ideas from "outside"	Internally shared values and norms producing few "surprises" in implementation

ᵃ For many of these ideas, especially those associated with what we have called the "internally cooperative vision," we have relied on David H. Maister, "The One-Firm Firm: What Makes It Successful," *Sloan Management Review*, Fall 1985, pp. 3–13, and an unpublished manuscript titled "Hunters and Farmers" written by Maister in 1985.

talking about mutually successful strategies adopted by highly successful firms who are among the most formidable competitors in their respective industries.

Target Market. For example, both visions target smart, hard-working, and ambitious people. In addition, however, each looks for something else. A firm with an internally cooperative vision needs team players, people who can get along well with their associates. Hewitt Associates, a leading benefits consulting organization, explicitly looks for people who are SWANs, who are *s*mart, *w*ork hard, are *a*mbitious, and are also *n*ice.[19] This requires people with somewhat less ego-driven behavior than at, say, Salomon Bros., where the emphasis is said to be primarily on self-reliant, competitive individuals rather than those who are nice.

Service Concept. Both internally cooperative and competitive visions emphasize service to external customers. But while firms with an internally cooperative vision stress financial success as well as fulfilling work lives for their associates, the internally competitive firm is more likely to stress satisfaction through financial success alone. "Farmer" firms regard the firm as more than the sum of its individuals and emphasize having members of the organization regard themselves as being with the best firm.

In contrast, "hunter" firms concentrate on building an environment that is exciting for the best individual performers in an industry. Members of the organization often cite their opportunities to work with the best individuals. In both farmer and hunter firms, the key to achieving the service concept lies in elements of their respective operating strategies.

Operating Strategy. Recruitment, selection, development, promotion, and rewards are quite different in firms with internally cooperative and competitive visions. Both screen carefully. But farmer organizations place relatively greater emphasis on personality and human nature while the hunters give greater weight to technical skills and competitive drive in addition to the character and values which both types of firms seek.

The internally cooperative vision places relatively greater emphasis on organized, firmwide personal training and development. Firms emphasizing it often can be identified by their well-known company "universities." Among the most well-known of these are Arthur Andersen's St. Charles, Illinois, Center for Professional Education, Disney's Disney University, and McDonald's Hamburger University. Arthur Andersen's Center, for example, sleeps 1,200 people and is the site of roughly 300,000 person-days of training per year. Senior executives in these organizations often point to the internal "university" as the glue that unites managers in a large, multinational company. Firms with internally competitive cultures emphasize development as well. But it is more likely to be personalized and individual, with less time given to formal programming of training activities and more emphasis placed on the development of technical skills.

Farmers promote from within whenever possible; hunters often look for the best people at all positions, whether they are inside or outside the firm. People leave the "one-firm firm" reluctantly, often on the occasions when asked to do so. In contrast, there is regular turnover of personnel in the internally competitive firm, with a certain amount of "churn" planned and fostered by an "up or out" promotion tradition.

Hunters are more opportunistic in their growth strategies, with fewer constraints on growth through the acquisition of other companies. Among farmers, there is a greater emphasis on controlled growth from within. This requires restraint and the acceptance of only that amount of new business that the firm can manage with a stable, modestly growing group of associates.

The internally competitive vision often can be identified through its emphasis on incentives for individual performance, often leading to fewer meetings and less sharing of ideas. Leadership is by example, with the lore of the organization built around individuals who have done audacious things in the past. Competition is often employed as a vehicle for change. For example, two or three teams are simultaneously assigned to "big idea" projects at Citibank. The best team's ideas win.

In contrast, firms with internally cooperative visions can be identified by their emphasis on incentives for group performance, sometimes based on the performance of the entire firm. Meetings designed to encourage the sharing of ideas are the norm. Leadership is more often centered around building group consensus for a new idea. This is the way change is achieved.

Competitive Advantages. Internally competitive firms often are highly entrepreneurial and opportunistic, relying on the best ideas they can find, either inside or outside the firm. In contrast, internally cooperative firms are often followers rather than pioneers. But they bring strong firmwide resources to bear on a problem and often are characterized by an ability to implement complex efforts requiring superior interfunctional coordination.

As Maister has pointed out, both groups of firms described above are formidable competitors. Both are likely to outperform competitors who do not have clear internal strategic service visions.[20] They are the ones who are most capable of mobilizing human resources so critical to most service firms.

CHANGING THE VERY ROLE OF MANAGEMENT

Earlier we spoke of the impact of change on first-level and middle managers under particularly effective efforts to alter the way work is organized in outstanding service organizations. What we didn't emphasize sufficiently is

Table 12–2 STRUCTURE OF ORGANIZATION AND CONTROL BEFORE AND AFTER AU BON PAIN'S PARTNER/MANAGER PROGRAM

	Before	*After*
Headquarters	Operationally oriented	Strategically oriented
Role of controls	Prescribe goals and behavior for store managers	Set outer limits on store management behavior and quality of service
Reward system	Primarily salary, based on size of store	Primarily incentives, based on controllable profit
Role of middle management	Policing first-level managers	Coaching and supporting first-level managers
Role of first-level (store) manager	Employee/follower	Owner/leader

that all roles are changed. Again, Au Bon Pain provides an example of this in action.

The Partner/Manager Program at Au Bon Pain gave store managers extraordinary incentives to exercise more control over their stores' profits. For this reason, it was felt that the role of district managers (if they were to be retained at all) could be changed from that of police and controllers to idea-generators for increasing sales and reducing costs, trainers for associate managers, and relief help during busy store seasons. With less urgency for district-level control, the number of stores supervised by a district manager could be increased from three or four to eight or ten. As Ron Shaich, president of Au Bon Pain, put it: "I expect that 90% of the problems we used to deal with at headquarters, the managers would now figure out on their own."[21]

But in addition to changing reward systems, controls, and the roles of store and middle managers, as suggested in Table 12–2, the senior managers at Au Bon Pain saw their own jobs change. They were able to concentrate increasing amounts of time on strategic decisions around issues of primary importance in an organization that had found a way to support the accelerated growth program that it could now pursue.

Why would an organization go to such lengths to change so many things? One explanation is that its managers saw a future of growth restricted by an environment that would make it increasingly difficult to attract outstanding management talent. This is one dimension of a vision of the future that we will explore further in the next chapter.

13

Conceiving
Future Breakthroughs

Y ou've heard what they say about being able to get anything you want at any time in New York City. A friend from Des Moines, Iowa, tells a story of working late one night in a Greenwich Village apartment while spending a summer in New York, having an aching hunger at 3 A.M. for Hungarian food from a favorite restaurant around the corner, debating with his wife about the sanity of going for a walk at 3 A.M. to find food, and somewhat self-consciously starting out. Not only did they find Hungarian food, but their favorite restaurant was open. And there was a line of people on the street waiting to get in.

Martin Trust will get you any kind of garment you may want for your retail shops through his design and sourcing service, Mast Industries. This includes copies, or "knock offs," of existing garments as well as garments of original design. He does this for The Limited, the largest specialty retailer of women's fashions in the United States, as well as for other retailers. A "knock off" purchased in Milan, Italy, today can arrive at Mast Industries' design headquarters in Andover, Massachusetts, tomorrow, where it is immediately disassembled, "copied" into the computer-aided design system, and then altered using visual computer display units. Parts of the garment are then redrawn by computer for a range of sizes, with the resulting "patterns" transmitted electronically to Mast's contract factories in Hong Kong or elsewhere and printed out there prior to computerized cutting and machine sewing. Finished garments are air freighted nonstop from Hong Kong to The Limited's distribution center near the international "port-of-entry," Columbus, Ohio. Computerized pre-processing by the U.S. Customs Department and The Limited's distribution personnel can have the garments inspected, priced, packaged, and ready-to-ship to U.S. retail outlets in 48 hours after their arrival from Hong Kong. If there is a real rush to get a garment to market and the fabric is available at the Hong Kong factory when the order arrives, the entire process from Milan clothes rack to Bakersfield, California, can be completed in ten days.

Through a process called "selective binding," publishers can now economically produce books and magazines bound expressly for small groups of customers. Eventually, it is assumed that it will be economic to do this for individuals. This kind of service already is available electronically. CEEFAX in Great Britain, for example, allows subscribers to receive an electronic newspaper with paging capability by which a viewer can turn to the desired topic displayed on a television monitor, with material updated much more frequently than the conventional daily newspaper can do it. A couple in Milton, Florida, have carried the concept to its limit. John and Karen Hefty, through their firm, Create-A-Book, Inc., create, print, and bind personalized books for children that utilize each child's name, friends, hometown, and other personal information in the story at a cost of $8.95 to $16.95 per book. Already, the books are created and sold through several hundred U.S. dealers equipped with personal computers, laser printers, industrial-strength staplers, and paper cutters.

Arguments over whether to allow nonessential retail stores to open on Sundays have receded with the rush to 24-hour, seven-days-a-week service. BayBanks, a New England-based regional banking organization, has extended the concept to finance. Its mortgage loan representatives are on a 24-hour, seven-days-a-week call system that rivals anything from the medical community. It requires that they wear beepers to that customers desiring financing can reach them at any time, any place. Closely related to the ideas of having things or information any time is the concept of "time shifting." By means of answering machines (a form of voice mail) and electronic mail, people have reduced time spent in "telephone tag" and developed their capability to do business on a 24-hour basis in increasingly global markets open somewhere all the time.

The most recently introduced major entry to the home information services market in the United States, Prodigy Services Co., a joint venture of Sears and IBM, has significantly reduced the cost of home shopping, electronic mail, banking, and other services to potentially heavy users of these services. It can be accessed from any home in the United States through personal computers. The French, however, probably are most advanced in this regard, with more than 10% of all French homes equipped with such capabilities through the Minitel system in which the PTT, the government's telecommunications arm, supplies the equipment and charges only for time used on the system. Similarly, high-technology health care, such as kidney dialysis, that previously required repeated hospital visits, is now being provided increasingly in the home through lower-cost, more universally accessible technology.

A combination of such computing and communications devices as affordable personal computers, printers, desk-top publishing units, voice mail, electronic mail networks, duplicating equipment, and facsimile (FAX) transmitters and receivers has made the office of the future accessible to the home. As a result, it has been estimated that the number of U.S. white-collar workers working full time in home offices increased by 50% between 1987 and 1989, accounting for nearly 5% of such people.[1] Of these, only a small number could be called telecommuters, people actually substituting totally their home for their regular office desk. But one estimate suggests the number of full-time telecommuters will reach 5 million by 1995 in the United States alone.[2] A combination of labor shortages, changing social patterns, increasingly difficult commuting, and even government incentives to discourage commuting should only encourage the trend.

And, if the office can be at home, so can retail outlets. Now, we have Home Shopping Network and the countless records and gadgets sold on UHF frequencies. Several consumer information services offer ''mall-type'' shopping via personal computer in the home. The combination of catalogs and toll-free 800 numbers bring the shopping experience of L. L. Bean, Lands' End, and Eddie Bauer right to your easy chair—no driving, no parking, no waiting (maybe three telephone rings), knowledgeable and friendly order-takers, guaranteed satisfaction, and, if needed, gift wrapping. Overnight delivery is available for an extra charge.

But home is what you make it. Now that electronics have freed the office from the office, the cellular phone and similar services have freed the office from the home. In Sweden, one enterprising company located 75 miles from Stockholm has outfitted a rail car with phones, fax machines, and personal computers in order to entice professionals to make the 85-minute commute from Stockholm twice each day. Ann Larsson, an MBA from Stockholm, commented, ''I wouldn't still be with the company if it weren't for the train.''[3] A growing number of field-based representatives have rigged up autos and vans with cellular phones, laptop computers, and facsimile machines to allow them to operate out of mobile offices. It should be no surprise that Los Angeles is the fastest-growing market for cellular phones. Thousands of commuters appear to be substituting the world's largest mobile office for what has been termed the world's largest parking lot, the Los Angeles freeway system. (During one recent two-hour commute the president of a southern California advertising agency reported that she received

20 phone calls and several faxes and was thinking about installing a second cellular telephone in her van.)[4]

TOWARD THE WORLD OF "FUTURE PERFECT"

Increasingly we want any thing, any time, and any place, something that Stanley Davis has labeled "future perfect."[5] And we want it now. Revenues of fast-lubrication auto service outlets tripled between 1987 and 1988 in the United States.[6] Within hours, an auto windshield can be replaced in Canada by a repairer in a mobile van. H & R Block, the tax preparation firm, offers a program in which clients, for a small fee, can have their taxes filed electronically for fast processing by the Internal Revenue Service (IRS). Those especially impatient can obtain a refund-anticipation loan, repaid when the IRS transmits their refund. We saw earlier that Citicorp Mortgage is pioneering the 15-minute home loan. Overnight guaranteed mail service is a way of life. But it is being replaced by facsimile machines that transmit documents and replies in minutes. And fax is being challenged by electronic mail that is even faster.

The migration toward having any thing, any time, any place, now is clear. It will not be reversed. The motivating forces, suggested in Figure 13–1, are strong. Nor will it include everybody, even though it may indirectly affect everyone. It will produce interesting combinations of behavior even among those who are on the leading edge of these trends. It will be a mixed blessing with many potential problems. That's why this chapter is devoted to an exploration of the forces behind this migration, what it means for the service sector, the management of services, and the quality of work life in services, all of which will shape breakthrough services of the future.

UNDERLYING FORCES

Forces explaining inexorable trends toward instantaneous, continuous, universal delivery of anything include the discovery of the value of information, an accelerating development and adoption of technology of particular relevance for services, the development of global markets for services, changing social patterns, and rising customer expectations.

DISCOVERY OF THE VALUE OF INFORMATION

As discussed in Chapter 10, information is the oil of the service sector. Only relatively recently have growing numbers of managers begun to fully realize this.

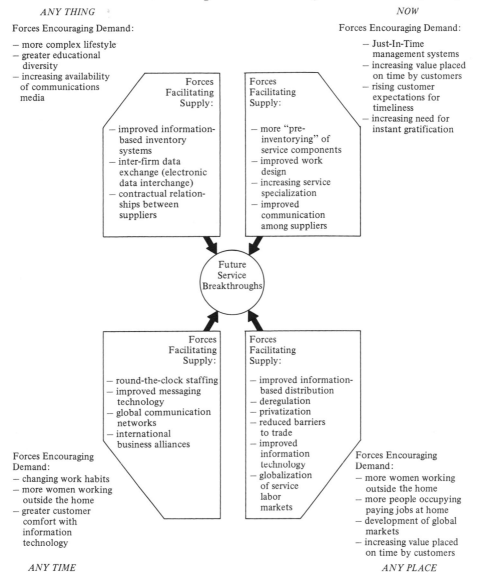

ANY THING

Forces Encouraging Demand:

— more complex lifestyle
— greater educational
  diversity
— increasing availability
  of communications
  media

Forces
Facilitating
Supply:

— improved information-
  based inventory
  systems
— inter-firm data
  exchange (electronic
  data interchange)
— contractual relation-
  ships between
  suppliers

NOW

Forces Encouraging Demand:

— Just-In-Time
  management systems
— increasing value placed
  on time by customers
— rising customer
  expectations for
  timeliness
— increasing need for
  instant gratification

Forces
Facilitating
Supply:

— more "pre-
  inventorying" of
  service components
— improved work
  design
— increasing service
  specialization
— improved
  communication
  among suppliers

Future
Service
Breakthroughs

Forces
Facilitating
Supply:

— round-the-clock staffing
— improved messaging
  technology
— global communication
  networks
— international
  business alliances

Forces
Facilitating
Supply:

— improved information-
  based distribution
— deregulation
— privatization
— reduced barriers
  to trade
— improved
  information
  technology
— globalization
  of service
  labor
  markets

Forces Encouraging
Demand:

— changing work habits
— more women working
  outside the home
— greater customer
  comfort with
  information
  technology

Forces Encouraging
Demand:

— more women working
  outside the home
— more people occupying
  paying jobs at home
— development of global
  markets
— increasing value placed
  on time by customers

ANY TIME   *ANY PLACE*

FIGURE 13–1 Factors Influencing the Nature of Future Service Breakthroughs

It is just beginning to dawn on the majority of managers that information is a significantly different kind of fuel than oil, that it has truly magical properties that other valuable resources don't provide. Harlan Cleveland has reminded us of these properties by pointing out that information is infinitely expandable; it does not drain our resources as our steel-and-auto economy of the past has; it can be substituted for capital, labor, and physical materials;

it is infinitely more transportable than goods; it is diffusive, and the more it leaks the more we have; and it is shareable, suggesting that information by nature is shared, not exchanged, and therefore multiplies theoretically without limit.[7] Contrasts drawn by Cleveland between characteristics of information and more conventional goods are summarized in Table 13–1.

Breakthrough service managers do not equate information with data. Anyone can capture data. But until we process it and identify the relationships it contains, we may have little useful information. As we have seen, breakthrough services not only capture data, they process and study it to: (1) learn more about certain products and processes than anyone else, creating enhanced value for the resulting service, (2) capture and learn from customer complaints leading to service improvements, (3) reorganize preferred customers and their needs, and (4) develop new information-based products and businesses.

Sears, Roebuck has collected more data about retail shopping habits than any other retailer in the world. But American Express knows more about retail shopping behavior than anyone else, because its system enables it to remember and study shopping patterns from time to time. Sears probably has wasted more data than American Express has collected. But American Express has to remember, because it places no credit limit on its green, gold,

Table 13–1 IMPORTANT DIFFERENCES IN THE CHARACTERISTICS OF INFORMATION AND GOODS

Information Is:	*Goods Are:*
Expandable without any obvious limits	Finite, bound by available resources
Compressible into summaries for easier handling	Only in some cases collapsible to a limited degree
Substitutable for capital, labor, or physical materials	Substitutable only in some cases for other goods
Transportable at least at the speed of light	Transportable at much slower speeds and with much greater difficulty than for information
Diffusive and hard to contain, especially that containing high proprietary value	Capable of being owned, hoarded, and kept from use
Shared among people, with an expansion of the total as it is shared	Exchanged between people, with no expansion of the total supply as a result of the exchange

SOURCE: Based on Harlan Cleveland, "Information as a Resource," *The Futurist*, December 1982, pp. 34–39, and Harlan Cleveland, "The Twilight of Hierarchy: Speculations on the Global Information Society," *Public Administration Review*, January–February 1985, pp. 185–195.

and platinum credit cards. It has to be able to identify and check on unusual purchasing behavior as a safeguard against the use of stolen cards.

Consider the value of the database American Express is creating and the different constituencies who will want access to the data. Service establishments accepting the American Express card can gain estimates of market share by different geographical regions. They can also gain a better understanding of the demographics and spending habits of their customers. As purchased items are coded, this information becomes valuable to product manufacturers. The database also provides information about the demographics of customers for the manufacturer's product. Advertising agencies and marketers could learn a great deal about the purchasing habits of members of various market segments for products and services. The value of the information of the sort collected by American Express and similar organizations may be greater than the finance exchange function it now provides. But who will own, control, and distribute this information is still an unresolved issue.

UPS handles more small packages than any other company in the world. As a result, it has collected a great deal of data about small package handling. A major competitor, Federal Express, on the other hand, has developed a remembering information system that enables it to analyze shipping patterns at the customer level, gearing its sales calls and incentive programs to such customer shipping patterns.

Airlines collect and store an immense amount of data in the form of schedules, reservations, and passenger manifests. Nearly all of it is discarded and forgotten (and until recently, no airlines knew passengers by their first names). American Airlines has taken advantage of this incredible waste on the part of its competition, as anyone knows who has received complementary "frequent flyer" miles because of an extreme delay of an American Airlines flight or has been upgraded on a crowded flight without requesting it because of the frequency with which he or she travels on American.

Most successful service businesses are information-centered. At the leading edge, managers recognize this and do away with conventional thinking that they are in transportation, financial services, or medicine. This requires a continuing stream of allocations for data collection and information base building, analysis, and communication. Most often, these allocations are expensed rather than capitalized by accountants. Even when these investments are capitalized, they are depreciated like investments in machines. Unlike breakthrough service managers who have made such investments, the accountant may not realize that the resulting asset often is an appreciating, not a wasting, one. To recognize this would require a complete rethinking of the concept of depreciation, one more potential result of the discovery of the value of information.

ACCELERATING ADOPTION OF TECHNOLOGY

The service sector (excluding government), which produced 74% of the U.S. private sector gross national product in 1987, was found at that time to own about 85% of the country's computers, telecommunications equipment, and other information-centered high technology.[8] Information developed by Stephen Roach suggests that the share of total capital invested by service industries devoted to high-technology equipment increased by nearly two-and-a-half times between 1970 and 1985.[9]

Medical, communications, power utility, and transportation services have benefited from technological advances in materials research in areas such as pharmaceuticals, superconductivity, metallurgy, and space exploration. New equipment (methods technology) has supported the development of improved work methods and the very working environment itself in many services. But of all technologies, those associated with information handling have undoubtedly had the greatest impact on services in recent years.

While the popular view of services may be that of small-scale, labor-intensive businesses with unsophisticated management, James Brian Quinn, Jordan Baruch, and Penny Cushman Paquette point out that firms making up much of the U.S. service sector do have "the scale, capital intensity and technical sophistication to apply technology effectively."[10] And their managers know they need it.

Technological advances should have two major effects on services. First, they should enable the creation of services that are more responsive to customers. Earl Sasser and William Fulmer suggest that this is being achieved through: (1) diagnosis and identification of individual customer needs, (2) individualized execution and improvement of customer encounters, and (3) improved customer convenience.[11] There is little doubt that this has occurred. By combining two or more of the basic materials, methods, or information technologies, service firms have achieved significantly higher levels of service, often geared to the needs of individual customers or servers. For example, a combination of advances in methods and information technologies produced the automated teller machines which enabled customers to obtain the kind of financial transactions they desired when they needed them at many more locations. Citibank's managers, who placed the largest early bets on these technologies, were certain this would allow customers eventually to obtain economical, customized (or perhaps "customizing") service.

Technology should improve productivity as well. It is around this issue that significant debate has arisen recently, because conventional methods of measuring productivity, at least in the United States, suggest that productivity increases in the service sector lag U.S. manufacturers who have been spending less per dollar of production in recent years for technology. Stephen Roach puts it more bluntly: "There's been virtually no relationship between spending on information technology and productivity."[12]

Any number of explanations for the absence of productivity improvements have been advanced. Some argue that it is too early to measure the impact of vast investments in information technology on service productivity. One recent study of 400 companies, for example, showed that more than half had not started automating their offices until 1984 or later.[13] Others suggest that early investments were misguided, not specifically focused, not followed up by top management or, worse yet, ignored by largely disinterested senior managers. Another school of thought holds that information technology is not the key to productivity improvement in services anyway, that capital investment in technology is only a small part of the cost of, or reason for benefits from, improved information processing. As Cyrus Gibson puts it, "Real office productivity comes from changing the work itself, and that has nothing to do with technology."[14]

What is more likely to be the case is that managers are still learning how to apply information technology *and* we don't know how to measure productivity in services. Accounting for changes in quality is much more difficult for services than for products, and most of our measures do not account adequately for changes in value added per service worker from one year to the next. James Brian Quinn suggests that "Once they have been properly installed, the same technologies that created the new economies of scale often generate a secondary effect that might be called 'economies of scope.' "[15] For example, once it installed a high-capacity credit card processing system, J. C. Penney began processing "credit card transactions for Shell Oil and Gulf Refining and Marketing as a way to leverage its investment in its information network."[16]

Because economies of scope are associated with handling a much wider array of data, variety of services, or range of customers than before, they often are associated with improved quality in a service, particularly one that in part is based on relationships. Current productivity measures do not take into account the timeliness, round-the-clock availability, and universal geographic coverage that customers increasingly expect. In other words, services may change greatly from one year to the next, even though they continue to go by the same name for purposes of measurement.

Despite the uproar about lagging productivity in services, one comprehensive study of value added in U.S. services and manufacturing suggests that workers in services add greater value per capita than their counterparts in manufacturing.[17] And using improved methods of measuring British data, Richard Barras has found that the rate of growth in the real value of output per employee in services was nearly three times as great as in manufacturing in the British economy between 1960 and 1981.[18] This was in an economy in which the service sector purchased only 70% of computers sold there in 1984, a smaller percentage than in the United States.

THE GLOBALIZATION OF SERVICES

Two recent news items underscore trends toward the globalization of services. Aeroflot, the Russian national airline, announced that it had contracted with the Marriott Corporation's In-Flite Services Division to provide catering services. In New York? No. Aeroflot had agreed to a contract under which Marriott (now Caterair) assumes the management of Aeroflot's "hub kitchen" in Moscow.

Several weeks earlier, New York Life Insurance Company announced that it had established a new office for handling claims of its American policy holders that would enable it to reduce its claims handling costs while preserving service levels. In New York? No. In Shannon, Ireland. Every weekday afternoon, claims that have come in that day are placed on an Aer Lingus jet to Ireland, where there is a surplus of well-educated white-collar workers to process them.[19]

Just to underscore the point, two million Americans were watching the ABC Night Line television show at 1 A.M. the night of October 19, 1987, the stock market crash. The reason? To find out how the Tokyo Stock Exchange had responded the next day. If indeed we needed it, this was a vivid reminder of the extent to which the world service economy has become one, thanks largely to improvements in transportation and communications and the establishment of standards making possible the creation of worldwide networks for business transactions, networks that penetrate national borders and render national policies less important than global ones.

Breakthrough service firms don't necessarily follow the flag. Thus we find Scandinavian Airlines System training Texas Air (Continental Airlines) personnel. And one of the fastest-growing markets for the U.S.-based Service-Master Company is its management of support services for hospitals in Japan. It is this service to foreign customers in foreign markets that represents an increasingly attractive, albeit largely unmeasured, component of foreign trade.

The more important trend toward globalization is a force for the performance of service anywhere. And because of differences in time around the world, it has fostered 24-hour service, most recently in financial markets. New technologies have reinforced the trend by making it possible to locate information-intensive service operations literally anywhere, taking advantage of favorable labor or communications economies. In addition to the development of new technologies, the deregulation of service industries particularly in England and the United States, the privatization of many state-owned service businesses from Mexico to France, the reduction of barriers to trade in services, and more widely accessible labor markets are fostering globalization.

Deregulation and Privatization. Deregulation and privatization are contagious because they make it possible for firms to operate most effectively, making them more formidable competitors. To the extent they are allowed to compete across national boundaries with regulated or nationalized competitors, there is a strong motive to deregulate or privatize the latter. This has been especially true for transport, communications, and financial services where the very nature of the service spans national boundaries.

In fact, the unleashing of entire service industries to hone their competitive skills in several highly developed nations, along with perceived financial strengths and a ready international market for services that "follow the customer's flag," have made the governments of less developed economies fearful of lowering world trade barriers in services. Only recently have countries with highly developed service economies been able to bring the issue to the top of the agenda of GATT, the General Agreement on Tariffs and Trade, which officially sponsors such multinational negotiations. Among the levers bringing reluctant participants to the negotiating table are deregulation and privatization.

Lower Trade Barriers. Airlines may not pick up and drop off passengers traveling between two cities in a foreign country. Data may not be transmitted freely across some borders. And preferential treatment is given to domestic investment brokers, insurers, and others when foreign firms try to compete for such business. But the barriers are coming down.

This is particularly true on a regional basis, with the further liberalization of trade in goods and services in Europe by 1992 and the first steps toward a North American common market taken by Canada and the United States in reaching an agreement to liberalize trade between them.

The pressures for the elimination of global trade barriers in services will be greatest in those industries linked by necessity to worldwide networks. Already, telecommunications barriers have been breached. Barriers to financial services, an industry bound by global relationships, are coming down. And as airlines and other transport networks invest in each other and form partnerships to enhance their global reach, as United Airlines and British Airways, Continental Airlines and Scandinavian Airlines System, and Delta Air Lines and Swissair have done already, it will be more and more difficult to preserve old barriers.

Globalization of Service Labor Markets. The lowering of trade barriers will continue to encourage the crossing of national boundaries to hire labor, especially for information-intensive services not requiring personal contact with the customer. High-tech, "low-touch" service firms will increasingly scour the world for the places to locate their "factories." We should not assume that they will have complete mobility, however. Nor will they operate most effectively as nomads following the latest low-cost labor market. But this phenomenon will provide further encouragement to countries with low wage structures to both lower barriers to the cross-border transmission of information and develop low-cost multinational communications services. The increased potential for the flight of jobs from one country to another, just as capital flows quite freely and rapidly today, will further draw countries and trading regions together in their economic planning activities. While some labor, business, and government leaders fear the possible loss of jobs that this could entail, breakthrough managers see it as one more challenge to compete globally for jobs as well as business.

CHANGING SOCIAL PATTERNS

Time has become an increasingly scarce item in spite of technology that just a few short years ago was promising a leisure society. What happened? One recent study by the Louis Harris polling organization suggests that at least in the United States people are utilizing what should have been increased leisure time to work longer and longer hours. It found that between 1973 and 1988, time spent on a job, including keeping house or going to school, increased by about 15% in the United States. During the same period, time spent in leisure activities declined by 37%.[20] Some reasons advanced for these trends are the need to work longer hours to preserve or improve the standard of living; an increase in the proportion of self-employed, professional, and managerial people who traditionally have worked longer hours; and the absence of a federal law guaranteeing minimum vacation time. This raises a growing suspicion that, to the extent that work can be made more challenging, the line between leisure and work may be redrawn by many people. This will be particularly true if, through technology, more and more of the paid labor force can work in the home, simultaneously meeting job and family obligations. These factors may render discussions of the leisure society somewhat academic.

The demand for services grows directly with increases in the proportion of a population participating in the paid labor force and increases in the proportion of a person's time spent in that labor force. It results not only because a greater proportion of household tasks have to and can be contracted, but also because it encourages people to value their time differently. It has contributed to the demand for time- and location-responsive services from fast food to fast auto servicing to in-home taped video entertainment.

RISING CUSTOMER EXPECTATIONS

These factors help explain the push for any thing, any place, any time. In addition, of course, we want it now. In a sense, the "me" generation of the 1980s is becoming the "now" generation of the 1990s. In large measure, this is the result of rising expectations produced by recently escalating levels of service, particularly that delivered by technological means. For example, we expect to be able in the future to see the person we are talking to by telephone today *because* we can now reach anyone in the world by telephone with just a few moments' delay whether we are on the ground, at sea, or in the air. The video telephone and interactive television are natural extensions of our experience that encourage us to envision *and expect* further improvements. Similarly, affordable jet travel has implicitly led many to assume that any part of the world is accessible on short notice. This in turn leads to escalating expectations about travel in the future.

We measure response times now in nanoseconds (fractions of seconds) as opposed to the seconds, minutes, hours, or days of yesterday. This can have important implications for the design of the service delivery system. Anyone who has observed operators of computer-connected workstations become impatient with response times of more than several seconds has probably concluded that slow response time contributes to operator dissatisfaction with the job and poorer performance.

An entire generation of college students, young executives, and others has grown to expect a meal to be delivered in 30 minutes without any effort on their part, thanks to Domino's Pizza and its emulators. Domino's has catered to effortless instantaneous satisfaction of needs. This does not necessarily mean that people are becoming more sedentary. But expectations concerning food service have been changed forever.

We are being led to believe that we can, through new technology, new insights into nutrition and living patterns, and medical findings, increasingly take control of our own lives. It is perhaps the most positive outgrowth of the so-called "me" generation. Rising expectations of this kind have led to the greatest demand since the late nineteenth century for new services, ranging from information about how to organize our lives to weight-watcher programs and fitness centers, nearly all of which are more service- than product-intensive.

FUTURE TRENDS

The factors creating a ready pool to meet demands for increasing numbers of service workers in the recent past are receding. Population growth rates in all developed "service economies" are declining. In the most extreme cases, such as the German Federal Republic, the population is not replenishing itself. Further, the fastest-growing segments of these populations are among people reaching retirement age, those who have been consuming many more services (particularly leisure and medical) than they produce. Several countries are experiencing rapidly declining numbers of young people preparing to enter the labor force. Some, such as the United States, are exhausting rapidly the supply of women entering or reentering the paid work force. This will mean that service-producing organizations, the only ones seeking to fill newly created jobs, will have to tap new pools of talent.

Significant productivity increases could satisfy part of the demand for labor in the service sector. But, as suggested in Figure 13–2, productivity increases in nonmanufacturing businesses continue to lag those in manufacturing, at least by measures employed by the U.S. Bureau of Labor Statistics (BLS). Where significant increases in productivity in service industries have been found, they have been confined to less labor-intensive services such as communications.

At the same time, the BLS is projecting the greatest rate of increase in demand for information-intensive jobs requiring technicians, service workers, professional workers, sales workers, and executive and managerial employees, found mostly in the service sector. Many of these are grouped under the category of "services" (encompassing medical, educational, and other professional services) in Table 13–2, a category projected to provide 10 million new jobs between 1986 and 2000. The logical conclusion is that, unless a larger proportion of the labor force is equipped for these jobs in the future than in the past, critical labor shortages may develop in information-intensive jobs.

This is all occurring precisely at a time when the U.S. system of public

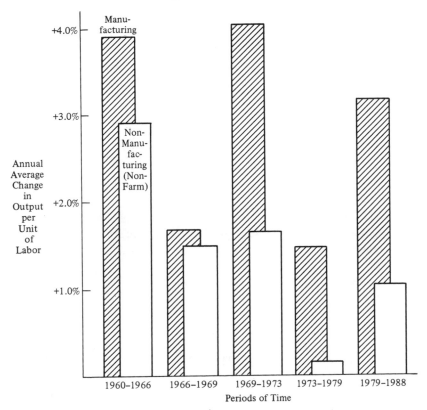

FIGURE 13–2 Productivity Trends in the United States, Manufacturing and Nonmanufacturing Industries, 1960–1988
SOURCE: For the periods 1960–66, 1966–69, 1969–73, and 1973–79, John W. Kendrick, *Interindustry Differences in Productivity Growth* (Washington, D.C.: American Enterprise Institute, 1982), pp. 12–13; for the period 1979–88, *Handbook of Labor Statistics, 1989* (Washington, D.C.: U.S. Department of Labor Bureau of Labor Statistics, 1989), p. 348. Because of possible differences in methods, the figures for 1979–88 may not relate exactly to those for preceding periods.

education is suffering a perceived crisis in its ability to produce functionally literate future members of the work force. In the United States, at least, these trends describe a disaster waiting to happen.

Increasingly the delivery of services of truly exceptional quality or low cost will demand greater attention to the relative roles of people and technology. As we have suggested earlier, it will dictate in some cases the replacement of people by technology. In other cases, it will require an investment in the selection, development, and rewarding of people designed to create a superior service delivery work force. It will force managers to seek greater latitude not only in how but also where they perform services.

Table 13–2 PROJECTED U.S. LABOR FORCE DEMAND AND SUPPLY, 1986–2000

	Labor Force Demand		
	1986 (000s)	*2000 (000s)*[a]	*Percentage (change)*
Goods Producing:			
Mining	783	724	−7.5%
Construction	4,904	5,794	+18.1
Manufacturing	18,994	18,160	−4.4
Total, goods producing	24,681	24,678	0.0%
Service Producing:			
Transportation and public utilities	5,244	5,719	+9.1
Wholesale trade	5,735	7,266	+26.7
Retail trade	17,845	22,702	+27.2
Finance, insurance, and real estate	6,297	7,917	+25.7
Services (medical, educational, and other professional)	22,531	32,545	+44.4
Government	16,711	18,329	+9.7
Total, service producing	74,363	94,478	+27.0%
Agriculture	3,252	2,917	−10.3
Private households	1,241	1,215	−.2
Nonfarm self-employed and unpaid family workers	8,086	9,742	+20.5
Total, all industries	111,623	133,030	+19.2%

THE LIMITS OF "FUTURE PERFECT"

Theoretically, we have the capability of achieving the world of "future perfect" today. Despite concerns to the contrary, we have been progressing

Table 13–2 PROJECTED U.S. LABOR FORCE DEMAND AND SUPPLY, 1986–2000 *(CONTINUED)*

	Labor Force Supply		
	1986 *(000s)*	*2000* *(000s)*	*Percentage* *(change)*
Men:			
16 to 24	12,251	11,506	− 6.1%
25 to 54	44,406	53,024	+ 19.4
55 and older	8,766	8,606	− 1.8
Total, men	65,423	73,136	+ 11.8%
Women:			
16 to 24	11,117	11,125	+ 0.1%
25 to 54	35,159	47,756	+ 24.5
55 and older	6,138	6,758	+ 10.1
Total, women	52,414	65,639	+ 25.2%
Total, men and women	117,837	138,775	+ 17.8%
White, 16 and older[b]	101,801	116,701	+ 14.6
Black, 16 and older[b]	12,684	16,334	+ 28.8
Hispanic origin, 16 and older[b]	8,076	14,086	+ 74.4
Other, 16 and older[b]	3,352	5,740	+ 71.2

SOURCE: Ronald E. Kutscher, "Overview and Implications of the Projections to 2000," *Monthly Labor Review*, September 1987, pp. 3–9.

[a] Projections for labor demand in the year 2000 are "moderate" (midrange) estimates.

[b] Total does not equal the total for men and women because Hispanics may be included in either the White and Black population groups as well.

regularly toward future perfect in the service sector. By any physical measure, in most service industries service is much better today than it was twenty years ago. This is true, for example, for the much-maligned airline industry. The "good old days," technically speaking, were not so great as we now imagine them.

The technological pieces for accomplishing future perfect rapidly are falling into place. But this doesn't necessarily mean it will happen, or that it should. Major impediments are the inherent nature of some services, customer preference, regulatory barriers, and the availability of qualified service providers and managers.

INHERENT SERVICE NATURE

As William Baumol and William Bowen, economists who have studied productivity in the arts, have pointed out:

> Human ingenuity has devised ways to reduce the labor necessary to produce an automobile, but no one has yet succeeded in decreasing the human effort expended at a live performance of a 45-minute Schubert quartet much below a total of three man-hours.[21]

Similarly, we could shorten a gourmet meal technologically from three hours to ten minutes. But customers seeking a pleasurable experience don't benefit from instantaneous delivery. Yet, other services are bounded by human capability itself. While we may program an electronic instrument to enable humans with no particular ability to learn to play music within minutes after picking it up, no effective ways have been found to make the acquisition of difficult skills, such as violin playing or Chinese speaking, easy or immediate. The best we may be able to do is to make it available anywhere, anytime, and in any form, primarily through communication.

CUSTOMER PREFERENCE

Research tells us that the very people to whom timesaving services are most important during the week are also the most likely to spend an entire weekend day preparing one fine meal or cultivating one rare rose. The human search for variety as a source of quality in living will, if anything, increase as people achieve the means for paying for it.

Opportunities for services designed as alternatives (or even antidotes) to "future perfect" continually are arising and are being identified by entrepreneurs who are students of human behavior as well as economics. Thus, new technology has not forced us all to eat lunch in ten minutes, it has broadened the range of alternatives we have for dining.

REGULATORY BARRIERS

The dramatic deregulation on both a domestic and international basis of many services in the past decade has created new opportunities for service improvement as well as economies in the delivery process. At the same time, it is a highly visible change that can be blamed for any failure perceived by customers or competitively disadvantaged service providers.

As we pointed out earlier in this chapter, deregulation is contagious. It unleashed competitive forces that have penetrated even the economic curtain between Western and Eastern Europe. These forces have been so strong in industries such as the U.S. airline industry that they have led to what some claim is destructive competition, the elimination of competitors, the creation of increasingly monopolistic conditions, and the eventual deterioration of the very competition and quality of service that was intended in the first place.

Rather than a push for increasing prosecution of antitrust and other competition-preserving legislation already on the books of most nations with free economies, many will call for the reregulation of service industries. To the extent that reregulation often leads to retaliation, it can be just as contagious as deregulation has been in recent years.

It is easy to see how reregulation could stand in the way of achieving the world of "future perfect," especially in multinational services. Its development bears watching.

AVAILABILITY OF QUALIFIED SERVICE PROVIDERS

If services are so much better technically than they were twenty years ago, why are we confronted with questions about why service is so bad these days? A careful examination of complaints suggests that nearly all are associated with people, not technology or the capabilities that it provides. Service is faster, more universal, and more diverse. But, we are told, that it is not being delivered in responsive and empathetic ways, and with assurance. And we are told that services often fall far short of our expectations, both in our initial encounter and during recovery from an initial shortfall.

The most critical resource of the coming decade will be people. Managers who have already concluded this are taking steps to tap new labor pools, including senior citizens, householders who otherwise would not leave the home, and individuals with two jobs. This requires that people be selected from these pools to match the human and technical skills demanded by both jobs and customers. It will require that breakthrough employers devote increasing attention to education designed to improve both on-the-job and basic literary skills, transportation for service providers, and ways of helping employees meet needs for child care, flexible working hours, and flexible working locations.

MANAGEMENT

The demand for people with general management talent will increase with the growth of multiunit service organizations. The empowerment of both customers and service providers will have a profound impact on the kinds of managers that will be sought in the service sector.

Increasing numbers of managers will be needed who can train and inspire service providers working with empowered customers. Services that are more transparent to customers, either because of physical visibility or improved access to information, have to be managed with a view to a greater emphasis on tangible evidence of quality as well as empathy in those situations where the empowered customer can't make the service work. While some kinds of demands on service providers will be lessened, others will be increased. This will require changes as well in determinants of performance and management emphasis.

In organizations stressing empowerment for service providers, the responsibilities of, and demands on, first-line managers will be increased. It will require people who can understand, interpret, relate, and translate facts into information and decisions. Further, it will require increasing numbers of managers who are able to achieve the transformation from an emphasis on supervision to that emphasizing support for others, who are able to delegate responsibility, and who are able to limit their activities to training, inspiring, cheerleading, and problem solving. This is not a package of skills that is found in great profusion, nor have we been training managers for this kind of environment. It suggests that the transformation to an empowered organization in many cases will be a slow one, with management the primary bottleneck.

In spite of concerns we have expressed in this chapter, there is a growing cadre of outstanding service managers who are pointing the way for the merely good among their associates. We have tried to document, through anecdote and comment, what they are doing that is truly remarkable to realize service breakthroughs. To underline and summarize their accomplishments, we next offer a set of characteristics that may serve as the basis for benchmarking individual efforts against those of the very best breakthrough managers.

14

Realizing
Service Breakthroughs

W e started this book with an analogy between service breakthroughs and
flights through the sound barrier. While that has a nice technological ring to
it, perhaps the analogy of a baby bird pecking its way out of a shell would
have been more appropriate. Consider the following examples:

Remarkable as Nordstrom's strategic service vision seems to us today,
few remember that the company got its start as a shoe store in Seattle. In
fact, some of its practices such as paying nearly all salespeople on a commission basis, innovative as they may be to fashion retailing, were and are
common practice in selling shoes. The company's inventory policies, featuring depth of assortments and excellent coverage of various sizes, are
much more common practice in the shoe business than in other forms of
fashion retailing. Nordstrom's management did not come upon its strategic
service vision by chance, but it was influenced at the start by some very
conventional practices in the business it knew best, shoe retailing.

In starting a chain of Japanese steak houses, Benihana of Tokyo, that have
set the standard for planning and design for many would-be competitors and
other restauranteurs, Rocky Aoki did not get it right the first time. While he
envisioned a meal prepared at a hibachi seating eight people which could be
paced by the cook practicing his or her craft in front of diners and literally
feeding them course by course, he designed his first restaurant with too few
seats in the bar. This was critical. Aoki knew that he wanted diners to be
"paced" by the chef to complete a meal in one hour or less so that he could
get maximum "turnover" of the seats and high utilization of restaurant
facilities and personnel. It wasn't until after he had built his first restaurant
in New York City that Aoki decided that the optimum waiting time for

patrons in the bar would be slightly more than 20 minutes, suggesting that he have about one seat in the bar for every three in the restaurant. He found that he had provided only half the required space in the bar and adjusted subsequent designs accordingly, just as he experimented with various other practices in the restaurant as he went along.

At Federal Express, one of today's shining service examples, Fred Smith decided that it would be necessary to build a wholly owned network of aircraft, pick-up and delivery equipment, and sorting hubs in order to provide maximum control and security if he were to offer a premium overnight package delivery service over long distances. This required an immense amount of capital and sizable incremental investments each time he decided to expand the frequency of service or the number of points served. Any one of a number of conditions could have put the company out of business. Several, including a rapid rise in fuel prices and a recession in the economy at about the time the company was rolling out its service, nearly did. In fact, the size of the aircraft around which the overnight delivery concept originally was designed could severely have hampered the profit potential of the company throughout its life. It wasn't until the relaxation of regulatory restrictions, with Fred Smith in the forefront of the lobbying activity, that the company was able to operate aircraft with which it could begin to make significant profits.

And how about the perfection of Disneyland? Walt Disney sank more than he had into its building. Attractions were not properly designed or built the first time. And operating procedures for which Disney is justly famous today were not in place.

As a result, on opening day, Disneyland experienced overloading on the Mark Twain sternwheeler, which nearly capsized as crowds moved from one side of the boat to the other to view attractions. There was a gas leak in Fantasyland, with flames coming through the asphalt street. And the vaunted cast members for which Disney is now famous didn't exist; instead food and merchandise shops were staffed by employees of companies that had leased the space. Outside contract operators staffed parking lot, crowd control, and custodial jobs. According to one account:

> From the way the crowd control employees yelled at the customers, it appeared that they assumed their mission to be cattleherding. . . . The custodial company's standards apparently stopped at cursory cleanliness. The security guards evidently thought that they had been retained specifically to protect Disney property from thugs, a description they liberally applied to anyone who came through the gate.[1]

Patrons complained about a pricing system that required them to pay both upon entering the park and for each attraction they experienced. There were not enough water fountains. Money was collected by runners using buckets to get money from the ticket booths to the bank before closing. According to Randy Bright, "When the weekly paychecks were issued, members of the management team were told not to cash theirs until they were certain that all of the hourly employees' checks were covered by the dwindling bank funds."[2] One newspaper headline trumpeted, "The $17 Million Dollar People Trap That Mickey Mouse Built."[3]

Someone with less conviction would have regarded Disneyland as a service disaster. For Walt Disney it was a laboratory. In his words: "I watch every bit of a big crowd and find out where we need to improve our crowd control conditions to make it easier to get around, and our shade areas and all the problems we have in the summer."[4] Fortunately for millions of children, young and old, Walt Disney and his staff literally lived with their customers, little-by-little improved the service concept, and slowly developed what now appears to have been an ingenious facility and management philosophy created in full blossom from nothing.

The point is that breakthroughs may occur with a bang but they are earned one "peck" at a time with a combination of foresight, hard work, and attention to many details as well as just one or two overriding concepts. Remember what Harry Dalton, the manager responsible for the path-breaking COSMOS shipment tracking system at Federal Express, said: "The only thing we know for sure is that we won't get it quite right the first time, but we'll come back and fix it."[5] Our objective here is to bring together those characteristics which have yielded today's service breakthroughs and will yield tomorrow's.

BENCHMARKING BREAKTHROUGH SERVICES

Throughout this book we have suggested those things we believe separate the very best from what we have called the "merely good" service providers. To underscore these observations (and our biases), we have summarized below the major points of this book in the form of contrasting beliefs and practices characterizing each type of service provider on a number of dimensions.

We have made no attempt to be comprehensive in our presentation. Nor will all benchmarks that follow be applicable to all services. We would caution too that breakthrough services may not reflect breakthrough practice or attitude on every dimension, although they rarely fall below the level of the "very good" on any one.

This set of contrasting descriptions is designed to provide the basis for benchmarking management practice in a service organization against both the "merely good" and the very best. Which of these observations best characterizes the service organization of interest to you?

CREATING BREAKTHROUGH SERVICES

Dimension	"Merely Good" Service Providers	Breakthrough Service Providers
Approach to the design of the service encounter	Regard the relationships in a service encounter as a series of trade-offs (higher quality vs. higher productivity, lower cost vs. lost customer loyalty, etc.)	Regard the relationships in a service encounter as a series of mutually reinforcing concepts (higher quality *and* higher productivity, lower costs *and* higher customer loyalty, etc.)
Emphasis on quality and value	Concentrate on producing services of the highest quality	Concentrate on producing services of the highest value to customers, taking into account quality in relation to price and other customer costs of service acquisition
Emphasis on sales-building efforts	Design marketing and service delivery efforts for sales growth	Focus marketing and service delivery efforts on building the loyalty of existing customers while also attracting new ones
Approach to building customer satisfaction	Measure customer expectations and meet or exceed them	Measure both customer and server expectations and meet or exceed both, recognizing the self-reinforcing relationship between server and customer satisfaction

DEVELOPING A VISION OF THE SERVICE BUSINESS

Dimension	"Merely Good" Service Providers	Breakthrough Service Providers
Definition of service concept	Define their service concept and their businesses in terms of services, processes, or even equipment by which they are delivered	Define their service concept and their businesses in terms of results produced for customers
Customer targeting	Identify target customers primarily on demographic dimensions (age, income, etc.)	Identify target customers primarily on psychographic dimensions (life-styles, perceived risks, etc.)
Operating strategy formulation	Formulate operating strategies to provide conventional "low cost" or "differentiation" advantages over competitors	Develop operating strategies that leverage value for customers over cost, often achieving both low cost and significant differentiation
Service delivery system design	Design service delivery systems that focus on reliable and timely service delivery	Design service delivery systems that offer customer assurance and tangible evidence of the service ("leave behinds," uniforms, etc.) as well as reliability and timeliness

BUILDING CUSTOMER LOYALTY

Dimension	*"Merely Good" Service Providers*	*Breakthrough Service Providers*
Measurement of purchasing behavior	Track repeat purchasing behavior of loyal customers	Track repeat purchasing behavior of loyal customers and follow up with those whose service usage has lapsed
Cost-value measurement	Generally support the idea that loyal customers are valuable	Seek to measure the value of customer loyalty and the cost of lost customers as the basis for budgeting efforts to preserve the existing customer base
Marketing budget patterns	Spend liberally to promote usage by old and new customers	Explicitly establish budgets for efforts to retain existing customers as well as engage in spending to promote usage by old and new customers
Strategy for serving existing customers	Develop methods for serving all customers more effectively, with general purpose of increasing repeat service utilization	Activate specific initiatives to develop customer loyalty through measuring and managing expectations, carefully managing the initial service encounter, "membership" programs, customer "training," and efforts to make customers better at what they do

FOCUSING AND POSITIONING A SERVICE

Dimension	"Merely Good" Service Providers	Breakthrough Service Providers
Sources of focus	Focus on serving specific groups of customers, primarily through marketing emphasis	Focus on serving specific groups of customers with an operating strategy and service delivery system designed specifically to meet their needs, often requiring restrictions to discourage unwanted customers
Focus in operating strategies	Attempt to develop new markets or businesses that share a service delivery system with existing ones	Expand into new businesses with dedicated service delivery systems and management
Scope of positioning efforts	Center their positioning efforts around promotional themes that seek to help customers differentiate them from competitors on important dimensions	Regard positioning as something to be achieved first through operating strategy and service delivery system design and secondarily through marketing efforts that seek to help customers differentiate them from competitors on important dimensions
Primary bases for establishing a "position" in relation to customers and competitors	Based on marketing research of customer needs and competitor capabilities, develop operating strategies to deliver superior service on dimensions important to customers	Based on marketing research of customer needs and competitor capabilities, seek "contrary" positions through operating strategies built on initiatives that run counter to "industry myths" and that change the way customers feel, live, or do business, altering the important dimensions of competition for an entire industry

DETERMINING THE TRUE COST OF POOR QUALITY

Dimension	"Merely Good" Service Providers	Breakthrough Service Providers
Management attitudes toward measurement	Realize the importance of measuring the cost of poor quality but do not have the means to do so in the firm's existing accounting system	Develop devices outside the accounting system for measuring service quality costs
Scope of effort	Devise means of measuring and tracking explicit ("hard dollar") costs of appraisal (inspection, testing, and system auditing), error prevention, and correcting complaints made by customers (so-called external failure costs)	Track not only explicit costs of appraisal, error prevention, and external service failures but also the internal (often "soft dollar") costs of poor service (lowered employee morale, increased turnover, and lowered productivity)
Use of information	Use measurements of the cost of poor quality to justify periodic programs to improve quality at points that the tracking system indicates are important	Use this information as the basis for budgeting and launching company-wide quality improvement efforts and tracking the value of quality improvements against the costs of such efforts
Emphasis on customer cost	Develop measures of customer costs that are limited to the cost of the defective service, which is reflected in the corrective action (often the replacement of the service)	Develop measures of customer costs that include the money, time, and emotional costs spent in replacing defective services or complaining about them, which is reflected in a corrective action that goes beyond merely replacing the defective service

DEVELOPING DEVICES FOR ACHIEVING TOTAL CUSTOMER
SATISFACTION

Dimension	*"Merely Good" Service Providers*	*Breakthrough Service Providers*
Uses of service guarantees	Use service guarantees primarily as marketing devices, providing a source of differentiation and assurances especially to new customers	Use service guarantees primarily as devices for achieving outstanding quality through improved error detection and eradication, and secondarily for marketing purposes
Type of service guarantee adopted	Introduce guarantees for specific, measurable aspects of a service to customers meeting carefully specified conditions, often developed by the firm's legal department	Introduce unconditional guarantees of total customer satisfaction, with evaluation dependent on customers' judgments, and placement and collection of claims made easy
Role of recovery initiatives	Often regard service recovery initiatives, procedures, and training as secondary to efforts to encourage servers to "do it right the first time"	Give high priority to service recovery initiatives, procedures, and training as a means of preserving total customer satisfaction even though performance on a particular dimension of service may be less than desired
Latitude given servers to provide service recovery	Provide strict guidelines indicating what a server may and may not do in a recovery situation	Empower servers to do what is necessary to effect immediate service recovery, with review after the fact primarily for learning, not control, purposes

MANAGING FOR QUALITY AND PRODUCTIVITY GAINS

Dimension	*"Merely Good" Service Providers*	*Breakthrough Service Providers*
Basic approach to quality and productivity improvement	Seek to improve quality through programs that reward the identification and correction of errors in service delivery	Seek to improve both quality and productivity through continuing efforts that motivate employees to "do it right the first time" and reward them for it as well as the identification and correction of errors in service delivery
Development and use of service standards	Measure customers' expectations and seek to develop standards for quality that meet or exceed them, using them as the basis for performance measurements and reward	Measure customers' expectations and competitors' performance and seek to develop standards for quality that exceed both, using them both as the basis for performance measurement and reward and as "bogies" to be continually improved upon
Selection of appropriate methods	Adopt a single, company-wide approach to quality and productivity improvement, often one utilized successfully elsewhere, thereby facilitating training, measurement, and the communication of results	Adopt the "what's right for us?" attitude, utilizing more than one approach to quality and productivity improvement, depending on (among other factors) the nature of the task being performed, its ease of description and measurement, and the ease with which causes of quality and productivity improvement can be identified

MANAGING FOR QUALITY AND PRODUCTIVITY GAINS *(Continued)*

Dimension	*"Merely Good" Service Providers*	*Breakthrough Service Providers*
Marshaling of resources	Often focus quality and productivity efforts around facility design, information technology, *or* the training and motivation of servers	Recognize the importance of calibrating and coordinating changes in facility design, information technology, *and* the training and motivation of servers in efforts to improve quality and productivity

MANAGING DEMAND AND SUPPLY

Dimension	"Merely Good" Service Providers	Breakthrough Service Providers
Emphasis in managing demand and supply	Attack the problem primarily by managing either demand (through marketing, pricing, or demand inventorying practices) *or* supply of services	Attack the problem primarily by managing both demand (through marketing, pricing, or demand inventorying practices) *and* the capacity to supply a service
Forecasting of demand	Track demand by analyzing past sales and transaction data under various conditions, using the result as an input for demand forecasting	Track demand patterns by capturing data for both actual customers and those who were not served because of capacity problems, using it as input to superior revenue control information systems
Capacity design	Determine the size of somewhat fixed capacity facilities, either by optimizing the cost of serving vs. not serving customers during peak periods or maintaining excess capacity to meet peak needs	In addition to using demand estimates to determine facilities of "optimum" size, look for ways to design flexible capacity by utilizing "floating" personnel, contracted services, high levels of organizational spirit, or other devices
Policies regarding customer queues	Seek to minimize customer waiting time during peak periods of demand	In addition to seeking ways to minimize customer waiting time during peak periods of demand, alter the customer's waiting experience through diversions that the customer finds relevant and useful, including the involvement of the customer in the service, with or without economic incentives

MANAGEMENT OF NETWORKS

Dimension	*"Merely Good" Service Providers*	*Breakthrough Service Providers*
Emphasis in network management	Regard networks primarily as operating facilities connected by communications or transport routes	Regard networks both in a physical sense and as individuals linked by a common name or by relationships in channels of distribution for services
Major consideration in network design	Seek to optimize the length and complexity of networks as well as the "connectivity" (service to points on the network) they provide	Take into account both the cost of building and operating networks and the cost to customers (in time and convenience) in using networks of various configurations to maximize the overall value of networks to customers
Strategies for building and expanding networks	Build and expand networks to accommodate reasonable levels of demand generated by marketing effort	Coordinate marketing, operations, and network construction and expansion to ensure the most effective use of existing network facilities before making necessary additions
Management of network utilization	Price and market services to produce short-term balanced usage of shared network facilities	Price and market services to produce long-term balanced usage of shared network facilities

MANAGING INFORMATION TECHNOLOGY

Dimension	*"Merely Good"* Service Providers	Breakthrough Service Providers
Attitude of leadership toward information	Regard information as an important resource for estimating and planning to accommodate demand as well as for internal control	Regard information as a primary device for delivering outstanding service as well as extending services to new dimensions and even into new businesses, often by making it available for direct use by customers
Strategy for developing information technology	Utilize the best "packaged" technology available from dependable sources, with the technology adapted to the task at hand where necessary	Set out to develop proprietary software in combination with available, proven hardware components, with the primary objectives of raising customer switching costs and tying customers to the server
Strategy for implementing information technology	Spend relatively heavily for technology in comparison with expenditures for training in its use	Spend relatively heavily for training in the use of technology in comparison with expenditures for the technology itself
Strategy for utilizing information technology	Utilize information technology as a means for empowering employees *or* customers, depending on the task being performed	Utilize information technology as a means of empowering employees *and* customers, often for the same task, as a means of providing a choice of methods to customers for accessing the serving organization and its information resource

MOBILIZING PEOPLE

Dimension	"Merely Good" Service Providers	Breakthrough Service Providers
Recruiting and selection of people	Work hard at finding the best people available, depending on the technical and human skills needed for a particular job	Work hard at sorting out the best people available *who find them*, spending less effort than the "merely good" at recruiting and selection but hiring better people as the "employer of choice"
Personal development	Through job-related training and promotion to progressively more demanding jobs, develop people, particularly at middle to upper levels of the organization	Through training both for the job and in "life skills" and through the expansion of existing jobs, help people to develop at all levels in the organization, with particular emphasis on those directly serving customers
Empowerment of people	Empower employees according to the needs of the job, often by making authority commensurate with responsibility, with bottom-up processes for suggesting change subject to higher management approval	Empower employees beyond the needs of the job as a matter of principle, often through assigning responsibilities that exceed authority, with individuals encouraged to act first and document actions later, all with the objective of creating an organization responsive to customer (and employee) needs

MOBILIZING PEOPLE *(Continued)*

Dimension	*"Merely Good" Service Providers*	*Breakthrough Service Providers*
Compensation and recognition practices	Pay at the upper end of the scale for comparable jobs in the industry, both in terms of salary and benefits, with a resulting modest amount of personnel turnover at all or most levels of the organization and recognition provided both in the form of pay increases and promotions	Pay "off the scale" for the industry, both in terms of salary and benefits, by creating fewer, larger, noncomparable jobs with compensation on a pay-for-performance basis, resulting in turnover largely from "self-selection" in entry-level jobs and low turnover rates in other jobs, with recognition provided in ways other than hierarchical promotion

ORGANIZING WORK

Dimension	"Merely Good" Service Providers	Breakthrough Service Providers
Shape of the organization and the nature of internal communication	Organize on a traditional pyramid shape with levels of management and responsibilities added to provide maximum opportunities for promoting, requiring long lines of communication for concurrence and approval of operating decisions	Develop a flat organization with few levels comprising jobs somewhat scaled in size to the growing capabilities of the individual as a form of both personal development and promotion, allowing for short and often informal lines of communication
Structuring jobs	Structure jobs according to the demands of various tasks, with a clear, often somewhat rigid definition of responsibility, if not authority	More often structure jobs according to the needs and capabilities of individuals to foster growth in both individuals and their jobs, with an implicit but not rigid definition of responsibility
Emphasis on continuity in contact with customers	Emphasize the importance of continuity in contact with customers most often by developing information systems to facilitate the transfer of responsibility for customer contact from one employee to another, with an acceptance of the inevitability of promoting good managers further and further away from customers	Emphasize the importance of continuity in contact with customers, primarily by devising ways, often through job expansion, of keeping good employees and managers in direct contact with customers as long as possible in their job progression

ORGANIZING WORK *(Continued)*

Dimension	*"Merely Good" Service Providers*	*Breakthrough Service Providers*
Means of support for front-line servers	Continually emphasize the importance of support for front-line servers through means ranging from management exhortations to headquarters staff to the creation of profit centers only at operating service facilities with authority there to purchase needed services	Emphasize the importance of support for front-line servers by "turning the organization upside down," making middle management largely a support as opposed to a control function, and organizing profit centers around front-line operating entities

ENVISIONING FUTURE BREAKTHROUGHS

Dimension	*"Merely Good" Service Providers*	*Breakthrough Service Providers*
Approach to new service design	Seek ways of improving services through existing methods	Continually monitor new methods of offering services that obsolete existing methods, both for defensive and potentially offensive reasons
Attitudes toward information	Understand how information-intensive services are different and seek to develop the most efficient information processing methods available	See information as the learning curve of service, and a significant source of competitive advantage and devise ways of capturing and using it as the basis for previously unavailable services as well as a highly mobile means of service delivery
Approaches to service delivery	Seek to expand the availability of services in terms of form, location, and time	Embrace the concept of "future perfect" and explore the development of service delivery systems that can deliver "anything, any time, anywhere, and now" and which themselves make use of such universal capabilities while incrementally improving existing services as well
Environmental scanning	Are among the first to react to environmental changes such as the evolving nature of the available work force, international market opportunities, and technological developments	Conduct continuous environmental scanning, allowing them to anticipate and take advantage of social, economic, and technological change

MANAGERS AT THE LEADING EDGE

These benchmarks suggest the ways in which leading service organizations got that way. They are led by breakthrough service managers who inherently hold as their goals the delivery of services that meet or exceed customer expectations time after time, providing total satisfaction and effective recovery in those rare instances when expectations are not met. They are living the strategic service vision both outside and inside their firms. They are living proof that the ideas discussed in this book can be implemented. They are doing it while we're talking about it.

We need more leaders of this kind. Mitchell Fromstein, John B. McCoy, Fred Smith, Jan Carlzon, Bill Marriott, Al Burger, and other CEOs we have mentioned provide it at one level in their respective organizations. The Gary Aronsons, Sylvio de Bortolis, and other unit operating managers provide it at a lower level in their respective companies. Collectively they all are the most critical resource of all. But a cadre of leaders with similar vision is forming. It is less interested in things than in ideas. People, both customers and service providers, are its primary concern. National borders mean little to it. And it is concerned, above all, with results. Consequently, our lives are being changed in ways we could not have envisioned a short time ago. Thanks to this cadre of inspiring, farsighted managers with the ability to develop and deliver breakthrough services, our lives will continue to be changed in ways we can only begin to imagine today.

Appendix

Illustrative Approaches to Transportation Network Design

In their simplest form, networks comprise nodes, routes, and the ways in which they are connected. Nodes are points at which information, passengers, or freight are received, sorted, and prepared for reshipment, if necessary. Routes connecting nodes are the links over which messages, people, or things are transported. And connectivity is a term used to measure the average distance, measured in terms of actual distance, number of links, or actual time, required to get from all points to all other points in a network.

For example, Figure A–1 shows three of the ways that six points (nodes) may be connected with each other. Assuming an equal likelihood that someone or something may be moving from any point to any other point (other than the "hub" shown as part of Network C), it is clear that Network C, the "hub and spoke" network, delivers the biggest "bang" (connectivity and service) for the "buck" (expenditure for network facilities and operation) of the three network configurations shown in Figure A–1. It costs less than the other two to operate. While it delivers slower average service times than the other two, it offers in effect five departures per day from each node to every other node. But this is only under the set of assumptions listed in the figure, assumptions that resemble characteristics of an airline route network. As the number of origins and destinations is increased, it is clear that service time in Network A increases rapidly and the cost of operating Network B increases rapidly, both in relation to Network C. This perhaps explains in at least a crude way why hub-and-spoke networks have had such appeal to airlines (if not to all passengers forced to use them).

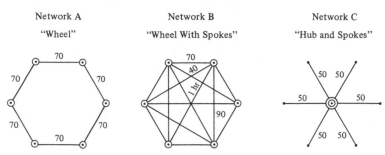

Network A — "Wheel"   Network B — "Wheel With Spokes"   Network C — "Hub and Spokes"

Key to the Diagram:

- • = network nodes
- ⊙ = network nodes at which "sorting" takes place
- ◎ = network sorting hub
- 50 = links between network nodes, with time to traverse the link shown in minutes

Assumptions:

Average operating cost per non-sorting node (including cost of capital) = $1,000 per day

Average operating cost per sorting node (including cost of capital) = $2,000 per day

Average operating cost per sorting hub (including cost of capital) = $4,000 per day

Average cost to traverse links = $10 per minute required to traverse the link

Average cost to maintain links = $10 per unit of distance (here stated in minutes) per day

Sorting time at regular network node at which sorting takes place = 30 minutes

Sorting time required at hub node = 60 minutes

Volume of traffic moving = one load per day in each direction between each network node with no volume generated at the sorting hub

Performance Results:

Cost of One Day's Operation:	A	B	C
Operation of nodes:	$12,000	$12,000	$10,000
Maintaining links:	4,200	12,300	3,000
Traversing links:	37,800	24,600	30,000
Total	$44,000	$48,900	$43,000
Average Service Time From One Node to All Other Nodes (in minutes):	180	114	160
Average Frequency From Each Node (times per day):	1	1	5

FIGURE A–1 Theoretical Comparison of Three Networks

Notes

CHAPTER 1
Creating Breakthrough Services

1. In a recent year, Carlzon estimated that each of the 10 million SAS customers came into contact with five SAS employees for an average of 15 seconds each time, producing 50 million "moments of truth." Jan Carlzon, *Moments of Truth* (Cambridge, Mass.: Ballinger Publishing Company, 1987).

2. Valarie A. Zeithaml, "How Consumer Evaluation Processes Differ Between Goods and Services," in James H. Donnelly and William R. George, eds., *Marketing of Services* (Chicago: American Marketing Association, 1981), pp. 186–190.

3. "Au Bon Pain—The Partner/Manager Program," Case No. 9-687-063 (Boston: HBS Case Services, Harvard Business School, 1987).

4. Conversation with Erie Chapman, May 14, 1988, and information presented in Ron Zemke and Dick Schaaf, *The Service Edge* (New York: NAL Books, 1989), pp. 144–148.

5. Patricia Sellers, "How to Handle Customers' Gripes," *Fortune*, October 24, 1988, p. 100.

6. Claudia H. Deutsch, "The Powerful Push for Self-Service," *The New York Times*, April 9, 1989, Section 3, pp. 1 and 15, at p. 1.

7. As reported in Sellers, "How to Handle Customers' Gripes," op. cit, p. 100.

8. Robert G. Eccles and Dwight B. Crane, "Managing through Networks in Investment Banking," *California Management Review*, Fall 1987, pp. 176–195, at p. 180.

9. See, for example, G. Lynn Shostack, "Planning the Service Encounter," in John A. Czepiel, Michael R. Soloman, and Carol F. Surprenant eds., *The Service Encounter*, (Lexington, Mass.: D. C. Heath & Company, 1985), pp. 243–253; Benjamin Schneider and David E. Bowen, "New Services Design, Development and Implementation and the Employee," in William R. George and Claudia E. Marshall, eds., *Developing New Services*, (Chicago: American Marketing Association, 1985), pp. 82–101; J. J. Parkington and B. Schneider, "Some Correlates of Experienced Job Stress: A Boundary Role Study," *Academy of Management Journal*, vol. 22, 1979, pp. 270–281; Warren G. Bennis, "Beyond Bureaucracy," in Warren G. Bennis, ed., *Amer-*

279

ican Bureaucracy, (Chicago: Aldine Publishing Company, 1970), pp. 3–17; Peter M. Blau, *On the Nature of Organizations* (New York: John Wiley and Sons, Inc., 1974), pp. 80–84; E. E. Lawler III, *Motivating in Work Organizations* (Monterey, Calif.: Brooks/Cole Publishing Company, 1973), pp. 153–165; and Eugene M. Johnson and Daniel T. Seymour, "The Impact of Cross Selling on the Service Encounter in Retail Banking," in Czepiel, Soloman, and Surprenant, eds., *The Service Encounter*, op. cit., pp. 225–239.

10. Susan C. Faludi, "At Nordstrom Stores Service Comes First—But at a Big Price, "*The Wall Street Journal*, February 20, 1990, pp. A1 and A16.

CHAPTER 2

Developing a Vision of the Business

1. From an interview by Sandra Vandermerwe with Jan O. Carlzon, recorded on March 10, 1987.

2. This section is based on portions of James L. Heskett's book, *Managing in the Service Economy* (Boston: Harvard Business School Press, 1986), especially pp. 5–43, and James L. Heskett, "Lessons in the Service Sector," *Harvard Business Review*, March–April 1987, pp. 118–126.

3. Material concerning Mark Twain Bancshares is based on the case, "Mark Twain Bancshares, Inc.," Case No. 385-178 (Boston: HBS Case Services, Harvard Business School, 1984) and conversations with Adam Aronson.

4. "Mark Twain Bancshares, Inc." a videotape of an interview by Joseph Badaracco with Adam Aronson, prepared by the Harvard Business School Case Services.

5. "General Electric Strategic Position—1981," Case No. 381-174 (Boston: HBS Case Services, Harvard Business School, 1981), p. 5.

6. J. J. Parkington and B. Schneider, "Some Correlates of Experienced Job Stress: A Boundary Role Study," *Academy of Management Journal*, vol. 22, 1979, pp. 270–281.

7. "Nordstrom," Case No. 9-579-218 (Boston: HBS Case Services, Harvard Business School, 1979), p. 22.

CHAPTER 3

Building Customer Loyalty

1. "Garber Travel Service, Inc." Case No. 9-677-210 (Boston: HBS Case Services, Harvard Business School, 1977), p. 7.

2. Patricia Sellers, "Getting Customers to Love You," *Fortune*, March 13, 1989, pp. 38–49, at p. 38.

3. Frederick F. Reichheld and W. Earl Sasser Jr., "Zero Defections: Quality Comes to Services," *Harvard Business Review*, September–October 1990, pp. 105–111.

4. Jan Carlzon, *Moments of Truth* (Cambridge, Mass.: Ballinger Publishing Company, 1987), pp. 45–46.

5. Philip Nelson, "Advertising as Information," *Journal of Political Economy*, July–August 1970, pp. 729–754.

6. M. R. Darby and E. Karni, "Free Competition and the Optimal Amount of Fraud," *Journal of Law and Economics*, April 1973, pp. 67–86.

7. Adapted from a larger set of hypotheses presented in Valarie A. Zeithaml, "How Consumer Evaluation Processes Differ between Goods and Services," in James H. Donnelly and William R. George, eds., *Marketing of Services* (Chicago: American Marketing Association, 1981), pp. 186–189.

8. Ibid., pp. 188–189.

9. James L. Heskett, "Lessons in the Service Sector," *Harvard Business Review*, March–April 1987, pp. 118–125, at p. 120.

10. The term, "service bookends," and the examples contained in this section were related to us by our late colleague, D. Daryl Wyckoff.

11. Christopher W. L. Hart, "The Power of Unconditional Service Guarantees," *Harvard Business Review*, July–August 1988, pp. 54–62, at p. 57.

12. From a videotape segment of "A Stitch in Time," *The Fifth Estate* (Toronto: Canadian Broadcasting Corporation, 1985).

13. See, for example, Claudia H. Deutsch, "The Powerful Push for Self-Service," *The New York Times*, April 9, 1989, Section 3, pp. 1 and 15.

14. Cindy Skrzycki, "Baldridge Award: Hard Work for High Honors," *The Washington Post*, April 18, 1989, pp. D1 and D6.

CHAPTER 4
Focusing and Positioning the Service

1. "ServiceMaster Industries," Case No. 9-388-064 (Boston: HBS Case Services, Harvard Business School, 1987, revised 1988), p. 2.

2. "Nordstrom," Case No. 9-579-218 (Boston: HBS Case Services, Harvard Business School, 1979, revised 1984).

3. "Why Rivals Are Quaking as Nordstrom Heads East," *Business Week*, June 15, 1987, p. 99.

4. "Shouldice Hospital Limited," Case No. 9-683-068 (Boston: HBS Case Services, Harvard Business School, 1983).

5. "Schlumberger," Case No. 2-384-087 (Boston: HBS Case Services, Harvard Business School, 1983).

6. Statements in this paragraph are based on the results of a study reported in "The Breakdown of U.S. Innovation," *Business Week*, February 16, 1976, pp. 56–68, at p. 58.

7. See Al Ries and Jack Trout, *Positioning* (New York: McGraw-Hill Book Company, 1981). This book was based in part on a series of articles that Ries and Trout had published several years earlier.

8. Christopher H. Lovelock, *Services Marketing* (Englewood Cliffs, N.J.: Prentice-Hall, Inc., 1984), p. 134.

9. G. Lynn Shostack, "Service Positioning through Structural Change," *Journal of Marketing*, January 1987, pp. 34–43.

10. Marshall McLuhan, *Understanding Media* (New York: McGraw-Hill Book Company, 1964).

11. James L. Heskett, "Rethinking Strategy in Services," in David E. Bowen, Richard B. Chase, and Thomas G. Cummings, eds., *Service Management Effectiveness* (San Francisco: Jossey-Bass Inc., Publishers, 1990).

12. Material in this section is based on Kenneth R. Harney, " 'Instant Commitment' Loans revolutionizing the Industry," *The Washington Post*, February 4, 1989, pp. E1 and E3, and a conversation with a representative of Citicorp Mortgage Corporation management.

13. Harney, op. cit., p. E1.

14. Ibid., p. E3.

15. Robert Townsend, *Up the Organization* (New York: Alfred A. Knopf, Inc., 1970).

16. Leslie Wayne, "Some Lessons from Avis for UAL Buyout," *The New York Times*, September 24, 1989, p. F-4.

17. Lovelock, op. cit., pp. 133–139.

18. See, for example, Christopher Flavin, "Electricity's Future," *The Futurist*, April 1985, pp. 36–44, and "Are Utilities Obsolete?" *Business Week*, May 21, 1984, p. 63.

19. See, for example, Monci Jo Williams, "Why Is Airline Food So Terrible?" *Fortune*, December 19, 1988, pp. 169–172.

20. This example is based on information contained in "Club Med (A)," Case No. 687-046 (Boston: HBS Case Services, Harvard Business School, 1986).

21. "Carrefour S.A.," Case No. 574-012 (Boston: HBS Case Services, Harvard Business School, 1973).

22. Susan Cary, "SAS Unveils Strategy with Cosmic Flair," *The Wall Street Journal*, April 28, 1989, p. B3.

23. James Cook, "Power for Profit," *Forbes*, November 28, 1988, pp. 78–79, at p. 78.

24. William P. Barrett, "No Frills," *Forbes*, November 14, 1988, pp. 52 and 56.

25. Ibid., p. 56.

26. Ibid., p. 52.

27. Shostack, op. cit.

CHAPTER 5
Determining the True Costs and Benefits of Service Quality

1. "Club Med (A)," Case No. 9-687-046 (Boston: HBS Case Services, Harvard Business School, 1986).

2. Ibid.

3. Christopher Kean, "Banking on Quality," *The Quality Review*, Spring 1987, pp. 8–11.

4. See for example, N. R. Kleinfield, "Keeping Hotels on Their Toes," *The New York Times*, June 25, 1989, Section 3, pp. 1 and 10.

5. Armand V. Feigenbaum, *Total Quality Control*, 3rd ed. (New York: McGraw-Hill Book Company, 1983).

6. Joseph M. Juran, *Quality Planning and Analysis: From Product Development through Use* (New York: McGraw-Hill Book Company, 1980).

CHAPTER 6
Developing Devices for Achieving Total Customer Satisfaction

1. This and other information in this chapter about the Henry Ford Community College is based on Robb Deigh, "Degree With Money-Back Promise," *Insight* magazine of *The Washington Times*, November 24, 1986, p. 10.

2. Liz Roman Gallese, "Counselor to the King," *The New York Times Magazine: The Business World*, September 24, 1989, pp. 18–20ff.

3. This section is based on Christopher W. L. Hart, "The Power of Unconditional Service Guarantees," *Harvard Business Review*, July–August, 1988, pp. 54–62.

4. *Ibid.*, p. 54.

5. "Bugs" Burger Bug Killers, Inc., videotape (Boston: HBS Case Services, Harvard Business School), 1988.

6. Advertisement, Lands' End, Inc., 1989 Catalog.

7. Christopher W.L. Hart, *op. cit.*, at pp. 56–57.

8. From an advertisement appearing in *The Wall Street Journal*, March 9, 1987, as well as in other publications.

9. A telephone conversation between one of the authors and a service representative from Lufthansa Airlines, March, 1988.

10. Menu in use at Allie's Restaurant, Bethesda Marriott Hotel, February 1989.

11. "Bugs" Burger Bug Killers, Inc., *op. cit.*

12. From a telephone conversation between one of the authors and an agent at Cititravel, October, 1988.

13. Advertisement by Virgin Atlantic Airways in *The Wall Street Journal*, April 3, 1989.

14. Quote from Smith and Hawkins in 1988 catalog. See also Paul Hawkins, *Growing a Business* (New York: Simon & Schuster, Inc., 1987).

15. Nickie McWhorter, "Money-back guarantee sets this college apart," *Detroit Free Press*, September 16, 1986, p. C-1.

16. Amar Bhide, "Hustle as Strategy," *Harvard Business Review*, September–October 1986, pp. 59–65, at p. 59. See also Brian Dumaine, "How Managers Can Manage through Speed," *Fortune*, February 13, 1989, pp. 54–59.

17. Irwin Machknick, "Rich Makes His Pitch," *The New York Times Magazine*, July 30, 1989, pp. 18–29, at p. 24.

18. Interview with Philip Bressler, March 1988.

19. Material in this section is based on Christopher W. L. Hart, James L. Heskett, and W. Earl Sasser, Jr., "The Profitable Art of Service Recovery," *Harvard Business Review*, July–August 1990, pp. 148–156.

20. This is a report of a trip experienced by one of the authors.

21. Phillip L. Zweig, "Banks Stress Resolving Complaints to Win Small Consumers' Favor," *The Wall Street Journal*, December 8, 1986, p. 29.

22. Technical Assistance Research Programs Institute, *Consumer Complaint Handling in America: An Update Study*, Part II, performed for the U.S. Office of Consumer Affairs, April 1, 1986, p. 50.

23. Patricia Sellers, "How to Handle Customers' Gripes," *Fortune*, October 24, 1988, pp. 88–100, at pp. 89 and 92.

24. Don Munro, "This Yankee's Not a Tightwad with Postage and Dollar Bills," *American Banker*, October 13, 1987, p. 16.

25. "Making Service a Potent Marketing Tool," *Business Week*, June 11, 1984, pp. 164–170.

26. Technical Assistance Research Programs Institute, op. cit., p. 48.

27. See "OTISLINE," Case No. 9-186-304 (Boston: HBS Case Services, Harvard Business School, 1986).

28. Sellers, op. cit., p. 92.

29. Interview with Jane Zezeris, Secret Service employee, March 1989.

30. Based on the actual experience of one of the authors.

31. "The Art of Loving," *Inc.*, May 1989, p. 36.

CHAPTER 7
Managing for Quality and Productivity Gains

1. See, for example, Gary Knisely, "Comparing Marketing Management in Package Goods and Service Organizations," in Christopher J. Lovelock, ed., *Services Marketing* (Englewood Cliffs, N.J.: Prentice-Hall, Inc., 1984), pp. 9–29.

2. "Boosting Productivity at American Express," *Business Week*, October 5, 1981, pp. 62 and 66.

3. "A Work Revolution in U.S. Industry," *Business Week*, May 16, 1983, p. 103.

4. *Handbook of Labor Statistics, 1989* (Washington, D.C.: U.S. Department of Labor, Bureau of Labor Statistics), August 1989, p. 348.

5. See, for example, Philip B. Crosby, *Quality is Free* (New York: McGraw-Hill Book Company, 1979), p. 17.

6. Leonard L. Berry, A. Parasuraman, and Valarie A. Zeithaml, "The Service-Quality Puzzle," *Business Horizons*, September–October 1988, pp. 35–43, at p. 37.

7. Jeremy Main, "Toward Service without a Snarl," *Fortune*, March 23, 1981, pp. 58–66.

8. Conversations with British Airways executives, July, 1989.

9. D. Daryl Wyckoff, "New Tools for Achieving Service Quality," *The Cornell Hotel and Restaurant Administration Quarterly*, November 1984, pp. 78–91, at p. 87.

10. Ibid., p. 88.

11. See "Florida Power & Light's Quality-Improvement Program," Case No. 688-043 (Boston: HBS Case Services, Harvard Business School, 1987).

12. Ibid., p. 3.

13. Theodore Levitt, "The Industrialization of Service," *Harvard Business Review*, September–October 1976, pp. 63–74, and Theodore Levitt, "Production-Line Approach to Service," *Harvard Business Review*, September–October 1972, pp. 41–52, at pp. 44–45.

14. Based on information in "Mrs. Fields Cookies," Case No. 189-056 (Boston: HBS Case Services, Harvard Business School, 1988), and Tom Richman, "Mrs. Fields' Secret Ingredient," *Inc.*, October 1987, pp. 65–72.

15. Cary Reich, "The LeBaron Phenomenon," *Institutional Investor*, August 1985, pp. 104–105.

16. This is at the crux of the problem of measuring productivity in services on a macroeconomic basis. Because of the difficulty of assessing the quality of service output, as suggested for medicine, for example, by the proportion of successful operations on humans, measurements are made in much the same way as for manufacturing, i.e., for medicine in terms of the number of operations performed per surgeon-hour of work.

17. Daniel Machalaba, "Up to Speed: United Parcel Service Gets Deliveries Done by Driving Its Workers," *The Wall Street Journal*, April 22, 1986, p. 1.

18. This is described in a manual published by Northern Telecom in 1985 entitled, "Managing with Productivity Indexing."

19. References to experiences at this company are based on the case, "The Paul Revere Insurance Company," Case No. 9-687-013 (Boston: HBS Case Services, Harvard Business School, 1986).

20. Ibid., p. 1.

21. A transcript of a filmed presentation by Patrick L. Townsend, "The Paul Revere Insurance Company, Interviews with Pat Townsend, Brad Gay, and Chuck Soule, April 22, 1987," Film No. 888-001 (Boston: HBS Case Services, Harvard Business School, 1987).

CHAPTER 8

Managing Demand and Supply

1. Valarie A. Zeithaml, "How Consumer Evaluation Processes Differ between Goods and Services," in James H. Donnelly and William R. George, eds., *Marketing of Services* (Chicago: American Marketing Association, 1981), pp. 186–190, at pp. 188–189.

2. A. K. Erlang, "The Solution of Some Problems of Significance in Automatic Telephone Exchanges," *P.O. Electrical Engineering Journal*, 1917, p. 189. For a review of queuing models and capacity planning, see James A. Fitzsimmons and Robert S. Sullivan, *Service Operations Management* (New York: McGraw-Hill Book Company, 1982), pp. 257–284.

3. David A. Maister, "The Psychology of Waiting Lines," in John A. Czepiel, Michael R. Soloman, and Carol F. Surprenant, eds., *The Service Encounter*, Lexington, Mass.: D. C. Heath & Company, 1985), pp. 113–123.

4. Richard C. Larson, "Perspectives on Queues: Social Justice and the Psychology of Queuing," *Operations Research*, November–December 1987, pp. 895–905, at p. 899.

5. Maister, op. cit.

6. Christopher H. Lovelock, *Services Marketing* (Englewood Cliffs, N.J.: Prentice-Hall, Inc., 1984), p. 280.

7. Philip Kotler and Sidney J. Levy, "Demarketing, Yes, Demarketing," *Harvard Business Review*, November–December 1971, pp. 74–80.

8. Bill Paul, "Big Electric Utilities and Consumers Push Conservation Strategy," *The Wall Street Journal*, December 8, 1987, pp. A1 and A23.

9. W. Earl Sasser, "Match Supply and Demand in Service Industries," *Harvard Business Review*, November–December 1976, pp. 133–140.

10. "Waffle House (G)", Case No. 9-672-101 (Boston: HBS Case Services, Harvard Business School, 1972).

11. Daniel Forbes, "Part-Time Work Force," *Business Month*, October 1987, pp. 45–47, at p. 45.

12. Ibid.

13. "Shouldice Hospital Limited," Case No. 9-683-068 (Boston: HBS Case Services, Harvard Business School, 1983).

14. William E. Fruhan, Jr., *The Fight for Competitive Advantage: A Study of the United States Domestic Trunk Air Carrier* (Boston: Division of Research, Harvard Business School, 1972).

15. Samuel M. Fuchs, "Revenue Control: Mining Gold at the Margin," *Airline Executive*, January 1987, pp. 32–34.

16. Ibid., p. 32 (words in brackets added).

17. Ibid., p. 33.

CHAPTER 9
Managing Networks

1. For a more detailed description of this strategy, see the case "Scandinavian Airlines System (SAS) (A)" (Geneva: International Management Institute, 1985).

2. PHH Corporation, 1987 Annual Report, p. 5.

3. From an interview with PHH Corporation executives, November 7, 1988.

4. Harlan Cleveland, "The Twilight of Hierarchy: Speculations on the Global Information Society," *Public Administration Review*, January–February 1985, pp. 185–195.

5. For a more complete description of CompuServe's business, see the case, "CompuServe, Inc. (A)," Case No. 9-386-067 (Boston: HBS Case Services, Harvard Business School, 1985).

6. Early experiences of Federal Express are described in more detail in the case, "Federal Express Corporation (A)," Case No. 9-674-093 (Boston: HBS Case Services, Harvard Business School, 1974).

7. Chris Welles, Seth Payne, Francis Seghers, and Tom Ichniowski, "Is Deregulation Working?" *Business Week*, December 22, 1986, pp. 50–55, at p. 51.

8. "Federal Express (A)," op. cit.

9. Caleb Soloman, "How Williams Cos. Turned Oil Pipelines to Conduits of Data," *The Wall Street Journal*, July 11, 1989, pp. A1 and A5.

10. W. Earl Sasser, Jr., "Match Supply and Demand in Service Industries," *Harvard Business Review*, November–December 1976, pp. 133–140, at p. 138.

CHAPTER 10
Managing Information Technologies

1. See "Banc One Corporation and the Home Information Revolution," Case No. 1-682-091 (Boston: HBS Case Services, Harvard Business School, 1982) and Constance Mitchell, "Banc One Breaks Mold and Gets Ahead," *The Wall Street Journal*, June 13, 1988, p. A10.

2. From an early Federal Express advertisement.

3. See, for example, John Dearden, "Cost Accounting Comes to Service Industries," *Harvard Business Review*, September–October 1978, pp. 132–140.

4. "Can Amex Win the Masses—And Keep Its Class?" *Business Week*, October 9, 1989, pp. 134–138.

5. See the discussion of demand-supply management in the airline industry at the end of Chapter 8, and Samuel M. Fuchs, "Revenue Control: Mining Gold at the Margin," *Airline Executive*, January 1987, pp. 32–34.

6. Daniel F. Cuff, "Builder of People Express Links Failure to Technology," *The New York Times*, October 31, 1988, p. D-4.

7. "American Hospital Supply Corporation: The ASAP System (A)," Case No. 9-186-005 (Boston: HBS Case Services, Harvard Business School, 1985).

8. W. Earl Sasser, Jr., and William E. Fulmer, "Personalized Service Delivery Systems," in David E. Bowen, Richard B. Chase, and Thomas G. Cummins, eds., *Service Management Effectiveness* (San Francisco: Jossey-Bass Inc., Publishers, 1990).

9. "Wither the Weather?" *High Technology Business*, June 1988, p. 11.

10. Shoshana Zuboff, *In the Age of the Smart Machine* (New York: Basic Books, Inc., 1988).

11. Ibid., pp. 277–283.

12. Tom Richman, "Mrs. Fields' Secret Ingredient," *Inc.*, October 1987, pp. 65–72.

13. Buck Brown, "How the Cookie Crumbled at Mrs. Fields," *The Wall Street Journal*, January 26, 1989, p. B1.

14. These facts and much of the information in this section are drawn from Barnaby J. Feder, "Getting the Electronics Just Right." *The New York Times*, June 4, 1989, pp. F-1 and F-8, at p. F-8.

15. Ibid.

16. Ibid.

17. Ibid.

18. Martin Starr, "The Performance of Foreign-Affiliated Firms in America" (New York: Center for Operations, Columbia Business School, 1989).

19. Brian Freedman, "Apparel Stores Display Above-Average Productivity," *Monthly Labor Review*, October 1984, pp. 37–42, at p. 38.

20. Lisa Scheer, "We Want to Be a Federal Express," *Forbes*, December 12, 1988, pp. 71–72.

21. Ibid.

22. A much more complete description of the process followed in the development of COSMOS at Federal Express can be found in Carl Nehls, "Custodial Package Tracking at Federal Express," in Bruce R. Guile and James Brian Quinn,

eds., *Managing Innovation—Cases from the Service Industries* (Washington, D.C.: National Academy Press, 1988), pp. 57–81.

23. Ibid., p. 81.

24. "Office Automation: Making it Pay Off," *Business Week*, October 12, 1987, pp. 134–146, at p. 138.

CHAPTER 11

Mobilizing People

1. This description of the company is based on information in "Fairfield Inn," Case No. 9-689-092 (Boston: HBS Case Services, Havard Business School, 1989).

2. Conversation with Michael R. Ruffer, President, Fairfield Inn, February 3, 1989.

3. "Behind the UPS Mystique: Puritanism and Productivity," *Business Week*, June 6, 1983, p. 68.

4. Robert Levering, Milton Moskowitz, and Michael Katz, *The 100 Best Companies to Work for in America* (New York: New American Library, 1984), pp. 131–137.

5. Baila Zeitz and Lorraine Dusky, *The Best Companies for Women* (New York: Simon & Schuster, Inc., 1988).

6. Based on interviews with Thomas Gould, President, and other executives of Younkers, March and August 1989.

7. "Nordstrom," Case No. 9-579-218 (Boston: HBS Case Services, Harvard Business School, 1979).

8. This quote as well as information that follows about The ServiceMaster Company Limited Partnership are taken from the case, "ServiceMaster Industries Inc.," Case No. 9-388-064 (Boston: HBS Case Services, Harvard Business School, 1987). The quote appears on pp. 4 and 5 of the case.

9. Ibid., p. 1.

10. Ibid., pp. 6–7.

11. Ibid., p. 6.

12. Douglas C. McGill, "Why They Smile at Red Lobster," *The New York Times*, April 23, 1989, Section 3, pp. 1 and 6, at p. 6.

13. Barbara Marsh, "Going for the Golden Arches," *The Wall Street Journal*, May 1, 1989, p. B1.

14. "Au Bon Pain—The Partner/Manager Program," Case No. 9-687-063 (Boston: HBS Case Services, Havard Business School, 1987), pp. 2–3. Much of the description that follows is paraphrased from the case.

15. Interview with Leonard Schlesinger, former Executive Vice President, Au Bon Pain, Inc., November 4, 1988.

16. "Nordstrom," op. cit.

17. Francine Schwadel, "Irate Nordstrom Straining in Labor Fight," *The Wall Street Journal*, April 6, 1990, pp. B1 and B4, at p.B1.

18. For a description of the importance of franchising to service businesses, see James C. Cross and Bruce J. Walker, "Service Marketing and Franchising: A Practical Business Marriage," *Business Horizons*, November–December 1987, pp. 50–58.

19. This point is made quite persuasively in Paul H. Rubin, "The Theory of the Firm and the Structure of the Franchise Contract," *Journal of Law and Economics*, vol. 21, April 1978, pp. 223–233.

20. Urban B. Ozanne and Shelby D. Hunt, "The Economic Effects of Franchising," Select Committee on Small Business, U.S. Senate, 92nd Congress, 1st Session (Washington, D.C.: U.S. Government Printing Office, 1971).

21. Marsh, op. cit.

22. Ibid., p. B1.

23. Rubin, op. cit., pp. 229–230.

24. Steven Greenhouse, "McDonald's Tries Paris, Again," *The New York Times*, June 12, 1988, Section 3, pp. 1, 14, and 15, at p. 15.

25. Teri Agins, "Benetton Is Accused of Dubious Tactics by Some Store Owners," *The Wall Street Journal*, October 24, 1988, pp. A1 and A8.

26. Rubin, op. cit., p. 232.

CHAPTER 12

Organizing Work

1. David H. Maister and Christopher H. Lovelock, "Managing Facilitator Services," *Sloan Management Review*, Summer 1982, p. 22.

2. For a more detailed description of this strategy, see the case "CompuServe (A)," Case No. 9-386-067 (Boston: HBS Case Services, Harvard Business School, 1985).

3. The following description is based on interviews during June 1986 at Walt Disney World, "A Note on the History of the Walt Disney Company," Case No. 0-687-103 (Boston: HBS Case Services, Harvard Business School, 1987) and the following articles: Howard Gold, "Can the Performance Match the Promise?," *Forbes*, January 27, 1986, p. 87; N. W. Pope, "Mickey Mouse Marketing," *American Banker*, July 25, 1979, pp. 4–14; and N. W. Pope, "More Mickey Mouse Marketing," *American Banker*, September 12, 1979, pp. 4–14.

4. *ServiceTrends Trends and Forecast, Customer Service Industry*, 1988 Annual Edition (Lexington, Mass.: The Ledgeway Group, 1988), p. 49.

5. Paul R. Lawrence and Jay W. Lorsch, "New Management Job: The Integrator," *Harvard Business Review*, November–December 1967, pp. 142–151.

6. Charles W. Moritz, "Customer Focus: The Key to the Future of Information Services," from a speech to the Advertising Research Foundation, March 18, 1986.

7. Richard B. Chase, "Where Does the Customer Fit in a Service Operation?" *Harvard Business Review*, November–December 1978, pp. 138–139.

8. C. Wickham Skinner, "The Focused Factory," *Harvard Business Review*, May–June 1974, pp. 113–121.

9. For a more detailed description of this situation, see "United Parcel Service (A)," Case No. 9-488-016 (Boston: HBS Case Services, Harvard Business School, 1987).

10. This is described in the case, "Chemical Bank (A)," Case No. 9-172-228 (Boston: HBS Case Services, Harvard Business School, 1972).

11. Interview with Mitchell S. Fromstein, October 1989.

12. "Scandinavian Airlines System SAS (A)," (Geneva: International Management Institute, 1985), p. 10.

13. Interview with Leonard Schlesinger, November 1988.

14. Shoshana Zuboff, *In the Age of the Smart Machine* (New York: Basic Books, Inc., 1988).

15. "Scandinavian Airlines System SAS (A)," op. cit., p. 10.

16. "Scandinavian Airlines System SAS (C)," (Geneva: International Management Institute, 1987), p. 2.

17. David H. Maister has termed these organizations "one-firm firms." See his seminal article, "The One-Firm Firm: What Makes It Successful," *Sloan Management Review*, Fall 1985, pp. 3–13. His work provides much of the basis for this section. However, the inferences made here should not be attributed to him.

18. David H. Maister, "Hunters and Farmers," unpublished manuscript, 1985.

19. "Hewitt Associates," Case No. 9-681-063 (Boston: HBS Case Services, Harvard Business School, 1981).

20. Maister, "Hunters and Farmers," op. cit.

21. "Au Bon Pain—The Partner/Manager Program," Case No. 9-687-063 (Boston: HBS Case Services, Harvard Business School, 1987), p. 7.

CHAPTER 13

Conceiving Future Breakthroughs

1. "The Portable Executive," *Business Week*, October 10, 1988, pp. 102–112, at p. 105.

2. Ibid., p. 104.

3. Ibid.

4. Julie Amparano Lopez, "Once High-Tech Toys, Cellular Telephones are Becoming Staples," *The Wall Street Journal*, August 11, 1989, pp. A1 and A10, at p. A1.

5. Stanley M. Davis, *Future Perfect* (Reading, Mass.: Addison-Wesley Publishing Company, Inc., 1987).

6. Warren Brown, "Jiffy Lube Considers Putting Itself Up for Sale," *The Washington Post*, February 28, 1989, pp. C1 and C12, at p. C12.

7. Harlan Cleveland, "The Twilight of Hierarchy: Speculations on the Global Information Society," *Public Administration Review*, January–February 1985, pp. 185–195, at pp. 186–187.

8. Stephen S. Roach, "America's Technology Dilemma: A Profile of the Information Economy," Morgan Stanley Special Economic Study, April 22, 1987.

9. Stephen S. Roach, "Technology and the Service Sector: America's Hidden Competitive Challenge," in Bruce R. Guile and James Brian Quinn, eds., *Technology in Services: Policies for Growth, Trade, and Employment* (Washington, D.C.: National Academy Press, 1988), pp. 118–138.

10. James Brian Quinn, Jordan J. Baruch, and Penny Cushman Paquette, "Technology in Services," *Scientific American*, December 1987, pp. 50–58, at p. 53.

11. Earl Sasser and William E. Fulmer, "Personalized Service Delivery Systems," in David E. Bowen, Richard B. Chase, and Thomas G. Cummings, eds., *Service Management Effectiveness* (San Francisco: Jossey-Bass Inc., Publishers, 1990).

12. "Office Automation: Making It Pay Off," *Business Week*, October 12, 1987, pp. 134–146, at p. 146.

13. Ibid., p. 138.

14. Ibid., p. 142.

15. Quinn, Baruch, and Paquette, op. cit., p. 53.

16. "Information Power," *Business Week*, October 14, 1985, pp. 108–114, at p. 108.

17. Quinn, Baruch, and Paquette, op. cit., p. 52.

18. Cited in Ibid., p. 53.

19. Edward B. Fiske, "The Global Imperative," *The New York Times*, April 9, 1989, Special Education Supplement, 18–19.

20. Suzanne Gordon, "Work, Work, Work," *The Boston Globe Magazine*, August 20, 1989, pp. 16–60, at p. 40.

21. William J. Baumol and William G. Bowen, *Performing Arts—The Economic Dilemma* (New York: Twentieth Century Fund, 1966), p. 164.

CHAPTER 14
Realizing Service Breakthroughs

1. Randy Bright, *Disneyland Inside Story* (New York: Harry N. Abrams, Inc., 1987), p. 111.
2. Ibid., p. 107.
3. Ibid.
4. Ibid., p. 113.
5. Carl Nehls, "Custodial Package Tracking at Federal Express," in Bruce R. Guile and James Brian Quinn, eds., *Managing Innovation—Cases from the Service Industries* (Washington, D.C.: National Academy Press, 1988), pp. 57–81, at p. 81.

Index